Michel

Guérard's

CUISINE

GOURMANDE

Michel Guérard was born at Vétheuil in 1933. Drawn early to cooking, he served his apprenticeship with Kléber Alix at Mantes. He subsequently worked in the Hotel Crillon at Paris and with Jean Delaveyne at Bougival. In 1965 he opened his own restaurant, the Pot-au-Feu at Asnières, which rapidly acquired an international reputation. Since 1972 his base has been at Eugénie-les-Bains in the Landes, where he developed Cuisine Minceur to meet the needs of guests at his wife's spa hotel. His restaurant, which serves both gourmande and minceur menus, has recently achieved the coveted third Michelin rosette.

La maison d'Eugénie.

Michel Guérard's

CUISINE GOURMANDE

Edited and adapted
by
Caroline Conran

ISBN 0 333 31930 3

MICHEL GUÉRARD'S CUISINE GOURMANDE
first published 1978 by
MACMILLAN LONDON LTD
4 Little Essex Street, London WC2R 3LF

First published in 1981 by
PAPERMAC
a division of Macmillan Publishers ‑Limited
London and Basingstoke

Associated companies in Auckland, Dallas,
Delhi, Dublin, Hong Kong, Johannesburg, Lagos,
Manzini, Melbourne, Nairobi, New York,
Singapore, Tokyo, Washington and Zaria

Translation by Caroline Conran and Caroline Hobhouse
Photographs by Sarah Moon and Michael Yavel and drawings by
Michel Guérard, Susan Campbell and Patrice Costergent

Printed in Great Britain by
BUTLER AND TANNER LTD,
Frome and London

CONTENTS

LIST OF ILLUSTRATIONS

Colour plates

Introduction

by

CAROLINE CONRAN

Introduction

IT IS ONLY two years since Michel Guérard, master chef and presiding genius of his now famous three-star restaurant at Eugénie-les-Bains, in the pretty farmland of the Landes, wrote his first book introducing *Cuisine Minceur*, the revolutionary method that he evolved for producing exquisite food for those people like himself, who passionately loved food but wanted to remain slim and healthy. It was a tremendous success, and has quite changed many cooks' general outlook on cooking. But it is not the only reason that Guérard is admired in France by the brilliant fraternity of top chefs, which includes such great names as Paul Bocuse, Jean Delaveyne and the Troisgros brothers. These three-star chefs have between them changed French cooking radically. The new style of cooking which they have evolved together over the years is called Nouvelle Cuisine, and its principles are that food should have a 'lyrical lightness'; taste more of itself and be enhanced by, rather than smothered by, its accompanying sauces or gravies. Heavy hors d'œuvres – those large slices of dense dull pâté wrapped in solid pastry – have given place to beautiful and luxurious fish pâtés, delicate but rich 'salades composées' and light soups. Pastry has become like feathers, and new combinations of aromas and flavours are being introduced to a very conservative audience of food-lovers. The band of chefs involved in this new cooking have had the most enormous influence, not only at home in France but throughout the West and in Australia; there has been a real renaissance of interest in French cuisine and the eyes of the world are very much focussed on the goings-on in the great kitchens where new ideas steam up from huge copper pots. And the most original and innovative of them all is undoubtedly Michel Guérard, who stands right at the front of this culinary revolution. Fortunately for us, he is one of those rare people who can not only create – and he is truly original in his thinking – but can also communicate his ideas to others.

Small, dynamic, charming and kind, his love of cooking is highly contagious, and unlike the chefs of the previous generation, whose specialities were jealously guarded secrets, meant for a small and select audience of customers and admirers only, he wants to share everything, exchange ideas, let people know how to achieve his original and exquisite dishes for themselves. And, far from looking down on us home cooks, he has a very high opinion of our powers and capabilities.

This book, written for enthusiasts, with a genuine regard for the limitations of cooking at home in an ordinary kitchen, is the complete antithesis of his previous book. Already nicknamed Cuisine Grosseur by friends who have tried some of the recipes, it is a collection of his best and favourite gourmande recipes – for those who can sometimes commit themselves completely to the pleasure of cooking, without having to stint on time, butter and trouble. It is true to say that if you want the authentic flavour of French food, you can achieve it with this book. Start with the apple-tart **(No 138)**; make the pâte feuilleté as it is described in Michel Guérard's recipe, soak the apples in lemon juice, and drench the tarts in the required quantity of butter and sugar as they cook. The result is staggering, beyond description. It instantly transports you into a really good French restaurant, complete with white tablecloths and an efficient madame to keep everything running unobtrusively smoothly.

Many of the recipes are the author's own brilliant versions of old favourites, many are new and fascinating. There is an infallible fish mousse, **(No 53)**, a perfectionist's chicken-liver terrine **(No 36)** and a most unusual recipe for duck-ham, **(No 27)** which introduces a completely new food to the cook's basic repertoire.

There may be variations between what we can buy in the way of ingredients and what is available in France, but curiously enough these seem to make no radical difference in most cases, since good substitutes answer very well, and it becomes apparent that the methods used, and the care taken over each step of a recipe are what really count.

Of course, we cannot readily buy such esoteric ingredients as fresh foie gras, fresh truffles or freshwater crayfish outside France. Michel Guérard is aware of this and has suggested substitutes for almost everything that might be difficult to come by. I go into this in further detail on pages 14–18.

Equipment

On the whole the equipment used in this book is exactly the same as the everyday equipment you will have in your kitchen anyway. We have assumed that most cooks will have a standard range of saucepans, casseroles, knives and other gadgets (the kind of equipment you would find in a well-equipped French kitchen is illustrated on pages 12–13) and have specified items of equipment in the recipes only when they are unusual or important. In order that the finished dish will be aesthetically as well as gastronomically pleasing,

Michel Guérard sometimes specifies a certain colour for a serving-dish or plate, but although it may not look so pretty, the food will taste just as good in any suitable dish.

You may however, be somewhat stumped when it comes to steaming; some of the recipes specify wire racks that fit inside ordinary pans or small enamelled iron cocottes. In these recipes (steamed potatoes **No 110**, Fishmarket in a Casserole, **No 68** etc.), you may use a steamer or a fish-kettle to achieve the same result, or improvise by placing a small roasting rack in a large saucepan and covering it with a sheet of aluminium foil pierced with holes.

Another luxury that not many kitchens will run to is a set of tiny frying-pans, which are used for cooking and serving certain vegetables such as the Fried Potatoes and Carrots **(No 113)** and the Gratin Dauphinois **(No 114)** – a recipe, incidentally, of such simplicity and splendour that you need never try cooking this great dish any other way. These can equally well be made in larger pans or gratin dishes; simply allow a little longer for them to cook. Where the recipes advise using a wooden spatula, which is a fine blade of wood, extremely useful for stirring things delicately without breaking them, a small wooden spoon, carefully used, will do quite well.

The potato-peeler the author refers to, called in French a 'couteau économe', is the swivelling kind that takes off the peel in the thinnest possible strips.

One expensive piece of equipment which you may not own is a food-processor such as a Magimix or Robot-chef. These powerful machines with flat bowls and large strong-bladed cutters will take a great deal of work out of making light airy mousses and purées of such things as raw fish or cooked vegetables, and they are also marvellous for slicing, shredding and puréeing and pastry-making. If you can obtain one they are well worth having, if not, use a liquidiser and mixer. An electric ice-cream maker or sorbetière is useful, but not essential.

Oven temperatures

Chefs like to cook at great speed and over a very high heat. They use much hotter ovens than is usual in a domestic kitchen and since the oven is on all the time, it is likely to give a greater blast of heat as the food goes in. The timings given in this book, therefore, may seem to be on the brief side. Common sense will tell you whether the food is ready or not, but bear in mind also that Michel Guérard

Batterie de Cuisine

white porcelain soup bowls

egg-dishes

earthenware cocottes

oval ovenproof gratin dish

dishes for both cooking and serving

heavy enamelled iron casserole

terrine

non-stick frying pan

sauté pan

heavy ridged iron grilling pan

pans for frying, sautéing and grilling

strainer

colander

wire sieve

implements for sieving and straining

mandoline   liquidiser   mouli-julienne

tools for shredding, slicing and purées

bain-marie & saucepans   steamer   coussoussier

fish kettle

1 potato peeler
2 small knife
3 pastry brush
4 melon baller
5 channel cutter

pans for pouching and steaming

10

11

12

6 roasting fork
7 large kitchen knife
8 skimmer
9 ladle

scales and
measuring jug

14

15 16

13

10 forcing bag
11 wooden spatula
12 metal spatula
13 rolling pin
14 steak bat
15 large whisk
16 small whisk

weights and measures and small hand tools

S.C

likes his chickens slightly rosy at the bone, his beans faintly crisp and his fish only just turning from raw to cooked.

Ingredients

Foie gras   Because he lives in the Landes, in south-western France, Michel Guérard regards foie gras – fat poultry livers – with considerably less reverence than most people. The farms surrounding Eugénie are famous for their production of foie gras – mostly duck livers. The locals regard their produce as particularly fine and are very scornful of the word Strasbourg in connection with the foie-gras industry, maintaining that most pâté de foie gras de Strasbourg comes from Czechoslovakia, and has done for years.

In the original French version of this book the foie gras of the Landes, mainly enlarged duck livers (weighing up to 600 g each (18 oz) – goose livers from Toulouse weigh up to 2 kilos (4½ lbs) – feature very largely in a chapter on the subject, which is clearly dear to the author's heart. He cooks it in many different ways, a tradition which had almost died and which the French will be pleased to see revived. However, he realises that outside France there are difficulties involved in obtaining this marvellous embodiment of richness, and for this edition he has recommended other kinds of liver as alternatives in all the recipes except the first, which deals with making a pure terrine de foie gras frais **(No 44)**. This is included partly for interest, and partly for the benefit of anybody who may find themselves in France, and wants to try cooking the marvellous stuff for themselves. (I did, incidentally, try using the first recipe with some absolutely fresh farm chicken livers, just three or four of them, and they tasted quite exquisite, served quite cold with hot fresh toast and butter.)

Freshwater crayfish (*Asticus asticus*)   Like foie gras, freshwater crayfish or écrevisses (krefte in Scandinavia and yabbies in Australia), those small fiery red crustaceans (dull brown or black until they are fished out and boiled), that thrive in chalkstreams, have always been symbolic of the best cooking in France – pike quenelles like feathers with a light crayfish sauce topped with a whole crayfish, or a pyramid of crayfish cooked in court-bouillon are pearls of great price in the repertoire of traditional chefs. Michel Guérard too uses them extensively and imaginatively in this book, in feuilletés, sauces, salads and paupiettes.

At first glance this may appear to mean that those who live outside

France cannot tackle certain recipes. But for those people who cannot obtain crayfish, Michel Guérard recommends fresh or frozen Dublin Bay or king prawns, or scampi. Moreover, it looks as though crayfish farming is in many countries, including Australia, an up-and-coming and lucrative new occupation. Evidently a new strain of 'signal' crayfish from America, resistant to the diseases that have wiped out most of the indigenous types, can be bred to an edible size in two years, and many fish-farmers are now planning to take up crayfish rearing as a sideline. Many of these will no doubt go straight to France but with any luck there will be enough good cooks in other parts of the world to ensure that a ready supply is available at home too.

Frogs' legs can be obtained frozen outside France.

Lard and bacon   A number of recipes call for 'lard de poitrine fumé', this is smoked streaky bacon and is sold in the piece. It is quite excellent and keeps well, so you can buy a large piece and slice off bits as you need them.

Where goose or duck fat is required you can substitute lard or pork dripping. To make lard (called saindoux in France) taste more interesting, it can be heated with a sprig or two of thyme, which is then removed. The lard is allowed to cool and used in the normal way.

Oil   Most French chefs use two oils exclusively, **olive oil** for salads and where a rustic Provençal flavour is required, and **arachide**, refined groundnut oil, where the oil is supposed to stay in the background. Instead of arachide you can use sunflower oil, but Michel Guérard does not like the flabby taste of corn-oil. In the same way that lard can be flavoured with herbs, oils can be given a more interesting taste by steeping them with herbs for a day or two before use.

Stock cubes   In this book Michel Guérard uses stock cubes consistently throughout all his recipes, instead of the traditional 'fonds'. This he does not only to save time, which it most decidedly does, but to give a lighter result. If you prefer to use your own home-made stock following the instructions on pages 58–65, make sure it is not too strong, or it will destroy the balance of flavours in the dish. If you are using stock cubes, either Maggi, which the author himself uses, or Knorr give good results.

Crème fraîche and fleurette cream   Crème fraîche, the cream used in the original French recipes, is treated with a culture to help it to keep well, and to give it a light, lively taste and a less cloying texture than ordinary cream. You can make crème fraîche at home according to the simple recipe which follows. It is no more difficult than making yoghurt. Alternatively, you can use ordinary double cream which gives a very satisfactory result in cooking.

Crème fraîche

Stir 1 tablespoon buttermilk into 500 ml (scant pint) of whipping cream in a saucepan over a gentle heat. Bring the temperature gradually up to 24°C–29°C (75°F–85°F), no hotter or it will not work; at this point the cream will still feel very slightly cool to the back of your finger.

Remove from the direct heat, pour into a bowl, cover and keep warm (at about 24°C (75°F)) either in a bath of water over the pilot light of a gas stove or in a warm airing-cupboard, etc. It will take from eight to twenty-four hours according to the temperature it is held at.

To whip crème fraîche, add one-third of its volume of cold milk, water or chipped ice, a little sugar to taste, and whisk.

Fleurette cream is less rich than crème fraîche or double cream. The nearest English equivalent is whipping cream, which contains a minimum of 35% butter-fat, while double cream contains at least 48%. It whips easily and gives a lighter result.

Butter   French butter is usually unsalted and rather more acid in flavour than ours. Use unsalted or slightly salted butter in all cases, unless you are making pâte feuilletée for savoury feuilletés, in which case it is not important.

Vanilla sugar   You can buy vanilla sugar in small packets weighing 10 g (just over $\frac{1}{4}$ oz) each or you can make it yourself. Home-made vanilla sugar is not quite as strong as the commercial kind, so add a little more and take the equivalent amount out of the remaining unflavoured sugar required in the recipe.

To make vanilla sugar   Fill a 1 lb preserving jar or storage jar with caster sugar and put in a whole vanilla-pod. In a week or so you will have vanilla sugar; as you use it up, refill the jar with fresh sugar.

Pear liqueur (*Eau de vie de poire*)   This liqueur, specified in the recipes for Caramelised Pear Pastries (**No 141**) and Light Pear Soufflés (**No 134**) may seem an extravagant purchase. However, as a liqueur it is quite delicious, and much more interesting, as well as less stultifying, than brandy or port to drink after a good dinner.

Seaweed   This is used by Michel Guérard to add moisture and a pungent, iodiney flavour to some of his fish dishes.

The recipes for Fishmarket in a Casserole **(No 68)** and Bass cooked in Seaweed **(No 61),** suggest that one can obtain the right variety from the fishmonger, but this may be difficult outside France. The varieties to use are the finer types with small bubbles or bladders that are commonly found on the seashore. If you cannot gather it for yourself, you may be able to order it from your fishmonger if he is an understanding type and deals in the kind of shellfish and crustaceans which are sent to market packed in seaweed. Wash it thoroughly before using it, as it is a good harbour for all sorts of small sea-creatures.

Wild mushrooms   Certain edible fungi beloved of the French are specified in the recipes, namely ceps, morels and millers. They are all to be found growing in Northern Europe by those who have an absolutely clear idea of what to look for, but if you are in any doubt about a wild mushroom or fungi – leave it alone.

Ceps (French, *cèpes*, Latin, *boletus edulis*). There are several varieties, but basically a cep is a fleshy, round-topped fungus with a thick, fleshy stalk, spongy yellowish or whitish pores underneath and a suede-brown, slimy-soft bulbous cap, to be found beneath pine trees and at the edges of forest rides. Ceps must be picked and eaten young. Discard the spongy pores as, at any rate to my taste, they are a bit too slimy. Ceps are also available – and very good – dried, the best place to look for these is an Italian grocer (or Italian airport), where they are called Porcini.

Morels (French, *morilles*, Latin, *morchella esculenta*). These spongy looking dark brown or beige fungi are rare. They are very distinctive in appearance, their uncommon honeycombed structure being ideal for the harbouring of sand and grit, so wash them very carefully. Dried morels are sold only in very top grocers as they are exceedingly expensive. However, their flavour is so special that they are worth an occasional fling. Soak them in warm water for half an hour before using.

Millers (French, *mousserons*, Latin, *clitopilus prunulus*), are found in shady pastures or ferny banks and have a strong smell of flour. They are an opaque dirty white with soft thick white flesh, and are somewhat trumpet shaped. They are also available dried. As they are rather uncommon, it might be easier to substitute ordinary field mushrooms.

Chinese (and Japanese) mushrooms. The matsu mushroom (*tricholoma matsutake*), the shiitake (*lentinus edodes*) and the wood ear (*auricularia polytricha*) are all available dried from Chinese supermarkets. They need soaking before use in warm water.

17

Dried mushrooms are so delicious, adding a deep warm flavour to gravy or sauce, that it is surprising we do not make greater use of them. Although expensive, they are also very light, and what seems a tiny amount will swell to quite a decent bowlful when soaked. Use the liquid afterwards for flavouring, but strain it as a certain amount of dirt will almost always collect at the bottom of the dish while they are soaking.

Salad plants The very special salads in this book have little in common with the limp head of lettuce leaves which so often passes as a salad, and Michel Guérard specifies some unusual plants like red chicory, lamb's lettuce or corn salad (mâche in France), dandelions and purslane. There are not many places outside Italy where the rose-coloured chicory, beloved of the Italians for its bitterness and by the author for the beauty of its colouring, can be bought, so substitute ordinary chicory or obtain seeds from a specialist seed-merchant and grow it yourself. The other small salad plants can be replaced with fresh wild dandelions and with the thinnings of lettuce beds; they add freshness, prettiness and variety to the salad bowl.

Measurements

Since the introduction of metric measurements in the kitchen in Britain and elsewhere, cookery-book writers have been faced with all sorts of headaches, as it is now necessary to give two different measurements at once.

In this book the usual business of converting pounds and ounces to grammes has been reversed, but the problems remain the same.

The difficulty lies in finding sensible equivalents – one ounce actually equals 28·350 grammes, for example. So to prevent situations where the reader is supposed to measure out 0·353 of an ounce (10 grammes), and so on, we have followed the usual practice of rounding the quantities up or down to the nearest number of ounces or pints.

However, even so, some measurements are distinctly fiddly, so we suggest taking the (eventually) inevitable plunge and obtaining metric scales and measuring jug – you can then use Michel Guérard's original measurements.

If this is impossible, use your own judgement as to whether it is important to be exact or not.

Australian Metrication
The recipes in this book were originated in metric measures. The Imperial equivalents given throughout the book follow the British conventions of typography and rounding up and down. In Australia, the Metric Conversion Board recommends different conventions. For example the Australians work to 1 oz = 30 g, whereas the British work to 1 oz = 25 g. The best advice we can give is that you should use metric scales and measures, and only use the Imperial measures as a rough guide.

Conversion Tables

WEIGHT

1. Exact equivalents (to two places of decimals)

Metric	*British*
25 g	0·88 oz
100 g	3·53 oz
1 kg	2·20 lb
British	*Metric*
1 oz	28·35 g
8 oz	226.78 g
1 lb	0·45 kg (453·6 g)
1½ lb	0·68 kg (680·40 g)
2 lb	0·91 kg (907·2 g)

2. Approximate equivalents

Metric	*British*
25 g	1 oz
50 g	1¾–2 oz
75 g	2½ oz
100 g	3½ oz
200 g	7 oz
500 g (0·5 kg)	1 lb 2 oz (18 oz)
1000 g (1 kg)	2¼ lb (36 oz)

LIQUID MEASURES

1. Exact equivalents (to two places of decimals)

Metric	*British*
250 ml (0·25 litre)	0·44 pints
500 ml (0·50 litre)	0·88 pints
1 litre	1·76 pints
British	*Metric*
½ pint	0·28 litres
1 pint	0·57 litres

2. Approximate equivalents

Metric	*British*
150 ml	$\frac{1}{4}$ pint
250 ml	scant half pint
300 ml	$\frac{1}{2}$ pint
500 ml (0·5 litre)	scant pint
750 ml	$1\frac{1}{4}$ pints
1000 ml (1 litre)	$1\frac{3}{4}$ pints
1·5 litres	$2\frac{1}{2}$ pints
2 litres	$3\frac{1}{2}$ pints

OVEN TEMPERATURES

Temperature equivalents for oven thermostat markings

Degrees Fahrenheit (°F)	*Gas Regulo Mark*	*Degrees Centigrade* (°C)
225	$\frac{1}{4}$	110
250	$\frac{1}{2}$	130
275	1	140
300	2	150
325	3	170
350	4	180
375	5	190
400	6	200
425	7	220
450	8	230
475	9	240
500	10	250

Michel

Guérard's

CUISINE

GOURMANDE

For Aimée Boulanger, my grandmother

FOREWORD
by
MICHEL GUÉRARD

Foreword

It was at Vétheuil, where I was born, that I started my hectic career as a gourmet. I was five years old at the time and every day, without fail, I would visit the town's only restaurant, a few chocolate éclairs'-throw from our house. I would take up my position outside the kitchens and start singing my favourite song at the top of my voice – until someone opened the window. My friend the cook would then appear and send down a shower of pastries left over from the night before. He never failed me, but I have never been able to decide whether this largesse was the result of his fondness for children or a particular aversion to my songs.

Saturday was our great day. Ten scruffy lads in short pants, we sat on the cold stone steps of the town hall, waiting for the Lady Bountiful who each week would invite us to rifle the inviting window of the boulangerie-pâtisserie. The first time I followed my older comrades on this raid my career as a gourmand nearly came to an end for good. During the previous week I had spent hours with my nose pressed to the plate-glass window in feverish anticipation and had finally plumped for a pastry oozing with pale cream – partly because it looked so good, but mostly because it was enormous. When the moment came, I crammed it into my mouth, eyes shut in ecstasy. Immediately they filled with tears, as my gorge rose in revulsion. I was about to swallow a huge chicken vol-au-vent, as cold as death! The humiliation was, however, nothing to the shock to my taste buds, and I realised at that moment that fate intended me to be an apostle of good food.

How could I fail to become a cook-gourmand with a childhood presided over by a grandmother who took such loving care to concoct delicious little meals for me by the fireside on winter evenings? I can still remember the strong summery scent of wild almonds, wafting from the apricots, taken from their frugal jars and ranged in caramelised waves on the tarts, as they came hot from the oven, and watching with shivers of pleasure the caps of the plump stuffed apples rising between my two stockinged feet propped up at the open oven door. Later, in Normandy with my mother, I learned to listen to the musical murmur of ragoûts acquiring their musky flavours beneath their golden oil, to dip my finger into stews brimming over with intoxicating aromas, to watch over wild rabbits as they were toasted to a deep golden brown by the heat of the fire. The war came and I enlisted in my new career. Every Thursday I would set up my own field of the cloth of gold – a tent made of old sacks and other gorgeous cast-offs. I would receive a clamourous crowd of friends whom I would entertain with little cakes which I had carefully made in secret the night before, using the skin of boiled milk. We would round off the meal with a purée of blackberries, and then, stained blue like Sioux warriors with the juice, would go in search of fallen flying-bombs or jettisoned empty fuel tanks to make into canoes. At this point, having followed the other members of the family into the church choir, I nearly gave up cooking for good. Perhaps inspired by the perfume of the incense I decided to become a priest – or even a bishop! And then, one day, I somehow found myself on the stage of the village hall and decided my vocation was to be an actor.

But dreams have to stop, and my apprenticeship abruptly forced me to grow up. It was a cold, unforgiving time, illuminated with rare moments of joy and exciting things to learn, but also full of despair, of discipline and of rebellion.

I found there the 'Maison des Autres'. Kléber Alix, my master, taught me to be ambitious to please and to succeed through sheer quality, but also to be humble and not to take myself too seriously. From now on, I patiently followed the dark and sunny roads to experience.

Then came the blessed period of my 'papas-gâteaux', those who helped me as though I were their son or younger brother. The bonds that grew up between us were almost conspiratorial, in a friendly way which was at once secret, warm, ripe and creative. They were called Jean Delaveyne, Paul Bocuse and the Troisgros brothers; they were also known as 'the others' – my friends.

For as you will gave gathered, cooking is as much an affair of the heart as a profession. A mixture of enthusiasm and sympathetic magic in which rigid disciplines, together with complete freedom of the imagination allow one to do really creative work. This generous profession comes to life amidst clouds of richly scented steam and there follows its course of spontaneous, if fleeting, creativity.

And I hope that when I come to be invited with my fellows to the Lord's table behind those other clouds, I shall have the courage to ask Him whether He will let me serve for eternity as an apprentice in the great angels' kitchen. And above all, to let me taste His latest creation!

Michel Guérard

THE PRINCIPAL METHODS
of COOKING

Whatever method you may use, whether traditional – either on an open fire or a grill, or roasting, sautéing, frying, boiling, steaming, braising or poaching – or modern, cooking means the transition of food from the raw to the cooked state, a phenomenon which changes its outward appearance – its colour, its texture and its flavour – and releases a surge of scents to stir the appetite. And the agent of the transition is *fire* in all its many guises – wood, coal, gas, electricity. . . .

IN THE BEGINNING

WAS THE EARTH,

THEN MAN

WHO DISCOVERED FIRE,

AND SO BEGAN TO COOK

THE TWO GREAT LAWS

1 Cooking by Sealing

Sealing and browning

The method consists of crisping and browning the surface of the food all over, by applying heat either with or without fat or oil. The purpose is to seal and imprison all juices and nutritious elements inside the food to be cooked. It is used in grilling, roasting, sautéing and frying.

Sealing without browning

The same result can be achieved without browning the food by cooking it in boiling liquid or steam, or in a non-stick pan. The method is used for poaching eggs and for cooking pasta, vegetables, fish, chicken and meat.

2 Cooking by Exchange

Exchange with browning

This consists of pot-roasting or braising meat, poultry, game and offal, first sautéing them briskly in hot fat or oil, to retain their juices and nutritive elements, and then moistening them to half their depth with wine, basic veal, chicken, game or fish stock or any other aromatic stock: the making of the basic *fonds blonds* also follows this principle.

The juices sealed inside the food are gradually released to combine with the cooking liquid and at the same time the food absorbs, and is enriched by, the various flavours of the liquid itself – hence the term 'exchange'.

Exchange without browning

This is the same as the preceding method but with one difference; the food may be sautéd in fat or oil but *not* coloured (*i.e.* stewed gently in butter, as in a fricassée), or soaked in water to remove every trace of blood, in the case of offal, and blanched for a few minutes if necessary, then sautéd in a non-stick pan before adding the moistening liquid, which will become the base of the sauce or gravy, by the process of exchange.

On the other hand, unlike meat, the braising of fish is not started by sautéing, but simply by placing the fish on a dish which may or may not be lightly buttered, and then moistening it to half its depth with fish fumet, or with cold white or red wine and placing it in the oven covered with greaseproof paper or aluminium foil to prevent burning. This last is an excellent example of cooking 'by exchange without browning' as the fish quickly releases its juices and flavours into the fumet, which in return helps the food to become succulent during its cooking, by 'exchange'. This method is also used for the cooking of basic veal or fish stocks, consommé and the poaching of fish in a well-flavoured stock (court-bouillon), started cold and gradually brought to simmering point.

COOKING ON AN OPEN FIRE OR BARBECUE

Man's first attempts at cooking were done on a wood-fire, and it is still a good place to start learning the art of cooking. I have written the next few pages specifically for all devotees of the open fire, for the young and weekend cooks. *With a little ingenuity they can cope with almost any form of cooking on an open fire.*

Cooking on a grill

This method is concerned with sealing and browning the meat on the top of a fire or stove. The source of heat comes from glowing embers, burning vine prunings or brushwood, fruitwoods and other woods (avoiding those that are resinous) or charcoal, and the only equipment needed is the grilling rack, on which you place whatever is to be cooked.

There are also, of course, effective modern grills which work by gas, electricity, infra-red rays, or which are simply a solid disc of iron, ridged on the top and slightly at an angle, with a handle on one side, which is put straight over the source of the heat, but nobody has yet managed to reproduce the wonderful effect of wood-smoke on food.

Red meat

The grill must be clean and very hot, and the meat should previously have been allowed to come to room temperature and then brushed rather lightly with olive or arachide oil.

The piece of meat is put on the grill and sealed on one side, then turned half-way round on the same side, to obtain a criss-cross pattern or 'quadrillage', and also to give it a light browning and form a crust on the surface. The other side is then treated in the same way.

Grilling 'bleu' – very rare

The meat is only left on the grill very briefly: test it by pressing it lightly with one finger on the crusted surface. If it offers no resistance, and remains soft, it is now 'bleu'. To make sure the meat is hot all the way through, take it off the heat, and put it on one side, covered, in a warm place for a few minutes.

Grilling 'saignant' – rare

If you leave the meat on the grill rather longer, a light beading of clear rose-coloured juice appears on the upper crust. Lightly press the meat with your finger. If it meets with a slightly pliant resistance, it is now 'saignant'.

Grilling 'à point' – medium rare

More thorough cooking needs a less fierce heat; keep the steak away from the hottest part of the fire; the upper surface will become heavily dewed with clear beads of juice. Pressing it with your finger, you will meet a firmer and stronger resistance than before; it is now cooked 'à point'.

Grilling 'bien cuit' – well done

If you prolong the cooking, the beads of juice become rosy-brown pools all over the surface of the meat. The finger now meets a very strong resistance; the meat is now 'bien cuit'.

White meat and poultry, game – kebabs (brochettes) – charcuterie

The fire should be less hot, but the grill itself must be well heated before the food to be cooked is placed on it. Meat should not be left too long on the grill, as it has a tendency to become dry. In fact it is essential to finish the cooking before the meat has lost its succulence. A chicken, for example, should not be allowed to whiten all the way through, but should still show a very pale rosy colour along the wish-bone, the sign of its being beautifully cooked, with a lovely melting quality to the flesh. Pierce the breast with a needle, which should slide in almost of its own accord, and allow a bead of almost colourless juice to seep out.

If the subsidiary ingredients of a kebab (brochette) include mushrooms, green or red peppers, bacon, etc. it is sometimes a good idea to part-cook them beforehand by blanching in boiling water (unsalted for bacon). The main ingredients – meat, poultry, offal, fish – are usually marinated before cooking (with oil, thyme, a bayleaf, parsley, slices of lemon, coarsely-ground pepper, etc. For marinade recipes see pages 88–9).

Fish

The fish, which are sometimes marinated in oil beforehand, are first brushed very lightly with oil.

Oily fish (sardine, mackerel, herring, salmon) are more delicious cooked on a grill as it helps them to lose some of their oiliness.

The grill is oiled to prevent the skin sticking when the fish are turned and should be:

> Very hot for small fish.
> Very hot for larger fish, which are usually given a quick turn on the grill to produce a criss-cross pattern or 'quadrillage' and then put in the oven to finish cooking.
> Hot for large fish which are to be cooked entirely on the grill.

Flat-fish (brill, turbot, skate, sole, plaice) should be grilled first on the white side and then on the dark.

Round fish (herring, mackerel, red mullet, bass, sardine) are put on the grill, all facing the same way, with their dorsal fins to the left, and then reversed.

Certain of the larger fish (salmon, hake, halibut) can be cut in steaks or 'darnes' before grilling.

However, rather than cutting a salmon into steaks (the old French word 'dalle', meaning tiles or slabs, is more appropriate) it can be cut lengthwise along the back into strips about 5 cm (2 inches) thick. The skin is important and must be left on. The skin is then slashed in a trellis pattern and the fillet placed skin-side down on the grill and cooked without turning. The grilled skin gives the flesh a pleasant smoky flavour and keeps it amazingly succulent and tender. If you like, the salmon can be marinated in a Scandinavian marinade (page 89) before cooking. Oysters, scallops, cockles, clams, and other edible shellfish all open of their own accord when put on the hot grill. They can be eaten just as they are, or with a few turns of the peppermill and some chopped herbs. (In the Roussillon, in south-west France, they cook snails, already purged and cleaned, directly on the grill; they are served with little sausages, also grilled, 'boudin catalan', bread dipped in oil and Roquefort cheese.)

Grilling – Shortcuts and sleights of hand

One of the properties of salt is to extract the juices from meat and so to prevent it from browning and forming a crust. It is therefore better to salt all smaller pieces of red meat half-way through the cooking. With larger pieces, where the meat is to be cut in slices after cooking, or with a large fish, which is going to be filleted before serving, it is essential to salt a second time after carving or slicing, adding at the same time some freshly-ground pepper. This is because the salt can never reach the heart of the meat or fish during cooking. This also applies to larger joints which are going to be carved: leg of lamb, rib of beef, loin of veal, loin of pork, saddle of lamb, and so on.

When you turn the meat during cooking, avoid sticking a fork into it, or you will lose valuable juices.

Larger pieces must be grilled more slowly to allow time for the heat to reach the centre, so keep them away from the hottest part of the fire. You can speed up the cooking by slashing the skin in several places, for instance with a leg of lamb or a fish.

If the piece to be grilled is uneven in thickness, keep the thin part further away from the heat than the thick part.

If you are not worried about excess calories, the grilled meat or fish can be brushed after cooking with a little brush or a 'plumet' (made out of a small bunch of chicken feathers) with a little oil or melted butter, which makes it shiny and appetising. Grilled meat or fish is usually served with the side which you have cooked first uppermost. After use and while still hot, the grill should be scoured with a metal brush to remove all the bits and pieces, which will otherwise burn next time you use the grill and give a bitter taste to the food.

Enclosed cooking on an open fire

The food is wrapped in greaseproof paper or aluminium foil and pushed into the hot ashes. The method is also called 'en papillote'.

Dry-cooking

Potatoes, mushrooms, asparagus, etc.
Rabbit, pigeon and smaller birds, etc. (decked with parsley, chives, thyme, bayleaves, etc.)
Apples, bananas, etc. (accompanied by vanilla pods).

Cooking with moisture

In this case a little liquid – red or white wine, or well-flavoured stock – is poured into the foil case or paper bag, before it is closed, to cover or moisten the food to be cooked. The parcel can then be put on the grill, or even in the glowing embers; the liquid will be absorbed by the food, and at the same time prevent the paper from burning.

Steaming over an open fire

Cover the grill with a layer of seaweed soaked in seawater, or with the wild succulent herbs (cresses, wild mint, brooklime) that grow in the watermeadows. Place the fish on top and cover with another layer of the same plants. It will not take more than twenty minutes to cook a sea-bass weighing 800 g (1¾ lb).

The lazy way of cooking on an open fire

Larger pieces of meat, such as a rib of beef, leg of lamb, etc., can be cooked on a fire without using a spit. All that is necessary is to brown the meat all over on the grill, giving it the usual grid pattern, and then to place it very close to the fire on hot, but not glowing, ashes, being careful to slip a piece of aluminium foil underneath it first. This method of cooking takes longer than any other, because the temperature is that of a very cool oven. Turn the joint from time to time, and don't be afraid to keep your leg of lamb there for two to three hours, according to its size. When you finally cut into it you will be staggered by its tenderness and the uniform rosiness of the meat.

Cooking in smoke on an open fire

For this method, a good fire is built up with a deep bed of glowing embers. Put the wire grill on, to heat up, and then brown the chosen food (meat, poultry, or fish) without cooking it.

As soon as this is done the embers are smothered with damp branches or sawdust (oak, alder, poplar or fruitwood, never resinous woods). The sealed food, on the wire grill, is then laid on top and covered with a domed metal meat cover or other suitable 'cloche' and the hot smoke gently cooks the food, permeating it with a myriad elusive woody scents and flavours.

(It is important not to confuse this method of cooking with the process of smoking fish such as salmon, trout and sturgeon, and poultry such as goose, chicken and duck, which after seasoning (and sometimes marination) are exposed to cool smoke. Tepid or cold smoking is similar to 'boucanage' or smoke-drying, one of the most important methods of preservation in the past.)

To sum up – cooking over an open fire can give one's imagination a free rein; all lovers of cooking and, in my opinion, all cooks worthy of their salt should dabble in this kind of cookery at least once.

ROASTING

The roast

Roasting a food means cooking it by the direct action of heat, without moisture, turning it frequently. It is another way of cooking by 'sealing and browning'. To obtain the sealing and crusting of the food, it is necessary, as in grilling, to coat the meat sparingly with fat and oil (one-third butter, two-thirds oil). Roasting can be done in the oven, on a spit and even, in an emergency, in a large uncovered cocotte or braising-pan.

Roasting in the oven

The oven (which ideally should have a vent for the fumes to escape), should be heated beforehand, the temperature depending on the type of joint to be cooked and its size. The temperature should be high enough (240°C/470°F/Mark 9) to sear the food thoroughly and conserve all its juices.

The food (meat, poultry, game, fish) is very lightly coated with fat and oil, put, unsalted, into the oven either straight in the roasting-tin (à la ménagère) or in a shallow oven dish called in France a lèche-frite, with a rack to keep the meat above the level of the fat or sauce, or else on a bed of broken and lightly-browned bones.

When the sealing and browning of the food is completed, slightly lower the heat of the oven and baste from time to time with the juices which collect in the bottom of the roasting-tin, until it is cooked. Now, it can be salted. White meats, poultry, game, and large fish, need a more moderate temperature, after the initial sealing, to cook successfully and retain their succulence.

Roasting on the spit

On a spit the cooking takes place over the fire, with the food uncovered, entirely surrounded by dry air, and rotating continuously. A roast cooked in this way is for some people more toothsome than one cooked in the oven.

The technique of cooking on a spit is the same as that of cooking in the oven, except that it is necessary to baste the joint more frequently with the juices which collect in the dripping tray below, to prevent the outside from drying out.

Roasting shortcuts and sleights of hand

• A joint, bird or fish, roasted on a spit or in the oven, is cooked by sealing and browning; the high temperature crusts the outside of the meat, imprisoning all its juices. These juices are driven inwards towards the heart of the meat through the complicated network of tiny blood vessels, allowing it to cook in its own juices without losing essential nutrients.

• If you cut into the joint immediately after it is cooked, you will find, first, an outside layer which is very well-cooked, then another less well done, and finally, the heart which is 'bleu', and contains all the juices, which will run out. *Therefore it is essential to let the meat rest.* If the meat is taken from the oven or fire and kept warm on a dish, covered with a domed meat cover, large bowl or a layer of aluminium foil, the fact that the heat is no longer exerting its inward pressure towards the centre of the joint will allow the juices, by an inverse process, to flow back towards the outer layers of the roast, giving it an even rosy or red hue according to the length of the cooking. At the same time, the muscular fibres, contracted by the heat, relax and expand again, giving the meat the desired tenderness. *It is therefore preferable to finish the cooking of, say, a leg of lamb an hour before you sit down with your guests.*

• Salt the meat during the cooking and salt it again as each slice is carved, adding a few turns of the peppermill.

• Avoid piercing the roast with a fork while it cooks.

• Certain of the drier meats, such as game, are improved by being covered with a waistcoat of bacon or pork fat, which is removed before the end of the cooking to allow the meat to brown. Hare, rabbit and game birds, such as pheasant and partridge, can also, if necessary, be larded by inserting little strips of pork back fat into the flesh with a larding needle.

• If certain parts of the meat, bird or fish are particularly delicate or easily burned (the knuckle of a leg of lamb, the tail of a fish for instance), protect them with aluminium foil.

The juices from the roast

The roasting juices are never better than they are at home, because the home cook instinctively keeps them simple and straightforward, whereas the professional cook often tries to make an elaborate sauce with them – something over-sophisticated, and, in my opinion, quite wrong.

Every piece of meat, poultry or game or even fish which has been roasted in the oven in a nice large dish, will have left in the bottom of that dish enough juice to make the gravy.

• Remember to coat the joint with two-thirds oil, one-third butter – 30 g (1 oz) for every kilogram (2¼ lb) of meat (oil can withstand higher temperatures than butter and helps to prevent burning).

• Put an unpeeled clove or two of garlic into the dish with the joint. Always preheat the oven.

After it has been cooking for ten minutes, baste the roast with the juices which have already collected in the tin, and turn it over when the top is nicely browned. Continue to baste, and turn frequently. Take the roasting-tin out of the oven, remove the roast and keep it hot on a covered dish; make sure that the juices covering the bottom of the tin are sufficiently concentrated (do not on any account allow them to blacken, as this gives the gravy an irreparably bitter taste).

Spoon off most of the fat (about a quarter should remain with the juices and will amalgamate with the gravy when boiled). 'Deglaze' the pan, that is, add twice as much water as you wish to make gravy and scrape up all the particles caramelised on the bottom of the tin with a spoon, dissolving them in the hot water. Allow the gravy to boil and reduce (leaving roughly two tablespoons per person).

Strain the gravy through a sieve, crushing the cloves of garlic with the basting-spoon if you like it slightly garlicky. You can, at the end of the cooking, incorporate several little dabs of butter which are mixed in by shaking the dish with a rotary movement to give the gravy a velvety texture (see page 68 for technique). A few drops of very good red wine vinegar will also bring out the character of the gravy.

How to improve the roasting juices

You can put a few broken-up veal bones round a joint of beef, or veal, or lamb bones round a leg or a loin of lamb, or one or two crushed chicken carcases round a chicken, and let them brown while the meat is cooking. When the time comes to make the gravy, you can replace the hot water with light veal, lamb or chicken stock.

SAUTÉING

Sautés are a quick method for making dishes in savoury sauces. Their instant cooking by sealing is similar in principle to grilling and roasting, in that it consists of the rapid cooking – in an open pan, a shallow sauté pan, or, failing that, a frying-pan, the bottom of which is covered with oil and butter, half-and-half (allow about 15 g ($\frac{1}{2}$ oz) a person) – of small pieces of meat, offal, poultry, game, fish, or vegetables, which on contact crisp and brown, enclosing all the juices. The difference lies in the finishing of the dish.

Sautéing – basic recipe

Once sautéd and browned on both sides, seasoned and cooked (bleu, saignant, à point, or bien cuit, as with grills, see page 35), take the pieces out of the pan and put them to keep warm on a hot dish. Pour off all the fat into a bowl. Deglaze, that is pour into the pan the liquid specified in the recipe – white wine, red wine, vinegar, madeira, port, sherry, vermouth, armagnac, or brandy – two tablespoons of wine or two teaspoons of spirits per person. The liquid is brought to the boil to dissolve the caramelised juices stuck to the bottom of the pan. Allow it to reduce by three-quarters of its volume. Add three to five tablespoons of concentrated veal, chicken, game or fish stock, according to what is being cooked. Allow to reduce by half.

Remove the pan from the heat and add nuts of butter (30 g (1 oz) per person), or some cream (50 g (1¾ oz) per person) blending them into the sauce by shaking the pan with a rotary movement. The sauce should never drown the meat, it must be a 'sauce courte' which just covers whatever you have cooked and spreads delicately round it. The meat or fish, once cooked, should be put on one side to keep hot, and should never be boiled in the deglazing liquid (spirits, wine, stock) which would transform the dish into a ragoût.

Two examples

Sautéd beef with red wine

Pièce de bœuf sautée au Bordeaux

For two people
Take the cooked piece of meat (500 g, about 1 lb, of entrecôte in a piece) out of the pan.
Leave a little fat in the bottom and soften a tablespoon of chopped shallots in it.
Deglaze it with 4 tablespoons of Bordeaux or other red wine.
Allow to boil and reduce by three-quarters of its volume. Add 8 table-spoons of concentrated veal stock (**page 58**).
Allow to boil and reduce by half. Add 60 g (2 oz) of fresh butter, and remove the shallots or leave them in, whichever you prefer.
Cover the piece of meat with the sauce. You can then decorate it with two rounds of poached marrow.

Sautéd veal escalope with cream

Escalope de veau sautée à la crème

For one person
Follow the same procedure but deglaze with vermouth or port without adding the shallots.
Add 2 large tablespoons of double cream.
Allow to reduce by half and lightly coat the escalope.

Shortcuts and sleights of hand

• The sauté method, to be absolutely perfect, should be done at the last minute.

• The size of the sauté pan should correspond with the quantity of meat to be cooked. If the base of the pan is not entirely covered by the food to be sautéd, the fat will rapidly start to burn in the space between the pieces of meat, and give a bitter taste to the sauce.

• Small pieces (tournedos, cutlets, escalopes) are cooked fast in an uncovered pan.

• Larger pieces, needing longer cooking (thigh and drumstick of chicken, pieces of rabbit), are cooked covered once they have browned.

How to succeed with fish à la meunière

Cooking 'à la meunière' is suitable for fish (trout, young pike, turbot, red mullet, sole, John Dory, hake, etc.) or foods such as brains; it is a form of cooking similar to sautéing, but is finished without deglazing. For example, take trout.

Truite à la meunière

Put butter and oil, half-and-half – about 20–30 g ($\frac{3}{4}$–1 oz) altogether in a frying-pan, or oval sauté pan roughly the size of the fish – this mixture ensures that the butter will not brown too rapidly. If you like you can add a whole, unpeeled, clove of garlic. The flavour of the garlic stays in the background, and adds subtle undertones to the dish.

Put the pan over the heat. Wipe the fish with absorbent kitchen paper to dry it. Season with salt and pepper and then lightly dip both sides in flour. Tap to remove excess flour.

Lay the fish in the hot fat. Let it cook over a gentle heat for about 4 minutes on each side, until it turns an attractive pale straw colour. Remove the fish and keep it hot on a serving dish. If it has been properly cooked, the small amount of butter remaining in the pan will still be pale gold. Increase the heat and add a further 50 g ($1\frac{3}{4}$ oz) of butter to transform it into 'beurre noisette'; the butter will become a golden-brown and stop 'singing' (because the water content has evaporated). Squeeze in the juice of a lemon which will make the butter froth up, and pour it immediately over the fish, having first removed the clove of garlic.

Fish should be cooked in the minimum of fat, and should keep its essential flavour of river or sea when it is cooked, rather than being used to mop up quantities of butter.

DEEP FRYING

Frying is a method which involves 'sealing and browning' and consists of plunging a food into a bath of hot fat or 'deep fat', brought up to a maximum temperature of 170°C/335°F (arachide oil, olive oil, lard, or rendered and clarified beef or veal kidney fat), and keeping it at this temperature until the food is cooked. Butter and margarine are not used because they break down and burn at these high temperatures. To make the process easier, the food to be cooked should be very dry, and the pieces small enough for the heat to penetrate to the centre fairly rapidly. It is also important to throw in only a small quantity at a time, so that the temperature of the fat is not suddenly lowered.

Deep frying without coating

Potatoes: pommes frites, straw potatoes, matchstick potatoes, chips of various kinds, soufflé potatoes.
Choux pastry: fritters of various kinds (beignets, pets de nonne).
Shortcrust: carnival fritters.
Bread doughs: brioche fritters.
Herbs: parsley, sorrel (these must be fried at a low temperature to conserve their colour).
Small birds: small chickens, ortolans, quails.

Deep frying after coating

1   In flour

Small fish, Larger fish cut in slices (steaks).
Method: Dip the food in milk, then season with salt, and dip in flour, tapping to remove surplus flour.

2   In breadcrumbs

Chicken, Fish, Veal Escalopes.
Method: The food is coated with beaten egg mixed with oil, and
then covered with dried breadcrumbs.

3   In fritter batter

Fruit fritters – (apple, apricot, banana), Vegetable fritters – (cauliflower, salsify), Meat fritters – (brains), Fish fritters – (brandade de
morue or purée of salt cod).

4   In flaky pastry

Truffles.

How to make successful chipped potatoes

The potatoes (a firm yellow variety for preference) are cut into sticks
of varying thicknesses – from 1 cm ($\frac{1}{2}$ inch) thick for Pont Neuf potatoes to 3 mm ($\frac{1}{8}$ inch) thick for matchstick potatoes – then washed
in cold water and dried in a cloth.
Heat the oil or fat in a deep-frying pan until it reaches at least 150°C/
300°F. Test the temperature by throwing a chip into the oil; if it
rises to the surface almost immediately (in twenty-five seconds), the
oil is ready.
Plunge the chips in the frying-basket and let them cook for seven
to eight minutes. To test them, take out one chip and let it cool.
If it is soft enough to crush between your finger and thumb, the chip
is cooked.
Take them out with a slotted spoon or straining skimmer (or simply
in the frying-basket) and turn them on to a dish covered with a cloth,
or with absorbent kitchen paper.
Raise the temperature of the oil to 170°C/335°F (but do not let it
start smoking) and plunge the chips back, in the frying-basket, mov-
ing it round so that the chips stay separate. Two or three minutes
is enough to make them golden-brown and crisp.
Take them out of the oil again, and put them once again on their
dish, on which you have put a fresh cloth or absorbent paper.
Sprinkle with fine salt, (or, better still, freshly-ground salt from a salt
mill) tossing them around.
It is the second dip in hotter oil which gives the chips their imper-
meable crust. They become puffed-up by the volatilisation of the
water trapped inside (the principle also used in making pommes
soufflés).

It is essential to be able to control the temperature of the oil, which should never rise above 170°C/335°F. (Use an electric deep-frying pan with a thermostat or a special thermometer.)

Editor's note   In England, Desirée or King Edward are two good chipping varieties.

How to fry small-fry successfully

A fisherman friend, whose unusual profession is the re-stocking of the lakes and ponds of France with fish, has given me all sorts of obscure information about freshwater fish, including a beautiful way of frying small-fry. He doesn't flour them before frying, but simply strings them, like pearls on a necklace, on a reed from the riverbank, leaving them in the sun for a moment to dry; then he fries them. The result is a unique lightness.

COVERED COOKING

Covered cooking means cooking foods by sealing or by exchange (sometimes both together) either in their own juices or in an aromatic liquid which intensifies their flavours. Aromatic steam is formed, penetrating the food, which in turn releases its juices to enrich the accompanying liquid.

Cooking in steam

This form of cooking is by sealing alone, since the enriched steam of a flavoured or plain bouillon is used to cook the food, without it giving anything back in return. It is also possible to use plain salted water as the basic liquid.

The method requires a vessel about the size and shape of the food to be cooked – a saucepan, a fish-kettle or a couscoussier are all suitable – which is quarter-filled with liquid – either flavoured or not, free of fat or not, according to what is required. A wire rack or pierced metal plate is put inside the pan over the boiling liquid allowing the steam to reach the food and cook it. If bouillon is used, any that remains can form the basis of an accompanying sauce.

There are also two simple and unique ways of steaming using the same principle.

First, the food to be cooked is placed on a bed of seaweed (for salt-water fish) or wild herbs (for freshwater fish) and covered over with another layer, and then moistened with a few tablespoons of boiling liquid to start the cooking and help induce the steam.

Second, you can follow the same procedure for a leg of lamb, or a ham, replacing the seaweed with sweet-smelling hay.
It is not possible, when cooking with seaweed or hay, to use the liquid as the basis for a sauce.

Cooking in a bladder or bag (en vessie)

Cooking in a bladder – a kind of cooking by exchange – is another form of steaming. The bladder is used as a cooking utensil in which the food, which may be stuffed or not, is hermetically sealed (chicken, pot-au-feu – and why not leg of lamb?). Put a few tablespoons of really good, fruity stock – either chicken or beef, to which can be added one or two tablespoons of port, madeira, the liquid from a tin of truffles, or a whole truffle, fines herbes, dried mushrooms – in with the food to be cooked. The pig's bladder should be well washed and turned inside out to prevent any disagreeable smells or flavours escaping or exuding during cooking.
The food is then slipped inside and the bladder is sewn up with a needle and strong thread. It must be pricked here and there with a needle to make tiny holes which act as safety valves – otherwise the bladder would come apart under the pressure. Then, *either*: submerge it in a pan of hot water, being careful to attach the end of the sewing thread to the handle of the pan, *or*: simply put it in the top half of a double boiler over steadily boiling water (a couscoussier or large steamer is ideal).
This method of steaming is rather quicker than others; a 2·5 kg (5½ lb) chicken will be tender and succulent in three-quarters to one hour.

Editor's note Instead of using a pig's bladder for cooking 'en vessie', it is much more convenient and almost as effective to use a plastic roasting bag. In this case do not prick the bag before cooking.

Cooking in paper cases (en papillotes)

Cooking 'en papillote' is another kind of cooking by exchange. Only the wrapping is different. The food may be **pre-cooked**: sweetbreads, boiling sausage, black pudding, andouillette, pork sausages, pig's trotters (either stuffed or plain), veal chop (covered with a mushroom purée or a mirepoix of vegetables), or **raw**: all fish and shellfish, small game-birds, ortolans, young rabbits, etc., slices (escalopes) of foie gras, potatoes, fungi (truffles, ceps, etc.), apples, bananas.

The food is hermetically sealed in a sheet of greaseproof paper or aluminium foil, oiled or not, which is folded round the food in the shape of an apple turnover or Cornish pasty, pleating the edges together so that the steam isn't lost.

Two examples

1. A whole peeled and cored apple, sprinkled with caster sugar and rum, together with half a vanilla pod and a nut of butter is enclosed in a little bag made of aluminium foil and pushed into the glowing embers (or into a moderate oven) – and cooked for 15 minutes.

2. A slice of raw salmon, seasoned, is placed on a sheet of greaseproof paper, and flavoured with a teaspoon of finely-chopped shallot and a tablespoon of vegetables – carrot, celery, mushrooms cut in julienne strips (see page 98); sprinkled with a tablespoon of fish fumet (page 62), a tablespoon of white wine and lubricated with a nut of unsalted butter.

Fold the paper over in the form of a turnover, and cook in a very hot oven on an oiled ovenproof dish for 6 minutes.

These two methods of cooking – 'en vessie' and 'en papillote' – are always very special, because they intensify and refine the flavours and aromas trapped inside.

In fact it is in these two methods – 'en vessie' and 'en papillote' – these 'made-to-measure' garments – that exchange during cooking is brought to perfection.

Cooking in a crust (en croûte)

The aim of this method of cooking, as in the preceding methods, is to concentrate the flavours of the food being cooked – to which can be added various other ingredients – herbs, mushroom purée etc., by covering it with a pastry crust, which may or may not be intended to be eaten, and which follows its contours exactly.

In an edible crust

In certain cases the food is sealed beforehand, so that the juices stay concentrated inside, and it should be cooled before enclosing it in the pastry. Examples: fillet of beef, saddle or leg of lamb (boned), chicken, capon, game (quail, woodcock, pheasant).

The meat or game is enclosed in pâte feuilletée (flaky pastry), brioche dough, shortcrust pastry or hot-water crust and baked in the oven. The food can also be put raw into any of the pastries mentioned above; this is the most usual way of doing a pâté en croûte. In either case the top crust should have one or two holes made in it, into which you insert little funnels made of paper, about the diameter of your little finger. These act as chimneys through which steam can escape, and prevent cracking and breaking of the pastry during cooking. The pastry is brushed with beaten egg before cooking to give it a good colour.

In a non-edible crust

The one used most frequently is made of a mixture of dampened coarse salt, and a little flour. You can, having first browned it in fat in a roasting-tin, bake a rib of beef (five or six ribs) entirely enclosed in a shell of salt, a slow and tenderising process.

Chicken baked in salt

Cover the bottom of a cast-iron casserole lined with silver paper, with a layer of coarse salt, put the chicken on top and bury it completely with another layer of salt.

Bake it, uncovered, in a hot oven; when the cooking time is complete (1 hour for a chicken of 1·5 kg ($3\frac{1}{4}$ lb)), ease the 'cake' of salt from its pot and take out the chicken, which will be just as crisp as if it had been roasted.

Cooking in clay

Among country people in some places, it is an old custom to use clay for cooking small birds and some poultry such as game fowl, bantams, guinea fowl and pigeon. These birds are gutted *without being plucked*, seasoned, sometimes stuffed and then covered completely with a layer of moist clay. They are then put in the embers of a fire, or baked in the oven (220°C/425°F/Mark 7), just as they are. The clay, during the cooking, forms a second, hermetically sealed oven. All that needs to be done before serving is to break the crust, in which all the feathers will have stuck, and release a bird as tender as you could desire.

BRAISING – RAGOÛTS

Braising is cooking 'by exchange' par excellence. First sealed all over in fat (except in the case of fish) the browned food, together with a mirepoix of vegetables, is moistened to half its depth with a well-flavoured liquid – light stock, wine, or concentrated veal stock (*see page 58*).

A heavy cast-iron casserole (or even better, a braising pan) is hermetically sealed to help the cooking, which should be *long, slow*, and *even*, gradually tenderising the fibres in the food and, with the help of the juices which run out, adding an extra succulence to the cooking liquid which becomes a rich and aromatic sauce.

How to braise successfully

Take, for example, a piece of braising beef (top rump). Ask the butcher to lard the meat (this operation consists of inserting six or eight long strips of pork back fat – about 1 cm (just under ½ in) across – along the grain of the meat, right through the joint to 'marble' the meat thoroughly). This fat will help enhance tenderness and flavour right through to the heart of the meat.

If you decide to braise an ox-cheek (not very popular, but still a marvellous piece for braising), its own naturally gelatinous texture is enough to keep the meat succulent without larding. Marinate your chosen piece of beef (*see* marinades **pages 88–9**) overnight to impregnate it with the aromas of the wine and the flavours of the vegetables and herbs.

Take the beef out of the marinade, wipe it dry with kitchen paper or a cloth, then heat a little oil in a heavy cast-iron casserole and brown the meat, together with, if possible, a knuckle of veal, to a deep golden-brown.

Once the meat has formed an even crust on the outside, remove it from the pan and put in the vegetables from the marinade, or even better, the same quantity of mirepoix together with a bouquet garni and two unpeeled cloves of garlic. Cook gently for 5 or 6 minutes, then place the piece of beef on top.

Add the liquid from the marinade, strained through a sieve, and boil it until reduced to half its original volume. Then pour in veal stock or light beef stock to come half-way up the sides of the meat.

Season very lightly, since the flavours intensify during the course of cooking. As the liquid comes to simmering point, cover the pan, and take care that the cooking remains gentle and even throughout. This can be done either in the oven or on the top of the stove, in which latter case put a wire gauze disc or simmering disc under the casserole. The meat is cooked when a skewer will pierce it effortlessly. Lift the meat on to a serving dish with the help of a skimmer.

The sauce, which has become very concentrated during the course of the cooking, must be strained and skimmed to remove every trace of fat. Use a ladle to pour the juices into a sieve, which can be lined with absorbent paper. Finally, let the sauce reduce further to obtain the exact thickness required.

General comments

Larger pieces of veal (saddle, loin, or whole leg) can be cooked in the same way, provided that the sealing is done without browning the meat at all (braisage à blanc). Veal sweetbreads (first soaked in cold water, but not necessarily blanched) can be sealed and browned or sealed 'à blanc' without being browned. Braised vegetables are usually put into an ovenproof dish, with fat or oil and herbs, and concentrated chicken stock or bouillon may be added. They are then covered with pork rind or fat bacon and cooked with the lid on.

The braising of fish is rather different – they are not cooked in a covered pot, but laid in a buttered dish and covered over with chopped shallots, moistened to half their depth with a half-and-half mixture of white or red wine and fish fumet **(page 62)** and cooked in the oven, covered either with oiled greaseproof paper or buttered aluminium foil.

As a rule, to keep it succulent, it is wise to baste the food several times with its own braising liquid during the course of cooking. Even when cooked for a very long time, braised foods always have a splendid flavour; the meat will fall to pieces and can be eaten with a spoon, 'à cuillère'. It was in this way that the Duc de Richelieu, towards the end of his life, somewhat toothless, but still a shameless gourmand, asked for his pigeons to be cooked.

Making a ragoût uses the same method as braising, but is used for meat or poultry that has first been cut in pieces (bœuf bourguignon, navarin of lamb, veal marengo). After having been sealed and browned, the pieces of meat are sometimes sprinkled with flour (which has preferably been browned in the oven, *see page* 66) to help thicken the juices.

POACHING

Poaching a food means immersing it in boiling liquid (water, light stock, stock, fish fumet, court-bouillon, or syrup). It can be done by putting the food into a cold liquid and bringing it slowly to the boil, into liquid that is gently simmering (shivering), or into liquid that is boiling furiously.

Starting with a cold liquid

This is cooking 'by exchange', with or without browning. Starting off with a cold liquid prevents sealing and allows the juices and flavours to be released to enhance the surrounding bouillon. Pot-au-feu is cooked in this way in order to impart the maximum flavour to the bouillon, somewhat to the detriment of the meat; so is concentrated veal stock **(page 58)** (although the bones are first browned in the oven) and fish fumet **(page 62)**.

If on the other hand you want to retain the moisture and flavour of the piece of food to be cooked, you should enrich the bouillon by adding seasonings, vegetables, wine, concentrated meat or fish glazes as seem appropriate. The food will thus be compensated for any loss of flavour. See for example the note on pot-au-feu **(No 98).**

Examples

Fish poached in court-bouillon or fish fumet; chicken poached in chicken stock; brains poached in a vinegary court-bouillon. If the food being cooked is going to be served cold, it is a good idea to let it cool in its own liquid, after cooking for a slightly shorter time than usual.

Pulses (haricot beans, lentils, split peas) which have first been scrupulously picked over and washed, and sometimes soaked beforehand, are started in cold water, which is then brought to the boil, skimmed, salted with coarse salt and flavoured with carrots, onions, a clove and a bouquet garni.

Starting with a hot liquid

This is cooking by sealing without browning.
Cooking in a hot liquid preserves intact practically all the flavour and nutritional value of the food.

Vegetables must be cooked uncovered in plenty of fast-boiling salted water.

Cooking fish 'au bleu'   For this dish the fish must start not only fresh, but actually alive. The fish is killed by a quick blow on the head, cleaned and sprinkled with vinegar (to give it its beautiful blue colour) and plunged straight into simmering court-bouillon.

Cooking boiled and poached eggs

Cooking fresh or dried pasta and rice   After cooking, take care to rinse the food in warm or even cold water to remove the starch, which would make it stick together.

Poaching fruit (pears, apples, peaches, apricots, raspberries, etc.) in a syrup, which is usually flavoured with vanilla.

Shortcuts and sleights of hand

How to cook haricot verts and keep their colour

It is important to know that some vegetables, of which the French bean is one, contain certain natural acids which on contact with heat start a chain reaction which changes their colour from a beautiful tender green to khaki. These acids are volatile and must be allowed to escape, so that they do not have time to alter the colour of the beans.

The best method is as follows: boil the water in a tinned copper or a stainless-steel pan (avoid metals which react with the water) and salt it with 20 g (¾ oz) of coarse salt per litre (1¾ pints). Throw the French beans into the fast-boiling water, they should be cooked as fast as possible and uncovered.

French beans should be eaten 'al dente', that is to say, offering a slight resistance when you bite into them. This method avoids over-cooking which destroys not only the colour, but the flavour and vita-mins too.

Very young French beans, freshly picked, are cooked in 4 minutes, a few minutes longer if they are larger and not so fresh. Scoop them quickly out of the boiling water with a slotted spoon and douse them in a bowl of iced water for 10 seconds; this immediately stops them from cooking any longer, and also removes some of the salt. They are deliberately oversalted to help cook them quickly and give them a fine colour.

How to cook tender asparagus

It is common knowledge that you don't eat the whole stalk when you are eating asparagus; the tips are fragile and the bottom of the stalk very stringy – so this part usually ends up left on the plate.

Here is a simple way of putting matters right: once you have washed and pared the asparagus, stand them, all tips level and pointing upwards, in a deep tin which is pierced all over with holes to make it into a sort of colander. All that is necessary is to lower the tin into boiling water in 3 stages, each one taking 3 minutes, or more according to the size of the asparagus. If it is very fresh and on the slender side, each stage will take 3 minutes, with first the ends, then the middles and finally the tips of the asparagus being cooked.

This means the ends, which are toughest, will have 9 minutes, the middles 6 minutes and the tips 3 minutes, and the sticks of asparagus will be evenly tender from top to bottom.

Thicker or less fresh asparagus will take longer, but the principle remains the same.

STOCKS, LIAISONS and SAUCES

The splendour of the French Cuisine springs from its sauces. A maker of sauces is a kind of magician; in his culinary alchemy he uses his basic 'stocks' as the rich medium in which he can make his sauces grow, and the velvety liaisons help him to bring them into full bloom. Sauces are one of the cornerstones of cooking.

THE THREE ESSENTIAL STOCKS

Editor's note

At one time stock-making in hotels and restaurants was a complicated ritual, involving much splitting of calves' feet and roasting of bones to obtain a few pints of what was admittedly a most savoury and richly-flavoured stock. But with the advent of the nouvelle cuisine with its light sauces and delicate flavours the most desirable stock became a far less concentrated affair. To the relief of most home cooks, the author has substituted in this book a quickly-made light dilution of stock cubes, a product which would have sent a shudder through the bones of any previous generation but which he assures us gives the necessary flavour without adding richness or heaviness. They can be used successfully in every recipe, but for those who prefer to make their own stocks this chapter gives the author's own recipes for the standard stocks and simpler variations on them.

Golden Veal Stock

Fond blond de veau

For one litre (1¾ *pints*) of stock

Ingredients
1 kg (2¼ lb) broken veal bones (shin and
    knuckle bones)
50 g (1¾ oz) uncooked ham
500 g (1 lb) beef trimmings
100 g (3½ oz) carrots ⎫
100 g (3½ oz) mushrooms ⎬ all cut into
50 g (1¾ oz) onions ⎪ mirepoix dice
15 g (½ oz) celery ⎭
1 chopped shallot
1 whole clove garlic, crushed
7 tablespoons dry white wine
2 litres (3½ pints) cold water
2 fresh tomatoes, deseeded
1 tablespoon tomato purée
1 bouquet garni
½ teaspoon chervil   ½ teaspoon tarragon

1   Brown the bones in a roasting dish in a very hot oven for 15 minutes, without fat ('à sec'). Turn them several times with a metal spoon whilst they are browning.

2   Add the ham, trimmings, carrots, mushrooms, onions, celery, garlic and shallot, return the dish to the oven and allow the vegetables to sweat (cook without browning) for 5 minutes.

3   Put the bones and vegetables into a saucepan or large deep pot, pour on the white wine and let it boil until it has almost evaporated. Add the cold water, fresh tomatoes and tomato purée, herbs and the bouquet garni.

4   Let it cook slowly, uncovered, for 3 or 4 hours. During this time, take great care to keep the surface perfectly clear of fat and scum, skimming regularly. Then strain the liquid, about a litre (1¾ pints), through a sieve into a bowl in which it can be kept until it is needed. To ensure that it is completely free of fat, put the cooled stock in the refrigerator for an hour or more. Any remaining fat will rise and solidify and can easily be removed.

Demi-glace

To give the stock made as described above a more substantial consistency, it can be very lightly thickened in the following way.

5   Stir a tablespoon of cornflour or arrowroot into 3 tablespoons of water or white wine. Gradually pour this mixture into the boiling veal stock, stirring with a wire whisk to obtain a smooth liaison.

6   Let it come gently back to the boil, and simmer until the stock has reduced by half. The stock will once again froth up at this stage, throwing up any remaining impurities, which will rise and form a greyish-brown scum on top; this can be skimmed off with a spoon.

Glace de viande

The same unctuous quality can be achieved without a thickening agent; it is simply a matter of simmering the basic veal stock gently on a very low heat, and skimming it regularly. The glaze is perfect when it will cover a spoon dipped into it with a smooth and glistening coat, and it will have reduced to about one-tenth of its original volume.

USES

Uses for basic stock

In many dishes served in their own sauce; either as the liquid used in the recipe, or as an extra ingredient in the cooking liquid: ragoûts, coq-au-vin, matelotes, fricassees, etc.

Uses for demi-glace

As a base for sauces in which either spirits or wine, heated and reduced, are used to dissolve, or deglaze, the caramelised juices which have stuck to the bottom of the pan in which meat was cooked, for instance, beef sautéd in red wine (*see page 43*).

Uses for glace de viande

Its light touch can improve a characterless sauce and make it succulent and generous.

Note   This stock can be made ahead of time and kept in a glass or plastic container to be used as needed. It will keep in the refrigerator for eight days, or in the freezer, or in small glass preserving jars (sterilised for 1 hour) which will keep some months in a cool place. Game stock and glace de gibier are made in exactly the same way as golden veal stock and glace de viande, but with bones and trimmings of game. In addition to the usual ingredients, five juniper berries and a sprig of sage are added.

Pale Chicken Stock

Fond blanc de volaille

For one litre (1¾ pints) of stock

Ingredients   1 kg (2¼ lb) of crushed chicken carcases and
    giblets (roasting or boiling chickens)
100 g (3½ oz) of mushrooms, sliced
100 g (3½ oz) of carrots, thinly sliced
1 chopped shallot
1 leek, sliced
1 small stick celery
1 whole clove of garlic, crushed
7 tablespoons dry white wine
2 litres (3½ pints) cold water
1 bouquet garni   1 clove
50 g (2 oz) onion, whole

1   Put the crushed carcases in a pan with the vegetables and garlic. Add the white wine, bring it to the boil and boil until it has almost totally evaporated.

2   Add the cold water, bouquet garni and the onion stuck with the clove. Allow to simmer gently, uncovered, for 3 hours, skimming frequently.

3   Strain the remaining stock through a conical strainer and put in a cool place until it is needed.

USES

As the liquid element in dishes cooked in pale sauces (blanquettes, fricassées, poules au blanc, etc.), in some soups and in the cooking of some vegetables (rice, lettuce, etc.).

Note   White veal stock is made in exactly the same way, replacing the chicken carcases with the same weight of veal bones (blanched by boiling 1 minute). Personally, I prefer the subtlety of chicken stock.

Golden Poultry Stock

Fond blond de volaille

This is made like golden veal stock **(page 58)** replacing the veal bones with browned poultry carcases (preferably duck). Do not forget to add a tablespoon of tomato purée.

USES

For the moistening of certain chicken or other poultry dishes (poulet au vinaigre, **No 73**, etc.).

Fish Stock or Fish Fumet

Fond ou fumet de poisson

For one litre (1¾ pints) of stock

Ingredients   1 kg (2¼ lb) fish heads and bones (sole, for
the best flavour, **or** turbot, brill, whiting:
avoid oily fish)
2 tablespoons arachide oil
25 g (1 oz) butter
100 g (3½ oz) onions, finely sliced
50 g (1¾ oz) mushrooms, finely sliced
1 chopped shallot
7 tablespoons dry white wine
1·5 litres (2½ pints) cold water
1 bouquet garni containing plenty of
parsley

1   Soak the fish bones in cold water to remove blood, unless they
are extremely fresh. If you use fish heads, remove the gills.

2   Sweat the vegetables and roughly-crushed fish-bones in the oil
and butter for 5 minutes without browning them.

3   Moisten with the dry white wine and boil until it has almost
totally evaporated.

4   Pour in the cold water, and add salt and the bouquet garni. Bring
it back to the boil, and allow to simmer, uncovered, for 20 minutes.
Skim the surface every time a layer of scum forms on the top of the
liquid.

5   Strain the fumet (there should be about 1 litre (1¾ pints) remaining) through a fine sieve into a bowl, pressing the bones gently with
a spoon. Cover and put in a cool place until it is needed.

Jellied fish stock – Glace de poisson
To obtain a concentrated fish glaze proceed in the same way as you
did for glace de viande. That is:

6 Simmer the fumet gently to reduce it, skimming frequently.

7 Remove from the heat when about 7 tablespoons of the syrupy, glossy liquid remain. Put in a cool place.

USES

Fumet is used to moisten fish dishes cooked with a small quantity of liquid, and braised fish. Jellied fish stock can be used in the same way as glace de viande, but with fish.

SIMPLIFIED METHODS OF MAKING THE BASIC STOCKS

Chicken stock cubes can not only be used effectively to replace classic chicken *fonds*, but they can also be used as a base for two other traditional stocks.

Simplified Veal Stock

Ingredients
1 tablespoon oil
1 large carrot
1 large onion
100 g (3½ oz) button mushrooms
1 calf's foot
bouquet garni, with plenty of parsley stalks
1 clove
1 large tomato
15 g (½ oz) dried fungi
1 teaspoon tomato purée
1 teaspoon arôme Patrelle (*optional*)
2 litres (3½ pints) cold water
3 chicken stock cubes
1 level teaspoon cornflour

1   Heat the oil in a saucepan and brown the carrot, onion and button mushrooms, all cleaned and cut into 1 cm ($\frac{1}{2}$ in) cubes.

2   Add the calf's foot cut into eight pieces, the bouquet garni, clove, tomato, cut in half, dried fungi (ceps, morels, etc.), one teaspoon of tomato purée and a teaspoon of arôme Patrelle. Add the cold water and the chicken stock cubes. Simmer, uncovered, for 2$\frac{1}{2}$ hours. Skim five or six times during cooking to remove the scum which rises to the surface.

3   At the end of this time, strain the remaining half litre (scant 1 pint) of bouillon through a sieve into a clean saucepan. Bring it back to the boil, whisking into the liquid a level teaspoon of cornflour mixed with a little water.
The veal stock is ready and it is almost demi-glace de viande. It is excellent! Put it in a covered bowl in the refrigerator and remove the layer of fat from the top on the following day.

Editor's note   Like the classic veal stock, this stock can be frozen, refrigerated for a limited period or stored in sterilised jars. Arôme Patrelle is a form of gravy browning only occasionally available outside France, and its purpose is mainly to colour the stock, so don't worry if you can't obtain it.

Simplified Fish Fumet

Ingredients	1 tablespoon olive oil
	1 large carrot
	1 large onion
	100 g (3$\frac{1}{2}$ oz) button mushrooms
	Broken-up bones of 6 sole or other firm white fish
	1 calf's foot, chopped in 8 pieces
	bouquet garni
	5 peppercorns
	1 clove
	2 litres (3$\frac{1}{2}$ pints) cold water
	3 chicken stock cubes

1   Heat the olive oil in a saucepan and add the carrot, onion and button mushrooms, all peeled and cut into 1 cm ($\frac{1}{2}$ in) cubes. Sweat the vegetables without letting them brown.

2   Add the broken-up fish bones, the calf's foot cut into eight pieces, the small bouquet garni, peppercorns and clove. Add the cold water and stock cubes.

3   Allow to simmer, uncovered, for 2 hours. Skim five or six times during cooking to remove the scum which rises to the surface. At the end of the cooking, strain the remaining 500 ml (scant 1 pint) of stock through a sieve.

This stock is astonishingly richly flavoured, and it can be diluted with 250 ml ($\frac{1}{2}$ pint) of water before use.

LIAISONS AND SAUCES

Liaisons using cereals and other starches

The required thickening of a basic liquid is obtained by the addition of starch found in various flours, which include wheat, maize (cornflour), barley, potato, rice and arrowroot. On contact with heat, in the presence of moisture, the starch will bring about the necessary thickening and create the liaison. This method of thickening sauces is disappearing, although, strictly speaking, it is, when subtly made, far more easily digested than any sauce thickened exclusively with butter and reduced cream. In any case, my personal opinions prevent me from using either of these methods in Cuisine Gourmande – and of course very rarely in Cuisine Minceur – so I am describing them mainly to show the basic principles involved.

Liaison with a cooked roux

Whether it is brown, light brown or white, a roux is a mixture of equal quantities of melted butter and flour, the combination of which will enable them to bind or thicken the chosen liquid. (If only half the quantity of butter is used, it will produce a sauce lighter in cholesterol.)

The change from white to brown roux is brought about by stirring it with a whisk over a moderate heat until it has reached the required colour. (The simultaneous heating of butter and flour together causes the browning of the roux.)

This can be achieved in another, better way which is both lighter and healthier – because it contains butter which has not been heated to high temperatures.

It is done quite simply, by melting the butter, as in the making of a white roux, and adding the same weight of toasted flour – that is, flour which has previously been spread out on a dish and cooked in a slow oven (150°C/300°F/Mark 2) to a chestnut-brown.

Sauce made with a White Roux

To make one litre (1¾ pints) of sauce

Ingredients   75 g (2½ oz) butter **or** 35 g (1¼ oz) for the
     lighter version of the sauce
   75 g (2½ oz) flour
   1 litre (1¾ pints) of liquid (milk, light
     chicken stock, light beef stock, fish
     fumet, etc., according to the dish)

1   Melt the butter in a saucepan (do not let it brown). Add the flour and whisk them together rapidly, to obtain a homogeneous paste.

2   Allow the roux to cool a little, then gradually add the boiling liquid, whisking all the time to prevent lumps.

3   Bring the mixture slowly back to the boil and let it simmer for 20 minutes; the sauce, rather heavy at the start, becomes lighter during cooking.

USES
Béchamel sauce, chicken velouté, fish velouté, sauce for civets, etc.

The process of 'crusting' – sprinkling with white flour and 'singeing' in the oven – pieces of meat which have already been sealed and browned, which is used in the making of ragoûts, stews (estouffades), and brown fricassees, works on more or less the same principle as the making of a roux.

Liaison with an uncooked starch

If a sauce seems too thin, it can be slightly thickened by adding a little potato flour mixed with cold water or white wine; gradually add the mixture to the boiling liquid to be thickened, stirring rapidly all the time. Add between two and eight tablespoons of potato flour to every litre (1¾ pints) of liquid. Allow to boil for about 15 minutes.

Liaison with a mixture of uncooked flour and butter or cream (beurre manié, crème manié)

To obtain the same result as in the above method, but giving extra velvetiness and flavour, a sauce can be thickened with beurre manié or crème manié. This is the equivalent of an 'uncooked roux'. Take either butter or cream, cold, mix it well with flour – one-third flour, two-thirds butter or cream – and add it to the simmering liquid in little bits, stirring all the time with a whisk until it has reached the required texture. It thickens almost immediately.

Liaison with egg yolks

This is done by beating egg yolks and mixing them with some of the liquid to be thickened. Return this mixture to the hot liquid and whisk over a moderate heat. On no account must it boil. Heating to more than 70°C (160°F) will coagulate the egg and cause it to separate.

USES

Velouté soups, sauce poulette, blanquettes, etc.

Liaison with blood or coral

Use the same method as above, replacing the egg yolks with blood from pork, game, fish (lampreys), etc., or the coral from lobster, etc. (sometimes mixed beforehand with crème fraîche or butter). Do not allow to boil. (*See* Sauce Américaine **page 77**).

USES

Coq-au-vin, civets of game, civets of fish, matelotes, homard à l'Américaine.

Liaisons using butter or crème fraîche

The liaison using butter is intended to thicken and, more important, to enrich the sauce and to make it more unctuous. It is simply a matter of slipping little dabs of butter into the sauce to be thickened, over a very gentle heat, whilst swirling the whole pan – a sauté pan in this case – round in a rapid circular movement.

Another equally effective method is to boil the two elements to be united (sauce and butter) over a fierce heat; this method will give a less creamy, but at the same time a glossier, sauce. To make a liaison with double cream or crème fraîche, all that is necessary is to bring the mixture (cream and sauce) to the boil and let it reduce.

A liaison using foie gras

Like the liaison using butter, this is a mixture of two-thirds tinned or freshly-cooked foie gras to one-third double cream, which is incorporated into the sauce, away from the heat, with a whisk.

The cream/foie gras mixture is made in a few seconds in a liquidiser, or simply by working them together with a fork.

Liaison by emulsion

A liaison by emulsion is a successful and homogeneous combination of two products that are naturally incompatible: for example, water and fat – oil, butter, cream, etc.

A third element – unrelated to either of the original products, but sympathetic to them – takes on the role of go-between, or catalyst and brings the two together. This element can be egg yolk, mustard, etc.

Cold emulsified sauces (mayonnaise and its derivatives) and hot emulsified sauces (béarnaise, hollandaise and their derivatives) are sometimes a bit risky for the cook at home; to make them less capricious, I have developed the detailed recipes you will find at the end of this chapter.

Liaisons using vegetable purées

This liaison, mainly useful in Cuisine Minceur, is made by adding a certain quantity of finely-puréed cooked vegetables to the liquid to be thickened. The vegetables are cooked either with the meat or fish whose sauce they are to thicken, or separately.

These purée-liaisons are rich in vitamins and are extremely digestible since the cellulose in the vegetables is broken down in the liquidiser after they have been cooked. The subtle and specific mixtures of vegetables which make these liaisons are based on completely new combinations of flavours.

It is also possible to experiment with new flavours based on selective combinations of fruits and vegetables.

Liaisons using yoghurt or fromage blanc

This is another liaison mainly useful in the art of Cuisine Minceur, but not used to excess, since yoghurt can leave a tart taste and non-fat fromage blanc can leave a slight sensation of dryness on the palate – which can to some extent be compensated for.

Other forms of liaison

Some liaisons are made with products made expressly for the purpose – such as alginates, made from seaweeds, or edible gums such as gum arabic, etc.

SOME STAR SAUCES FROM TRADITIONAL FRENCH CUISINE

Here are a few timeless recipes deeply loved in my country. First of all there is the ubiquitous Mayonnaise, then lightest of sauces, Béarnaise, and next their strongly-flavoured country cousin Beurre Blanc. L'Américaine, with its primitive taste, comes straight from the sea, and last, sensual and earthy, is Sauce Périgueux.

Editor's note Lighter, non-fattening versions of many of these sauces will be found in *Michel Guérard's Cuisine Minceur*.

Mayonnaise

Basic ingredients
1 egg
1 teaspoon dry mustard
salt
freshly-milled pepper (cayenne or white pepper)
200 ml ($\frac{1}{3}$ pint) oil (arachide, olive or whichever you prefer)
a few drops of vinegar (preferably wine vinegar or, if using olive oil, fresh lemon juice is better)

1 Separate the egg yolk from the white. Put the yolk into a bowl and add the mustard, salt and pepper – preferably white as it will not show up as black specks in the mayonnaise.

2 Beat with a whisk or stir with a wooden spoon. When the ingredients are well blended, pour in the oil in a thin stream, stirring energetically and flexibly all the time. As the sauce thickens progressively, gradually stir in the vinegar or lemon juice to thin it.

3 Beat in the remaining oil and taste for seasoning.

Shortcuts and Sleights of Hand

● Use egg yolks and oil at the same temperature (preferably room temperature).

● Do not add the oil too quickly.

● If the mayonnaise has curdled, mix it, a little at a time, into some French mustard.

● Keep the sauce in a cool place, but not in the refrigerator – the oil will seize up and the other ingredients will separate.

● Mayonnaise makes a succulent binding for macedoines of vegetables or meat. Made 'piquant', it is good with cold meat or fish, but it really becomes more interesting when other elements are added to give it character. Here are a few variations.

Sauce aïoli Mayonnaise made with olive oil, puréed raw garlic, and a little cooked, mashed potato.

Sauce antiboise Mayonnaise made with olive oil, garlic, coriander, chervil and parsley.

Sauce andalouse Mayonnaise with puréed tomatoes and little cubes of red or green pimento.

Sauce tartare Mayonnaise with capers, gherkins, onions, parsley, chervil and tarragon.

Sauce vendangeur Mayonnaise with red wine and chopped shallots.

Sauce vincent Mayonnaise with sorrel purée, parsley, chervil, watercress, chives and chopped hard-boiled eggs.

Béarnaise Sauce

For eight people

Ingredients for the reduction	7 tablespoons red wine vinegar 50 g (1¾ oz) chopped shallots 2 tablespoons chopped tarragon (out of season, use either tarragon preserved in vinegar (make your own) or frozen tarragon) 1 teaspoon chopped chervil salt 1 heaped teaspoon peppercorns, coarsely crushed
Ingredients for the liaison and for finishing the sauce	5 egg yolks 300 g (10½ oz) butter (plain unsalted or clarified) **or** double cream **or** whipping cream
Equipment	1 stainless-steel bain-marie 1 heavy saucepan or sauté pan of a suitable size 1 sieve

Depending on whether you have chosen to make the sauce with clarified butter, plain butter or cream, there are three different methods of procedure.

a To obtain clarified butter, melt the butter slowly in a pan, it will become transparent, like olive oil, and form a deposit of whitish milk solids on the bottom of the pan.

b When using plain unsalted butter, all that is necessary is to bring it to room temperature (20°C/68°F) without letting it get too soft, and to drop it in hazelnut-sized pieces into the 'reduction' ingredients. I like the second method better, because the presence of the milk solids gives the sauce a 'fruitier' butter flavour.

c The third recipe uses double cream or whipping cream – the latter gives a wonderfully light sauce.

In methods **b** and **c,** because the butter or cream is used at a lower temperature, the pan should be left over the heat rather longer.

1 Put the ingredients for the reduction (vinegar, shallots, pepper and herbs) in a heavy saucepan and bring them to the boil.

2 Reduce rapidly for 5 minutes (you should now have 2 or 3 table-spoons of liquid).

3 Allow it to cool, and in the meantime separate the egg yolks from the whites.

4 Add the egg yolks to the reduction, place the pan in a bain-marie over a gentle heat, and start beating the mixture vigorously with a whisk. Gradually raise the temperature to 65°C/150°F (the tempera-ture at which egg yolks start to coagulate – the back of your finger, when lightly dipped into the mixture, can easily stand the heat). The function of the whisk in this essential part of the operation is to keep the egg yolks at a uniform temperature as they coagulate, and to incorporate air to aerate the sauce and make it lighter.

5 The mixture now thickens and becomes creamy; when the strokes of the whisk leave clear traces on the bottom of the pan, start to incorporate – a little at a time – either the tepid clarified butter, the cold butter cut in little pieces, or the cream, whisking continuously.

Season and keep the pan, covered, over a gentle heat (60°C/140°F) on one side of the hotplate – take care not to let it stand in too hot a bain-marie. The sauce can either be served just as it is, or strained through a sieve, and freshly-chopped tarragon and chervil added.

Shortcuts and Sleights of Hand

• What can go wrong during the making of this recipe?

If the egg yolks become too thick, the temperature has risen too high; add a few drops of cold water.

• If the egg yolks froth up but do not become thick and creamy, the temperature is too low, increase the heat a little.

• Sauce béarnaise is a succulent accompaniment for: poached eggs, poached or grilled fish, grilled meat, and asparagus. It can also be varied almost infinitely by the addition of various complementary ingredients:

Sauce choron is béarnaise, enriched during or after whisking, with roughly-chopped tomato pulp (*see* **No 99**) – (two tablespoons of tomato to 300 g (10½ oz) of butter).

Sauce arlésienne has the same ingredients as choron, plus anchovy essence.

Sauce foyot is béarnaise enriched with two teaspoons of glace de viande (meat glaze).

Sauce paloise, a béarnaise in which the tarragon is replaced by fresh mint in the reduction ingredients.

Sauce tyrolienne is béarnaise in which the butter in the ingredients for the liaison is replaced by oil and a small amount of tomato purée to colour the sauce.

Sauce hollandaise is a béarnaise in which the reduction is replaced by plain cold water – one teaspoon – and the sauce is finished by adding lemon juice – half a lemon for every 300 g (10½ oz) of butter.

Sauce mousseline is a hollandaise sauce to which whipped cream is added at the end.

Sauce maltaise is a hollandaise sauce to which the juice and blanched, shredded peel of an orange are added.

Sauce moutarde is a hollandaise sauce to which mustard is added.

Note the action of whipping by hand with a wire balloon whisk, or with its modern counterpart, the electric beater, separates the molecules of the egg yolks and of the fatty substances in hot and cold emulsified sauces, enabling them to emulsify and become homogeneous and smooth. This whisking is of the greatest importance and can even, as in the following recipe for Beurre Blanc, allow you to leave out the main emulsifying ingredient, the egg yolk.

Beurre Blanc

For four people

Main ingredients	3 tablespoons water 3 tablespoons wine vinegar 2 heaped tablespoons chopped shallot 250 g (8¾ oz) unsalted butter at room temperature salt and pepper 1 teaspoon lemon juice
Equipment	1 thick sauté pan 1 small wire whisk

1 Put the water, wine vinegar and chopped shallot in a saucepan over a moderate heat. Bring to the boil and reduce for about 6 minutes until the mixture has a moist jam-like consistency. There should be about 2 tablespoons.

2 Lower the heat under the saucepan and allow the mixture to cool slightly.

3 Gradually add the butter, in little pieces, whisking energetically all the time. This process should take about 5 minutes, and the mixture will become creamy. Towards the end of the process, whisk a little faster, and slightly raise the heat under the pan.

4 Season, add the lemon juice and again lower the heat. When the sauce has cooled to 60°C/140°F it is ready to serve, but it can be kept warm in a bain-marie if it is not needed immediately.

This shorter method shows exactly how the tremendous agitation which takes place in a fast-boiling liquid is enough to make a spontaneous liaison between water and butter, taking the place of a whisk.

Beurre Blanc II

1   Use the same ingredients as before, but only evaporate two-thirds of the water and vinegar.

2   Allow to boil over a fierce heat and put a 250 g (8¾ oz) block of cold butter in the middle of the liquid.

3   This will gradually melt and be carried off into the seething liquid, thickening it as it does so.

4   The beurre blanc is now made, but to make it lighter still, add four tablespoons of cold water, at the last moment, whisking the mixture vigorously to a froth.

Suggestions for the home cook

* Some people strain the sauce to remove the chopped shallot, but I like to leave it as it is, because the shallot gives an authentic, rustic quality.
* To make this sauce even better, you can, after the butter has been added and the sauce cooled slightly, add either a heaped tablespoon of lemon or lime peel cut in julienne strips and blanched for 2 minutes in unsalted boiling water **or** 60 g (2 oz) fresh sorrel, shredded.

USES

Poached Lobster, Crawfish or Freshwater Crayfish **(No 57)**.
Salmon cooked 'en papillote' with braised vegetables **(No 60)**.
Grilled Sole with Oysters **(No 67)**.

Sauce Américaine

For six people

Main ingredients	1 raw lobster of 800 g (1¾ lb) 1 tablespoon olive oil 1 tablespoon arachide oil 1 tablespoon cold unsalted butter 2 diced shallots 1 diced carrot half an onion, diced 1 unpeeled clove of garlic, crushed whole 1 bouquet garni containing a sprig of tarragon 3 fresh tomatoes, skinned, deseeded and coarsely chopped 1 tablespoon tomato purée 3 tablespoons armagnac, **or** cognac 250 ml (scant ½ pint) white wine 250 ml (scant ½ pint) fish fumet **(page 62) or** water salt, pepper, a pinch of cayenne pepper
Ingredients for the liaison	50 g (1¾ oz) unsalted butter, crushed with the coral and tomali of the lobster **and** 1 level teaspoon flour (*optional*)
Equipment	1 large saucepan with low sides (sauté pan) 1 heavy-based saucepan

1 Kill the lobster according to the method described on page 215. Remove the tail and claws. Crack the latter with a blow with the back of a heavy knife to make it easier to remove the flesh after cooking. Cut the front part of the creature in half lengthwise. Discard the little gravelly pouch which lies inside the head. Remove the greenish part (intestines and coral) with a teaspoon and put it on one side in a small bowl.

2 Cut the tail into several slices.

3 Heat the oils and butter in a shallow saucepan (sauté pan). Allow the shallots, carrot, onion, garlic and bouquet garni to cook gently, without allowing to brown.

4 Remove them with a slotted spoon, draining them against the side of the pan to allow the oil to run back into it. Put in the pieces of lobster, sprinkled with salt and pepper, and allow the shells to redden.

5 Add the armagnac or the cognac and cover the saucepan: the alcohol should be boiled to reduce it by three-quarters and to impregnate the lobster with its flavour, without flaming it. (In my opinion, flambéing is pointless, and it also runs the risk of burning the delicate legs of the lobster, giving the sauce an unpleasant bitter taste.)

6 Cover the pieces of lobster with the mirepoix of vegetables, the fresh tomatoes, and tomato purée and season with salt, pepper and a pinch of cayenne. Moisten with the white wine and fish fumet. Allow to cook briskly, uncovered, for 10 minutes.

7 Remove the pieces of lobster (reserving the flesh for, perhaps, a lobster salad). Allow the sauce to boil, uncovered, and reduce to two-thirds of its volume.

8 Pour the sauce through a sieve into another saucepan. Incorporate the ingredients of the liaison – butter, coral, intestines, and flour (if used) – mixing them in vigorously with a whisk. Allow to boil for 2 minutes longer.

Note Like the three great stocks (*see pages 58–63*), this sauce can be made in advance and preserved (either by freezing or in sterilised preserving jars).
When made with lobster, the cost is high; to lower the price it is possible to use crab instead of that noble crustacean, the lobster, in which case it should be accompanied by bones of sole, heads of Dublin Bay prawns, freshwater crayfish, etc.

Truffle Sauce

Sauce Périgueux

For eight people

Basic ingredients
250 ml ($\frac{1}{2}$ pint) port
8 tablespoons armagnac or cognac
50 g ($1\frac{3}{4}$ oz) chopped truffles from a tin
4 tablespoons of the truffle liquid from the tin
500 ml (scant 1 pint) demi-glace (concentrated meat stock) (page 58)
50 g ($1\frac{3}{4}$ oz) unsalted butter (*optional*)
salt, pepper

1 Heat a saucepan, pour in the port and armagnac, bring them to the boil and reduce by three-quarters of their original volume.

2 Add the juice from the truffles, the chopped truffles, and the demi-glace. Season with salt and pepper and allow to cook over a low heat, simmering gently for 15 minutes. You can, if you like, incorporate the butter just before serving, adding it in little bits and swirling the pan round to mix it in.

Sauce au vin rouge de Bordeaux is made in the same way, but replacing the port and armagnac with the equivalent quantity of claret, replacing the truffle juice with a tablespoon of tomato purée and adding 2 finely-chopped shallots to the red wine.

Suggestions for improving your sauces

* *For a sauce which should be well-flavoured, but seems rather flat.*
Add a squeeze of lemon juice or a few drops of vinegar – something
sharp to liven it up.

* *For a sauce which has become tart or bitter, during cooking.* Add
a sprinkling of sugar, or a few drops of a fortified wine such as port,
and, if necessary, a little cream.

* *For a sauce which seems to lack character and is not a good colour.*
Add a little glace de viande **(page 58)** or glace de poisson, jellied fish
stock **(page 62)**, according to the dish, a turn or two of the peppermill
and sometimes a few drops of armagnac or cognac.

* When using wine in the making of a sauce, it is sometimes better
to reduce it by boiling, both to decrease the volume and evaporate
the alcohol. With white wine, it also eliminates any acidity, with red
wine it concentrates the bouquet. Spirits need the same treatment,
but on the other hand fortified wines, which have a more fugitive
flavour, are often better if added at the last moment.

Points to Remember

* In sauces based on a roux, lemon juice should be added after the
thickening and cooking – added at the beginning it will prevent the
liaison from working by slackening the mixture.

* In emulsified sauces, on the other hand, the lemon juice actually
encourages the coagulation of the egg yolks.

* The acids naturally present in most vegetables (with the exception
of spinach, cabbage and cauliflower) make milk unsuitable as a cooking medium, as they sour and curdle it.

Asparagus-filled Pastries with Chervil Butter **(No 38)** Freshwater Crayfish Pastries with Onions **(No 42)** Snails in Pots **(No 34)**

Salads, first courses and foie gras

Smoked Fish Salad with Crudités **(No 28)** Gourmande Salade **(No 24)** Duck-Breast
Ham Salad **(No 27)**

SPICES, HERBS and

MARINADES

Il est des Parfums frais comme des
  chairs d'enfants,
Doux comme des hautbois, Verts
  comme des Prairies
Et d'autres, Corrompus, Riches et
  Triomphants
Et chantant les transports de l'Esprit
  et des Sens ...

Charles Baudelaire
Les Fleurs du Mal

The Fascinating Flavours of Spices and Seasonings

Spices, seasonings and herbs, members of a vast family steeped in history, have long been sought and found in the most distant corners of the earth. But whether they are exotic aliens or domesticated natives, it is they that provide the poetry in cooking, with their scents of earth and sea, their fiery heat or cooling freshness, pungency or acidity, bitterness or sweetness.

Salt

Whether it's coarse or fine, sea-salt or rock-salt, this is the only mineral seasoning. It is the epitome of seasonings and is used everywhere and in almost every dish.

Acid flavourings

Lemons and their juice, wine vinegars made with red or white wine, sherry, champagne, alcohol etc., or fruit vinegars such as cider or verjuice (the juice of unripe grapes). All fruits and vegetables preserved in vinegar such as gherkins, pimentoes, capers, cherries, etc., come into this category.

Sweet flavourings

Sugar in all its forms – and its relations – honey and jam together with its partners; vanilla, cinnamon, chocolate, coffee. Most often used in the making of pâtisserie and puddings but sometimes in ordinary cooking; for example the cooking of peas, in the sweet-sour sauces beloved in the Far East, piquant sharp sauce where caramel is reduced with vinegar (used in canard à l'orange) and in the sharp fruit juices such as redcurrant used to intensify the flavour of game.

Vanilla deserves a special mention for its elusive and delicious flavour.

Store seasonings

These are carefully measured mixtures of different spices, which give their flavour to the finished product.

Curry powder: a harmonious blend of chilli, coriander, turmeric and other spices, it is used in 'Indian' dishes with rice, chicken or lamb.

Chilli powder

Soy sauce
English sauces: Worcestershire, tomato ketchup.

Wine and spirit flavourings

Wines and spirits, reduced and concentrated by evaporation, which accentuates and improves their flavours.

Pungent flavourings

Garlic, spring onions, chives, mustard, horseradish, radishes, leeks, onions, shallots.

When you want to flavour a roast with garlic, rather than spiking it with slivers of garlic, place unpeeled cloves under and alongside the joint, in the roasting-pan; the bouquet will be more subtle and kinder to the digestion.

Chopped garlic can be preserved in oil.
Chopped shallot can be preserved in white wine.

Spices

Pepper

Ground or whole, crushed, white or black (retaining the outer skin), pepper is used in nearly every kind of dish. It is best added near the end of the cooking so that it keeps its aroma.

Fresh or green peppercorns, subtle, exotic and mild, give a flavour all their own to any dish in which they are used. Dried, they can be used in much the same way as ordinary peppercorns and ground in a peppermill.

Paprika

Paprika, made from a certain type of red pimento, is used in Hungarian-style dishes such as goulash and for heightening the natural colour of roasted lobsters and other crustaceans.

Cayenne

Like paprika, cayenne is made from a type of red pimento. It replaces pepper or intensifies it in sauces such as Sauce Américaine, and is used where dark flecks of black pepper would spoil the look of the sauce – for instance in mayonnaise.

Nutmeg and mace

Nutmeg, the fruit of the tropical nutmeg tree, and mace, which is the dried aril, or outer covering, of the nutmeg, both have a strong full flavour. Nutmeg is usually used whole and grated, while mace is often used in powdered form. I prefer the latter for its flavour, which lies somewhere between nutmeg and cinnamon. Used with a light touch, it is the ideal complement for white sauces, pâté mixtures and stuffings and in a marinade for foie gras.

Saffron

Made from the styles of the saffron crocus, saffron should be a deep orange colour, without white streaks. The flavour is both muted and powerful, with full-bodied aroma. It is a particularly happy accompaniment to bouillabaisse, rice, fish soups and to any dish to which you want to give a distinctive flavour, chicken with mussels, for instance.

Cloves

The dried flower-buds of the clove tree, with powerful antiseptic properties and a strong flavour which should never be over-used. An onion stuck with a clove is useful to flavour certain stocks, blanquettes, pot-au-feu, consommés and marinades.

Coriander

Very useful for vegetables 'à la grecque'. I like to use coriander in Sauce Vierge **(No 3)** to accompany Bass cooked in Seaweed **(No 61)**.

Ginger

Except in the Orient, ginger is little used in savoury cooking. It is excellent in puddings and preserves.

Cinnamon

Young inner bark of a large Sri-Lankan tree. A sharp, hot sweet spice, which curiously, when mixed with sugar, 'warms up' certain dishes.

Herbs and Aromatics from the Green Domain of the Kitchen Garden

I am very fond of the kitchen garden, that green, secret and orderly place, a favourite refuge at every season of the culinary year. It is there that we find the magic touches that add freshness and humour to the most ordinary dish.

Parsley

Curly parsley – though it turns up all too often as a garnish – is delicious deep-fried and served with fried fish or rissoles. Personally, for flavouring I prefer to use the flat continental type of parsley because it has a finer and more pervasive bouquet. Either kind can be chopped finely or coarsely, and the stalks are used in a bouquet garni.

Chervil

Chervil, with its fine and delicate flavour, can be used, chopped, in a 'fines herbes' mixture, and the sprigs or little leaves are added to soups and even to salads.

Tarragon

A marvellous herb reminiscent of monastery gardens. Chopped with other herbs, it goes well with salads, and it is used in Américaine and Béarnaise sauces. It can be preserved in vinegar.

Basil

Its individual and heady flavour makes basil a herb to use sparingly, but what an inimitable 'musky' sunsoaked flavour! Its most traditional role is the traditional southern 'pistou' soups from Provence and Italy, but it has many other possibilities; especially in Italian cooking where it is served with pasta. It can be liquidised with a little olive oil and then sterilised in glass jars, or simply stored in the refrigerator. This method, using arachide oil, can also be used for parsley.

Rosemary

A Mediterranean herb, resinous and heavily scented. A useful ally in Cuisine Minceur, it should be used with moderation in the classic cuisine – with roast pork, in civets and in marinades. Don't overdo it. It shouldn't be used in great branches to flavour a fish, for example, as it will overpower the flavour.

Marjoram

Valued in the past for its medicinal virtues, marjoram is a delicate aromatic herb, with many uses, especially in Cuisine Minceur.

Mints

The fragrance and flavour of the mints – wild mint, spearmint and peppermint – have a piercing freshness. They are used on their own in desserts or in small quantities mixed with other herbs. Much prized in the Arab world, they make an excellent infusion, of particular interest in Cuisine Minceur. Mint sauce served with lamb or mutton is of course a classic in English cooking.

Thyme and wild thyme

One of three or four old friends in a bouquet garni. Strewn sparingly on roasts, especially on rabbit, thyme gives the gravy a pleasant delicate taste. Its flavour of flower borders and, in the case of the Mediterranean wild thyme, its fragrance of sunbaked stone, goes well with lamb and with some pâtés and stuffings.

Bay

Another old favourite for the bouquet garni. It is extremely strong, so half a leaf is often enough, especially if fresh. Treat cautiously, as in large quantities it can affect the heart.

Fennel and Dill

The delicate fresh leaves and the dried stalks perfume grilled fish, bouillabaisses and other fish soups. The swollen bulb of the fennel is the edible part of the plant and can be used in the same ways as celery or served 'à la grecque'.

Sage

A muted autumnal flavour, sometimes rather bitter, which goes well with fresh broad beans and with petits pois. It can be used to enliven roast or grilled pork and to wrap up small birds such as quails, before roasting. The young shoots can be eaten in salads.

Juniper

A restrained and genuine flavouring for game marinades; a traditional partner of choucroûte and used to give Genever gin its famous pungency.

Bouquet Garni

A symbol of French cooking, and frequently found in my recipes. It is made up of parsley stalks and sparing quantities of thyme and bayleaf, with a small sprig of celery, basil, tarragon, chervil or other herbs, depending on your own ideas at the time. The little bundle is tied with a twist of cotton and removed before the dish is served.

Remember ...

* All flavourings must be treated with tact and judgement. Excessive use of herbs and spices unbalances a dish, often irreparably.
* Flavour must not be allowed to swamp the taste of the main ingredient whether it be fish, meat, poultry or vegetable, but must enhance it.
* Heat intensifies flavour.
* Some herbs which were originally mainly medicinal are also used in cooking, especially in Cuisine Minceur. For instance, lime-blossom, hyssop, rosemary, thyme, mint, marjoram, etc.
* In pâtisserie, cocoa, coffee, vanilla, cinnamon, orange and lemon peel are the basic flavourings.

These few pages have been far from an exhaustive treatment. Most countries, including France, have a far wider range of herbs and flavourings than I have room to mention here.

Editor's Note

For further information on herbs and spices the following excellent books are invaluable: *A Modern Herbal* by Mrs M. Grieve (Penguin Books, 1976); *Herbs, Spices and Flavourings* by Tom Stobart (Penguin Books, 1977); *The Oxford Book of Food Plants* (Oxford University Press, 1969).

Marinades

In the past, the use of marinades in cooking was an ingenious way of preserving meat, making it tender and improving its flavour. Today these 'spiced baths' are still used to flavour such things as venison and other game and some meats, tenderising the flesh in the first case (with game animals, wild boar, venison, etc.) and in the second case (beef, mutton, etc.) imparting a hearty venison flavour to the meat.

The meat, whilst it is slowly soaking up the flavours of the marinade, should be kept cool, and turned over from time to time. The marinade is often used later, as the liquid for the sauce which will accompany the food which has been soaked in it.

Classic Uncooked Marinade

Ingredients
1 onion
2 shallots
half a carrot
a stick of celery, the length of your little finger
thyme, a bayleaf
parsley stalks
1 clove garlic
2 cloves
6 peppercorns
6 coriander seeds
a pinch of salt
500 ml (scant 1 pint) white **or** red wine
10 tablespoons wine vinegar
6 tablespoons oil

Slice the vegetables thinly and make a bed of half the vegetables and garlic, herbs and spices in the bottom of a suitable dish.
Put the meat on top and cover it with the rest of the vegetables, etc. Moisten it with red or white wine (depending on the recipe), vinegar and oil.

Classic Cooked Marinade

The cooked marinade speeds up the process of tenderising the meat. It is made with the same ingredients as the uncooked marinade. But the vegetables (onions, shallots, carrot, celery) must first be sweated in the oil, then add the wine, vinegar, herbs and spices and allow to simmer for half an hour.

Allow the marinade to cool before putting in the meat.

Tahitian Marinade

Raw fish prepared in the Tahitian manner are macerated in a little lemon juice and pepper which has the effect of partly 'cooking' them. Fish can also be marinaded before grilling in a mixture of oil, thin slices of peeled lemon, thyme, bayleaf, fennel, parsley stalks, basil, finely-sliced onion, chopped shallot, salt, pepper, saffron, etc.

Scandinavian Marinade

The Scandinavian way of marinating fish is equally fascinating – it consists of putting a layer of fresh dill between two boned, but not skinned, fillets of fish (salmon for example) and burying them in a mixture of salt, sugar and black pepper, and pressing beneath weights for twenty-four hours.

The exact ingredients are as follows: 225 g (8 oz) coarse salt, 300 g (10 oz) granulated sugar, 1 bunch of dill, 25 g (scant 1 oz) coarsely-crushed black peppercorns.

Guide to the practical

explanations and

suggestions contained

in this book

Sauces

How to improve the juices from a roast, page 42
Correcting your sauces, page 79
Making successful mayonnaise, page 70
Making successful béarnaise, page 72
Making successful beurre blanc, page 75
Making a lighter beurre blanc, page 76 and **No 67**
Making successful beurre rouge, **No 32**
Giving your sauces a fresh quality, **Nos 19, 40, 42**
Making a freshwater crayfish sauce without crayfish, **No 7**
Making a truffled butter sauce without truffles, **No 5**
Clarifying a jellied consommé, **No 20**

Fish, Shellfish and Crustaceans

How to be sure of quality and freshness, page 94
Cooking a fish 'à la meunière', page 44
Quick-smoking small fish, **No 28**
Making a melting fish terrine, **No 37**
Making a successful fish mousse, **No 53**
Cooking fish in seaweed, **No 61**
Cooking fish in salt, **No 62**
Shelling crayfish and lobster tails, **Nos 21, 29**
Killing crustaceans humanely, **No 57**
Filleting raw fish, illustration on page 97

Poultry and Game

Cooking poultry in a bladder or bag, page 48
Making a duck ham at home, **No 27**
Choosing a tender duckling, **No 36**
Boning poultry winglets, **No 70**
Telling whether a chicken is cooked, **No 74**
Detaching and slicing fillets of duck breast, **No 77** and see illustration
  on page 95
Keeping roast poultry and game moist, **No 83**
Choosing a tender young partridge, **No 84**
Preventing the flesh of hares and rabbits shrinking during cooking,
  No 85

Meat and Offal

Grilling successfully, page 34
Serving a tender roast, page 40
Choosing the raw livers for fresh foie gras, **No 44**
Keeping foie gras in the refrigerator, **No 45**
'Ripening' a duck or piece of meat, **Nos 78, 92**
Recognising good quality veal, **No 87**
Grilling out of doors, **No 90**
Grilling without a grill, **No 91**
Cooking a succulent ham, **No 96**

Vegetables

Using garlic as a vegetable, **No 76**
Peeling asparagus, **No 38**
Making a julienne of vegetables, illustration on page 98
'Turning' miniature vegetables, illustration on page 96
Cooking tender asparagus, page 55
Keeping French beans green, page 54
Replacing chestnut purée as an accompaniment to game, **No 102**
Making successful chips, page 46
   and keeping them crisp, **No 111**
Making successful potato purée, **No 112**
Preventing sliced potatoes from discolouring, **No 113**
Preparing artichoke hearts, **No 108**

Puddings

Making successful flaky pastry, **No 118** and illustration on pages 378–9
Making well-shaped choux puffs, **No 119**
Unmoulding babas easily, **No 120**
Making successful Crème Chantilly, **No 121**
Correcting a curdled Crème Anglaise, **No 128**
Making a quick pancake batter, **No 125**

How to be sure of the quality and freshness of fish, shellfish and crustaceans

1 Shellfish: Scallops, oysters, mussels, cockles etc.

- should smell freshly of the sea, with a hint of iodine;
- when knocked against each other, should give a dull sound, showing that the flesh is still swollen with sea water, and fills the entire shell;
- should be tightly closed, and if they are partly open, should immediately snap shut when touched;
- when they are opened and the top shell is removed, the wavy fringe round the edge should contract reflexively.

2 Crustaceans: Lobsters, crawfish, crabs of all kinds, freshwater crayfish and Dublin Bay prawns

- should be alive and vigorous, and lobsters and crawfish should flex their tails briskly when picked up;
- with two specimens of equal size, the heavier one is usually fresher;
- a female or hen lobster is at its most succulent and tender when it is carrying eggs.

3 Fish

- sea fish should smell freshly of the sea, with a hint of iodine;
- when just caught, the fish should be stiff;
- the flesh should be supple and luminous and the colours bright;
- a fresh fish will look you straight in the eye, and the eye, clear and brilliant, will completely fill the socket;
- the gills should be difficult to open and should be filled with damp fronds, brilliant rose-pink, clear red or reddish chestnut, according to the variety of fish;
- the flesh should not be soft, but firm and supple, and whether red or white fleshed, should shimmer with iridescence;
- finally, provided they have all these qualities, you should never soak fish in running water to whiten the flesh, as some people misguidedly do.

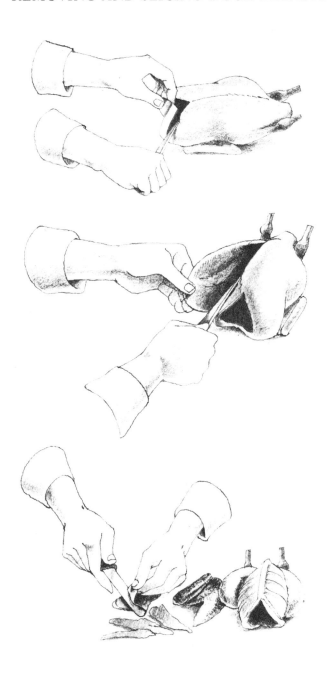

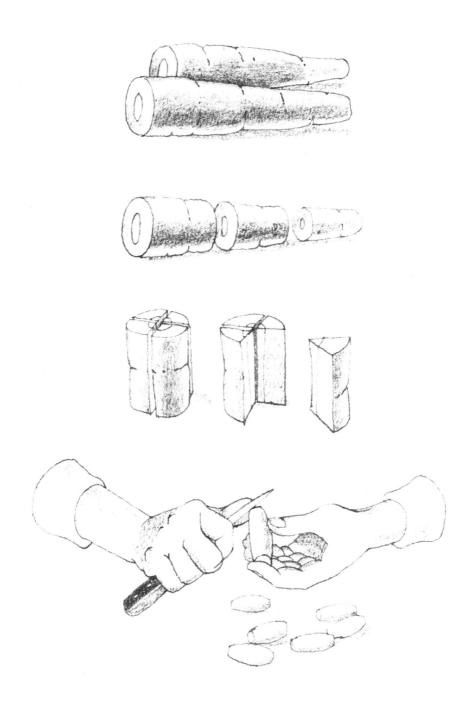

FILLETING A FISH

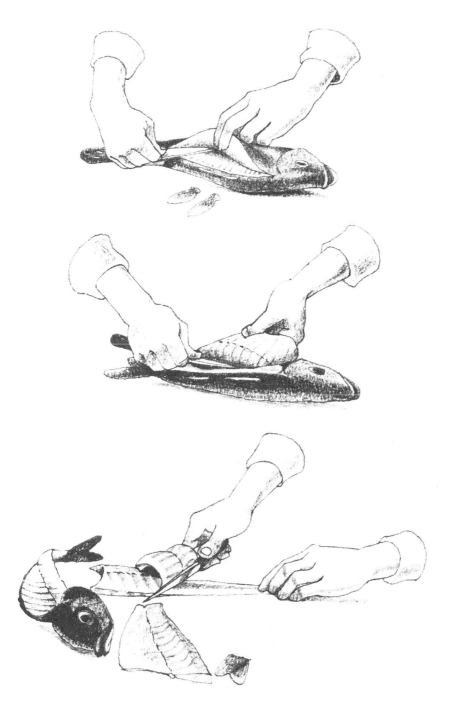

MAKING A VEGETABLE JULIENNE

SAUCES

1 Rouille

'The flavour of the Midi'

For six people

Main ingredients

2 eggs
1 litre (1¾ pints) water
2 tinned anchovy fillets preserved in oil
1 peeled clove of garlic
1 teaspoon tomato purée
2 raw egg yolks
1 teaspoon mustard
salt and white pepper
250 ml (scant ½ pint) olive oil
1 teaspoon lemon juice
¼ teaspoon harissa
a pinch of saffron

Equipment 1 liquidiser

Uses

Poached Lobster, Crawfish or Freshwater
    Crayfish **(No 57)**
Salt Cod Bouillabaisse **(No 66)**
'Fish-Market in a Casserole' **(No 68)**
All grilled fish

---

1 Check that the eggshells are not cracked, bring the litre (1¾ pints) water to the boil and carefully lower in the eggs. Allow to cook for 8 minutes. Remove with a slotted spoon and cool under running water. Remove the shells and take out the yolks. (The whites are not used in this recipe.)

2 Blend the hard-boiled egg yolks in the liquidiser for 1 minute, adding the anchovy fillets, garlic and tomato purée. Transfer to a small bowl and keep on one side.

3 Put the raw egg yolks into a larger bowl with the mustard, salt and pepper and mix well with a whisk. Then, add the olive oil in a thin stream, whisking energetically all the time. As the sauce thickens, add the lemon juice a little at a time to thin it out.

4 When all the oil has been absorbed, finish the 'mayonnaise' by adding the harissa, saffron and hard-boiled egg yolk mixture (2). Taste for seasoning.

White pepper is used instead of black to avoid black flecks spoiling the appearance of the sauce.

2 Court-Bouillon or Nage

'An aromatic poaching liquid for fish'

For four people or approximately 1·5 litres
(2½ pints)

Main ingredients	2 medium-sized carrots white part of 1 leek 30 g (1 oz) celery 60 g (2 oz) small onions 2 shallots 1·25 litres (2¼ pints) water 35 g (1¼ oz) coarse salt 5 strips of lemon peel 2 cloves of garlic, unpeeled 25 green peppercorns 1 clove 6 parsley stalks ⎫ ½ bayleaf ⎪ bouquet garni 1 small sprig of fennel ⎬ 1 sprig of thyme ⎭ 250 ml (scant half pint) dry white wine
Equipment	1 large stainless-steel saucepan
Uses	Freshwater Crayfish Soup **(No 21)** Roast Lobster **(No 56)** Poached Lobster, Crawfish or Freshwater Crayfish **(No 57)** Seafood Pot-au-Feu **(No 69)**

1   Peel and wash the vegetables. Channel the carrots with a special channelling knife (optional). Cut all the vegetables into paper-thin slices, and put them into the saucepan.

2   Add the water, salt, lemon peel, garlic, green peppercorns, clove and bouquet garni. Bring to the boil and simmer very gently, un-covered, for 30 minutes. The vegetables should be still slightly firm at the end of this time.

3   Add the white wine and boil for 30 seconds. Added at the end of the cooking, the wine adds a desirable freshness and body.

4   Keep in a cool place or in the refrigerator until needed.

3 Sauce Vierge

'A pure and simple olive oil sauce'

For six people

Main ingredients	3 whole tomatoes 2 cloves of garlic, unpeeled 2 tablespoons freshly-chopped chervil 2 tablespoons freshly-chopped parsley 1 tablespoon freshly-chopped tarragon 8 coriander seeds, crushed 200 ml ($\frac{1}{3}$ pint) olive oil salt and pepper
Equipment	1 stainless-steel saucepan
Uses	Poached Lobster, Crawfish or Freshwater Crayfish **(No 57)** Bass Cooked in Seaweed **(No 61)** Sea-Bream in a Salt Crust **(No 62)** 'Fish-Market in a Casserole' **(No 68)** Seafood Pot-au-Feu **(No 69)**

1   Remove the stalks from the tomatoes and, to make them easier to peel, plunge them in boiling water for several seconds, according to how ripe they are. Refresh them in iced water and peel with a vegetable knife.

2   Cut them in two and press them in the palm of your hand to expel pips and excess moisture. Then chop into little dice, $\frac{1}{2}$ cm ($\frac{1}{4}$ inch) across.

3   Mix the diced tomato with all the other ingredients in a bowl and, if the sauce is to be served hot, heat through in a bain-marie.

Suggestions for the home cook

* This sauce needs time to ripen and mature its flavour. It should be perfect after about 30 minutes in the bain-marie.
* It can equally well be eaten cold, with all kinds of salad and cold fish and poultry.

4 Fresh Tomato Sauce

Sauce coulis de tomates fraîches
'Universal and easy'

For four people

Main ingredients	300 g (10½ oz) fresh tomatoes 3 teaspoons olive oil 1 clove garlic, unpeeled 1 chopped shallot 1 teaspoon tomato purée 1 small bouquet garni 180 ml (⅓ pint) chicken stock made with ⅓ chicken stock cube and 180 ml (⅓ pint) water salt and pepper
Equipment	1 liquidiser
Uses	Foie Gras Pot-au-Feu (**No 49**) Stuffed Geese Feet (**No 79**) Tongue Pot-au-Feu (**No 97**) The 'Pot-au-Feu' Pot-au-Feu (**No 98**)

1   Remove the stalks from the tomatoes and plunge briefly into boiling water to make peeling them easier. Refresh in iced water and drain in a colander. Peel them, cut each one in two and press the halves gently in the palm of your hand to expel pips and excess moisture.

2   Heat the oil in the saucepan and allow the crushed whole clove of garlic and the chopped shallot to cook gently, without browning.

3   Add the tomato halves, the tomato purée, the bouquet garni and the stock. Cook, covered, on a moderate heat for 20 minutes.

4   At the end of this time remove the bouquet garni and purée the sauce in the liquidiser. Taste for seasoning. If the sauce is too thin, return it to the saucepan and allow to reduce and thicken.

5 Butter Sauce with Truffles

Sauce beurrée aux truffes –
'Earthy and succulent'

For four people

Main ingredients	40 g (1½ oz) tinned truffles 130 g (4½ oz) butter 5 tablespoons juice from the tin of truffles 7 tablespoons whipping cream salt and freshly-ground pepper 1 teaspoon lemon juice
Equipment	1 small stainless-steel saucepan
Uses	Foie Gras Pot-au-Feu (**No 49**)

1   Cut the truffles into julienne strips.

2   Heat 1 teaspoon of butter in the saucepan and soften the truffle strips in it for 2 minutes. Then add the truffle juice and the cream. Season lightly with salt and pepper and reduce by boiling until half the liquid has evaporated. This will take about 6 minutes.

3   While this mixture reduces, gradually add the remaining butter, in pieces, to the gently simmering liquid. Shake the pan with a continuous circular motion to homogenise the sauce; it will become thick and rich. Add the lemon juice and, if necessary, adjust the seasoning. Keep hot in a bain-marie until needed.

Suggestions for the home cook

* You can produce a marvellous and far less expensive sauce by replacing the truffles with mushrooms in the following way: peel 80 g (2¾ oz) of button mushrooms and cut them in julienne strips. Soften them in butter with a teaspoon of chopped shallot. Replace the truffle juice with 2 tablespoons of madeira or white port, together with 1 teaspoon of freshly-chopped tarragon, or ½ teaspoon tarragon preserved in vinegar, added to the sauce at the same time as the cream.

6 Cream Sauce with Chives

Sauce crème de ciboulettes 'A tender green herb garden sauce'

For four people

Main ingredients	4 tablespoons dry white wine 2 heaped tablespoons chopped shallots 2 tablespoons stock made with $\frac{1}{3}$ chicken stock cube diluted in $1\frac{1}{2}$ tablespoons water 350 ml ($\frac{1}{2}$ pint) whipping cream 1 level tablespoon Watercress Purée **(No 104)** 1 level tablespoon chopped chives 3 tablespoons cold water 100 g ($3\frac{1}{2}$ oz) butter 1 tablespoon lemon juice salt and pepper
Equipment	1 liquidiser
Uses	Sea-Bream in a Salt Crust **(No 62)** Sole Grilled with Oysters **(No 67)** Veal Tournedos with Chive Sauce **(No 87)**

1   Bring the white wine and the chopped shallot to simmering point in a small saucepan and reduce, uncovered, until there is about 1 tablespoon of moist purée remaining.

2   In another saucepan, boil the stock and cream until they have reduced to two-thirds of their original volume.

3   Meanwhile, liquidise the watercress purée, chives, cold water and white wine reduction (1) together. Pour in the stock and cream reduction (2) and the lemon juice, blend again for 30 seconds with salt and pepper. Keep warm in a bain-marie until needed.

7 Freshwater Crayfish Sauce

Sauce coulis d'écrevisses 'A rose-coloured sauce'

For six people

Main ingredients	2 medium carrots, peeled ½ onion, peeled 1 shallot, peeled 4 tablespoons olive oil 4 tablespoons arachide oil 1·5 kg (3 lb 3 oz) live freshwater crayfish (about 32 in all) or Dublin Bay prawns 1 unpeeled clove of garlic, crushed 1 small bouquet garni 3 tablespoons armagnac 3 tablespoons port 250 ml (scant ½ pint) dry white wine 3 raw tomatoes, peeled and diced (**No 99**) 1 tablespoon tomato purée salt and pepper 400 ml (¾ pint) double cream 1 teaspoon freshly-chopped tarragon
Equipment	1 shallow sauté pan and lid 1 pestle and mortar **or** liquidiser
Uses	Crayfish Feuilleté (**No 42**) Crayfish Millefeuille (**No 43**) Scallop Mousse (**No 53**) Lobster Cakes with Glazed Carrots (**No 58**)

1 Cut the carrots, onion and shallot into tiny mirepoix dice or, more simply, give them 15 seconds in the liquidiser.

2 Heat the olive and arachide oils in the sauté pan, throw in the crayfish and cook covered for 6 minutes to let them colour. Then, away from the heat, remove the crayfish with a slotted spoon, detach and shell the tails and put them on one side.

3 Put all but 8 of the crayfish heads (used later to decorate the dish) in the mortar and pound them roughly. Alternatively, they can be crushed in the liquidiser.

4 Return the pan to the heat and sweat the mirepoix vegetables (1) together with the garlic, bouquet garni and pounded crayfish heads. Do not let them brown.

5 Add the armagnac and port, cover the pan, and boil until they have reduced by half, impregnating the crayfish with their flavours.

6 Add the white wine, the diced tomato pulp, the tomato purée, salt and pepper. Boil for about 10 minutes until reduced by a third.

7 Add the cream and tarragon, and simmer for a further 10 minutes over a gentle heat.

8 Strain the sauce through a wire sieve, pressing down the crayfish debris and vegetables with the back of a small ladle so as to extract all the juices and flavour.

9 Store the sauce thus obtained, the shelled crayfish tails and the eight crayfish heads (for decoration) separately in the refrigerator, to be used together or separately according to the recipe. The sauce should be served hot.

Suggestions for the home cook
* An excellent and much less expensive sauce can be made using the same weight of small crabs – étrilles in France, velvet swimming crabs in England – cutting them in four before sautéing them (2).

Editor's Note
Small ordinary crabs could also be used as an alternative to crayfish or Dublin Bay prawns or swimming crabs.

8 Chilled Light Watercress Purée

Sauce mousse de cresson 'A pale green Chantilly'

For four people

Main ingredients	1 bunch watercress 2 leaves gelatine (30 g 1 oz) 2 teaspoons butter 1 heaped tablespoon chopped shallot 1 level tablespoon chopped tarragon 1 pinch chopped garlic 2 tablespoons dry white wine 350 ml ($\frac{3}{4}$ pint) whipping cream, very cold salt and pepper 1 teaspoon lemon juice
Equipment	2 bowls, of which one should be well chilled 1 small stainless-steel saucepan with a lid 1 liquidiser
Uses	Eel Terrine (**No 37**) Rillettes of Beef (*see* **No 94**)

Making the watercress purée

1 Pick over the watercress and wash in cold water; there should be about 60 g (2 oz).

2 Put the gelatine to soak and swell in cold water.

3 Heat the butter in a saucepan, and soften the chopped shallot for 1 minute, stirring with a wooden spatula. Add the watercress, tarragon, garlic and white wine, cover, and cook for 1 minute.

4 Add 150 ml ($\frac{1}{4}$ pint) cream, season with salt and pepper and reduce, simmering, uncovered, for 10 minutes.

5   Remove from the heat and add the drained leaves of gelatine, which will melt and dissolve on contact with the heat. Whisk the mixture well.

6   Pour the mixture into the liquidiser, add the lemon juice and blend for 1 minute to obtain a smooth green purée. Put the mixture in a bowl and chill in the refrigerator.

Preparing the whipped cream
7   Take the chilled bowl out of the refrigerator and whip the remaining cream gently with a balloon whisk for 45 seconds. The cream will become light and froth up to one-third more than its original volume.

8   Continue beating, faster, for 20 to 30 seconds. The cream will thicken, but should not become as thick as egg whites beaten to a firm snow.

Finishing the sauce
9   Add the whipped cream (8) to the watercress purée (6) and fold them carefully together using a wooden spatula. Taste for seasoning and chill in the refrigerator until needed.

Suggestions for the home cook
* Whipping the cream for longer than indicated in (7) and (8) gives greater volume and lightness, but the finished sauce will be less rich and velvety.
* Mixtures of other vegetables can also be prepared in the same way – for instance, leeks and fresh mint, asparagus and broccoli, etc.

9   Chilled Light Tomato Purée

Sauce mousse de tomates

Follow the same method as the preceding recipe **(No 8)**, but substitute 3 heaped tablespoons of raw tomato pulp **(No 99)** and 1 tablespoon tomato purée for the watercress. The result is a beautifully rosy sauce with a refreshing flavour. It goes well with Carp Terrine (*see* **No 37**) and Sardines Marinated in Red Wine **(No 59)**.

APERITIF CROÛTONS

10 Croûtons – Master Recipe

Les petits croûtons apéritifs

Replace the usual dreary offerings on bits of soggy toast with style.
Try cutting $\frac{1}{2}$ cm ($\frac{1}{4}$ inch) slices from a French 'baguette' loaf, butter-
ing them on both sides (you will need about 25 g (1 oz) butter for
8 croûtons) and browning them quickly on both sides in a hot frying
pan or simply grilling them.... You can then think up any number
of lovely fillings, but here are a few suggestions. All quantities are
for eight croûtons.

Hot croûtons

11 Croûtons with Cheese and Bacon
Croûtons au fromage et au lard

Blend 50 g ($1\frac{3}{4}$ oz) grated Gruyère, half a beaten egg, and 25 g (1 oz)
double cream in a liquidiser for 1 minute until you have a smooth
cream. Season with salt, pepper and a pinch of nutmeg. Spread the
mixture lavishly on 8 hot golden croûtons **(No 10)** and lay on top
of each a very thin slice, 3 cm ($1\frac{1}{4}$ inches) by 2 cm ($\frac{3}{4}$ inch) of smoked
streaky bacon. Grill for 1–2 minutes and serve immediately on a hot
serving plate.

12 Quail Croûtons
Croûtons à l'oiseau

Brown two small plucked and gutted quails, seasoned with salt and
pepper in a teaspoon of butter, then put them to roast in a very hot
oven for 3–4 minutes. During this time, make the croûtons **(No 10)**
and put a thin slice of fresh or preserved foie gras on each. Remove
the quails from the oven and cut each in four pieces. Put a piece
on each hot croûton, and season with a turn of the pepper-mill.
Decorate each croûton with a peeled and seeded grape, serve on a
hot plate and eat immediately, crunchy bones and all.

13   Quails' Eggs Croûtons
Croûtons à l'œuf de caille

Spread 8 hot golden croûtons **(No 10)** with Onion Purée with Grenadine **(No 100)**. Top with 8 little bouquets of watercress leaves seasoned with a few drops of lemon juice, then 8 quails' eggs fried for 15 seconds in 3 tablespoons of arachide oil. Season with salt and pepper and serve.

14   Pig's Ear Croûtons
Croûtons à l'oreille de cochon

Buy 200 g (7 oz) cooked pig's ear from the charcutier and cut in eight 3 cm (1¼ inch) squares. Roll the squares in flour, and then in a mixture of 1 beaten egg, 1 teaspoon chopped parsley, 1 teaspoon mustard, 1 teaspoon olive oil, salt and pepper. Finally, coat in breadcrumbs and fry briefly on both sides in a hot frying-pan containing 30 g (1 oz) beurre noisette (butter heated to a nut-brown colour). Put the fried squares on 8 hot golden croûtons **(No 10)** after spreading them with Dijon mustard.

Editor's note   You can cook your own pig's ears. Buy them from the butcher on or off the head, then braise gently in stock until tender – about 1½ hours.

Cold croûtons

15   Croûtons with Tomato and Chives
Croûtons à la tomate et aux ciboulettes

Drain 125 g (4½ oz) of raw tomato pulp **(No 99)**, put it in a bowl and mix with 2 tablespoons double cream, a tablespoon chopped shallot, 2 tablespoons chopped chives, a teaspoon of lemon juice and ½ teaspoon Tabasco. Season, and put the mixture in the refrigerator for an hour. Then, spread 8 hot golden croûtons **(No 10)** lavishly with this refreshing purée.

16   Anchovy Croûtons
Croûtons à l'anchois

Hardboil two eggs for 7 minutes only, refresh in cold water and shell. Cut them in 8 nice slices ½ cm (¼ inch) thick. Choose 2 small plum tomatoes and cut them in 8 similar slices. Put one on each of 8 hot golden croûtons **(No 10)**, season with salt and pepper and sprinkle with a teaspoonful of chopped chives. Put the egg slices on top, season them with freshly-ground pepper and finish with an anchovy fillet and a few drops of wine vinegar.

17   Fresh Salmon Croûtons
Croûtons au saumon frais

Take 30 g (1 oz) of fresh raw salmon and cut it into eight 3 cm (1¼ inch) squares. (They should be very thin and you may have to roll them flat between two sheets of kitchen foil.) Put them on a plate, salt them lightly and scatter over a tablespoon of chopped shallot, a teaspoon of lemon juice and another of olive oil and leave to marinate for an hour. Then place one on each of 8 hot golden croûtons **(No 10)** and decorate with 2 green peppercorns apiece.

SOUPS

18 Christine's Vegetable Soup

Soupe de tous les légumes du potager de Christine 'A splendid all-the-year-round soup'

Serve hot or cold

For six people

Main ingredients

2·5 litres ($4\frac{1}{2}$ pints) of stock made with 5 chicken bouillon cubes

---

First stage

75 g ($2\frac{1}{2}$ oz) carrots
20 g ($\frac{3}{4}$ oz) turnips
80 g ($2\frac{3}{4}$ oz) onions
} peeled and quartered

$\frac{1}{2}$ teaspoon celery
60 g (2 oz) white part of leeks, well-washed and cut in rounds
20 g ($\frac{3}{4}$ oz) shallots, peeled and halved
salt and pepper

Second stage

50 g ($1\frac{3}{4}$ oz) button mushrooms, quartered
50 g ($1\frac{3}{4}$ oz) watercress, washed and picked over
$\frac{1}{2}$ tomato, peeled and deseeded
$\frac{1}{2}$ lettuce heart, washed
25 g (1 oz) cucumber, peeled and diced
50 g ($1\frac{3}{4}$ oz) French beans, topped and tailed
salt and pepper

Ingredients for finishing the soup

$\frac{1}{3}$ clove of garlic, peeled and chopped
$\frac{1}{2}$ teaspoon tarragon, 1 tablespoon parsley
$\frac{1}{2}$ tablespoon chervil, $\frac{1}{2}$ tablespoon chives
250 ml (scant $\frac{1}{2}$ pint) whipping cream
20 g ($\frac{3}{4}$ oz) softened butter
salt and pepper

Equipment

1 couscoussier or steamer
1 liquidiser
1 medium-size saucepan

First stage

1 Put the stock in the bottom half of the couscoussier or steamer. Put the vegetables for the first part of the cooking – carrots, turnips, onions, celery, leeks and shallots – in the upper half. Salt and pepper lightly. Cover, bring the stock to the boil and let the vegetables cook in the steam for 15 minutes.

Second stage

2 Arrange on top of the first layer of vegetables, those for the second cooking – mushrooms, cress, tomato, lettuce, cucumber and French beans – and season lightly again. Cover, bring back to the boil and steam for a further 10 minutes.

Finishing and serving the soup

3 Heat the tureen or soup bowls.

4 Put the finishing ingredients – garlic, tarragon, parsley, chervil, and chives – in the liquidiser, and blend for 30 seconds.

5 Add all the vegetables from the steamer to the liquidised herbs and blend for a further two minutes, while gradually adding 200 ml ($\frac{1}{3}$ pint) of the chicken stock from the steamer, the cream and the softened butter. Check the seasoning.

6 Reheat the soup in the saucepan without letting it boil, and serve it immediately in a hot tureen or soup bowls.

7 If, on a summer's evening, you want to serve the soup cold, put it straight into an unheated tureen from the liquidiser (5), and put in the refrigerator until thoroughly chilled.

Suggestions for the home cook

* Because of the large number of different vegetables it contains, this soup may seem, at first, rather fiddly. But the cooking and blending is so simple that the result is worth a little effort. The soup is cooked in two stages because the vegetables require different cooking times.
* You can, of course, vary the selection of fresh vegetables according to the season.

19 Frogs' Legs Soup with Lettuce

Soupe de grenouilles à la laitue
'Fresh as a traditional garden of the past'

Serve hot or cold
For four people

Main ingredients	12 pale green leaves from the heart of a lettuce, making about 100 g (3½ oz) altogether
	15 g (½ oz) butter
	2 heaped tablespoons of chopped shallots, about 30 g (1 oz)
	1 heaped teaspoon chopped garlic
	10 g (¼ oz) parsley, with stalks removed, but not chopped
	4 tablespoons water
	600 ml (1 pint) whipping cream
	750 ml (1¼ pints) stock made from 1½ chicken stock cubes dissolved in 750 ml (1¼ pints) water
	2 heaped teaspoons Watercress Purée **(No 104)** (optional)
	12 pairs of frogs' legs
	2 egg yolks
	1 tablespoon of chopped chives
Equipment	1 stainless-steel saucepan with lid
	4 individual soup-bowls of white porcelain, heated

Editor's note
Frogs' legs, although not commonly eaten outside France, can now be obtained frozen from high-class grocers and delicatessens.

Preparing the soup

1 Wash the lettuce leaves in cold water, drain and cut them in half, discarding the central rib.

2 Melt the butter in a saucepan over a low heat, add the shallots and let them soften without browning for 1 minute, stirring with a wooden spatula.

3 Add the chopped garlic, the halved lettuce leaves, parsley and water. Cover and cook for a further minute.

4 Then, add the cream, stock and (if used) watercress purée. Season with salt and pepper and bring back to the boil.

Cooking and preparing the frogs' legs

5 Plunge the twelve pairs of frogs' legs into the boiling soup and allow to cook, covered, for 4 minutes. Take them out with a slotted spoon and put to drain on a plate. Let them cool, and then delicately pull away the flesh from the bones with your fingers.

6 During this time the soup should continue to boil away until it has reduced by about a third of its volume which will take about 15 minutes.

Finishing and serving the soup

7 Divide the meat from the frogs' legs equally among the heated soup bowls. They will reheat in the soup.

8 Whisk the two egg-yolks in a bowl, then add a few tablespoons of the hot soup, continuing to whisk. Reduce the heat to prevent the soup boiling and return the mixture to the saucepan, stirring well. Check the seasoning.

9 Pour the soup over the frogs' leg meat in the soup bowls and sprinkle with chopped chives.

Suggestion for the home cook

* To accentuate the fresh flavour already provided by the parsley and lettuce, add 3 tablespoons of cold dry white wine to the soup just before step 9.

20 Chilled Crab Consommé with Chervil

Bouillon d'étrilles en gelée au cerfeuil
'A clear fresh seafood soup for summer'

For six people

Main ingredients	2 kg (4½ lb) small swimming crabs **or**
	small ordinary crabs
	7 tablespoons olive oil
	2 carrots, peeled, chopped and diced
	1 onion, peeled, chopped and diced
	1 tablespoon chopped shallot
	1 whole crushed unpeeled clove garlic
	3 tablespoons armagnac
	3 tablespoons port
	250 ml (scant ½ pint) dry white wine
	2 tomatoes, peeled, deseeded and coarsely chopped (see **No 99**)
	2 tablespoons tomato purée
	1 small bouquet garni
	2 litres (3½ pints) stock made from 4 chicken stock cubes dissolved in the same amount of water
	salt and pepper

Ingredients for finishing the soup	3 egg whites
	13 leaves of gelatine (25 g (1 oz) in all)
	250 g (8¾ oz) tinned crabmeat
	2 tablespoons sprigs of chervil
	1 teaspoon tarragon

Equipment	1 large frying-pan
	1 large saucepan with lid
	6 large balloon glasses

Suggestions for the home cook

* You can add a few halved blanched lettuce leaves and even a few poached petits pois to the jellied consommé just before serving. It looks very pretty and adds an extra note of freshness.
* This recipe can, of course, be made the day before and kept in the refrigerator.

Making the consommé

1   With a large knife, cut the crabs in quarters, then season them with salt and a turn of the pepper-mill.

2   Heat half the olive oil in the large frying-pan and sauté the crabs in it over a good heat for 5 minutes, turning them so that they are browned on all sides.

3   Heat the remaining oil in a saucepan, add the carrots, onion, shallot and garlic and soften, without browning, for 5 minutes. Add the fried crabs, drained of their cooking oil, to the vegetables.

4   Deglaze the saucepan with the armagnac and port, bring to the boil and reduce by three-quarters of their volume. Add the white wine, and allow to reduce again by a half. Add the tomato pulp, tomato purée, bouquet garni and stock. Cover and cook over a brisk heat for 15 minutes.

5   Strain the bouillon through a conical strainer into a large bowl and squeeze the vegetables and crab debris with the back of a ladle to extract all their juices and flavours.

Clarifying the consommé

6   Salt the egg whites lightly and break them up gently with a fork in a small bowl. Slide them into a saucepan, and add the crab bouillon, whisking vigorously. Bring to a gentle simmer and allow to simmer for 20 minutes.

7   Meanwhile, soak the gelatine for 10 minutes in a little cold water to soften and swell it. Drain and dissolve it in the crab consommé.

8   Moisten a cloth and line the inside of a conical strainer with it. Strain the bouillon gently through it, into the rinsed bowl. Taste for seasoning and chill for 2 hours in the refrigerator.

Finishing and serving the bouillon

9   Cut the tinned crabmeat into dice 1 cm ($\frac{1}{2}$ inch) square and divide equally between the six glasses, dotting the crabmeat with half the sprigs of chervil and the chopped tarragon.

10   With the ladle, pile the just-set and trembling jellied bouillon into the glasses, and finish by decorating with the remaining sprigs of chervil. Serve very cold.

21 Freshwater Crayfish Soup

Soupe aux écrevisses de rivière
'A creamy soup with a mouthwatering
fragrance'

Serve hot or cold

For four people

Main ingredients	1 kg (2¼ lb) live freshwater crayfish, about 32 in all **or** fresh or frozen Dublin Bay prawns (scampi)
	4 tablespoons olive oil
	4 tablespoons arachide oil
	1 medium carrot { peeled and cut into tiny mirepoix dice
	1 onion
	1 shallot
	salt and pepper
	1 unpeeled clove of garlic, crushed
	1 small bouquet garni
	3 tablespoons armagnac
	3 tablespoons port
	250 ml (⅓ pint) dry white wine
	2 tomatoes, peeled, deseeded and chopped
	500 ml (scant pint) water
	1 tablespoon tomato purée
Ingredients for finishing the soup	7 tablespoons court-bouillon and vegetables **(No 2)**
	1 teaspoon chopped chervil
	1 teaspoon chopped tarragon
	200 ml (⅓ pint) double cream
	150 g (5¼ oz) softened butter
	1 tablespoon fresh chives, chopped
Equipment	1 shallow saucepan and lid
	1 liquidiser **or** 1 wooden pestle and mortar
	4 individual soup-bowls in white porcelain

Making the crayfish essence

1   Heat the oils in the shallow saucepan, throw in the crayfish and sauté them, covered, for 6 minutes, when they will turn a fiery red.

2   Remove the saucepan from the heat, take out and drain the crayfish using a slotted spoon and put them on a plate. Detach the tails, shell them and keep on one side.

3   Pulverise the crayfish heads coarsely in a mortar or liquidiser. Return them to the shallow pan and add the mirepoix of carrot, onion, and shallot, the bouquet garni, the garlic, salt and pepper, and sauté without browning, uncovered, for 5 minutes.

4   Add the armagnac and port and half-cover the pan. The mixture of spirits will boil, reducing by half and permeating the crayfish with its flavour.

5   Add the white wine, tomato pulp and tomato purée to the pan and allow to boil, uncovered, for 15 minutes, during which time it should reduce by half.

6   Sieve this sauce through a conical strainer, pressing the shells and vegetables with a ladle to extract the last drop of juice; keep on one side in a bowl.

Finishing and serving the soup

7   While the mirepoix and crayfish shells are cooking (4–6) divide the reserved crayfish tails (2) between the four soup-bowls and keep them warm in a low oven with the door open.

8   In the second saucepan, bring the 7 tablespoons of court-bouillon with its vegetables to the boil and add the teaspoon of chervil and the half-teaspoon of tarragon and allow to reduce by half. Then add the 200 ml ($\frac{1}{3}$ pint) of cream, the 150 g ($5\frac{1}{4}$ oz) butter cut in pieces and the crayfish essence (6), whisking all well together.

9   Allow to boil for 30 seconds, check the seasoning and pour over the crayfish tails in the soup-bowls. Scatter with chopped chives and serve.

(continued on the next page)

Suggestions for the home cook

* It is important to have the vegetables from the court-bouillon as they give this creamy soup a 'chewy' quality.

* To shell the crayfish tails, pinch the two harder rings at either end of the tail between your thumb and index finger until they crack. Remove them and pull the tail out whole from its bony casing, from the head end.

* The crayfish can be more simply cooked in boiling salted water, and the crayfish essence (6) replaced by 7 tablespoons of Sauce Américaine (page 77).

SALADS

22 French Farm Salad

Salade grande ferme
'The flavour of Roquefort sharpens
a simple salad'

For four people

Main
ingredients

1 large head of very well-blanched curly endive
40 g (1½ oz) softened butter
16 rounds of bread cut from a French
'baguette' loaf
1 peeled clove garlic
150 g (5¼ oz) smoked streaky bacon in
   three slices, each cut into little dice
80 g (2¾ oz) Roquefort cheese
1 heaped tablespoon of sprigs of chervil
   or freshly-chopped parsley
7 tablespoons of Vinaigrette or, better,
   Vinaigrette Gourmande **(No 24)**

Preparing the ingredients

1   Trim the endive with a small knife, detaching the leaves and cutting the largest in two or three pieces. Wash them carefully in fresh water twice and dry them first in a salad-shaker and then with a cloth.

2   Spread both sides of the rounds of bread with the softened butter. Heat a pan and brown the bread on both sides. Rub them with the clove of garlic and keep hot in a low oven with the door slightly open.

3   In the same pan, sauté and colour the bacon dice, without adding any fat, as their own lard will be enough.

Finishing and serving the salad

4   Dress the endive with the vinaigrette in the salad bowl, and coat it well, mixing it in with the salad servers. Crumble the cheese with a fork and add it with the croûtons to the endive, tossing them together well.

5   Scatter hot bacon and the chervil or chopped parsley over the salad and serve.

Suggestion for the home cook

* The best way to dress a salad properly is to toss it with your hands after pouring in the vinaigrette.

23 Lentil Salad with Anchovy Croûtons

Salade de lentilles aux croûtons d'anchoïade
'Lentils with the flavour of the Midi'

For four people

Main ingredients	200 g (7 oz) green lentils 1 litre (1¾ pints) cold water 1¾ teaspoons coarse salt 1 small bouquet garni A pinch of pepper 60 g (2 oz) diced onion 60 g (2 oz) diced carrot ½ clove garlic, peeled and chopped
Ingredients for the dressing	4 tablespoons arachide oil 4 tablespoons wine vinegar 1 tablespoon chopped shallot salt and pepper

Ingredients for the garnish	4 salted anchovies **or** 16 tinned anchovy
	  fillets
	1 egg yolk
	6 tablespoons olive oil
	12 rounds of bread cut from a French
	  baguette loaf
	1 tablespoon chopped capers

Equipment	1 stainless-steel saucepan with lid 1 liquidiser

Editor's note   Small green lentils will not need pre-soaking. Larger varieties will.

Cooking the lentils

1   Wash the lentils and drain them in the colander. Put in the sauce-pan and cover with 1 litre of cold water. (Unlike dried haricot beans, lentils don't always need soaking beforehand.)

2   Bring to the boil and skim if necessary.

3   Add the salt, bouquet garni, pepper, diced onion and carrots and the chopped garlic. Allow to cook gently, covered, for about 35 minutes. When they are cooked, drain them in the colander, remove the bouquet garni and leave the lentils in a cool place.

Preparing the anchovy paste

4   If using salted anchovies, wash them under the cold tap, to remove the salt, and separate the fillets from the backbones. To do this, take hold of each fillet at the tail end between your finger and thumb and peel it away from the backbone. Rinse the fillets again under the cold tap and dry on kitchen paper.

5   Blend the anchovy fillets with the egg yolk in the liquidiser for 30 seconds, gradually adding 4 tablespoons of olive oil. Pour into a bowl and set aside.

6   Brush either side of each round of bread with the remaining olive oil. Grill them till they are brown and crisp on both sides.

7   Spread one side of the grilled rounds of bread with the anchovy mixture (5).

Finishing and serving the salad

8   Make the dressing in a salad bowl as if it were a simple vinaigrette, mixing all the ingredients together thoroughly. Add the lentils and the chopped capers and mix well with salad servers. Pile the lentils into a shallow dome shape and arrange the anchovy croûtons round the edge like a crown.

Suggestions for the home cook

* The croûtons can be more simply made by covering each with a thin slice of tomato topped with a slice of hard-boiled egg and an anchovy fillet, instead of the anchovy mixture.
* To make this salad appear lighter, you can mix the lentils with some white haricot beans, soaked and then cooked in the same way as the lentils.

24 Gourmande Salad

Salade Gourmande
'The surprising harmony of vinaigrette and foie gras'

For two people

Main ingredients	170 g (6 oz) young, tender French beans, topped and tailed 12 fresh asparagus spears, well cleaned and trimmed **or** 12 tinned asparagus spears 4 beautiful leaves of salad such as red chicory, red endive, radicchio trevisano etc. 1 level teaspoon chopped shallot 60 g (2 oz) fresh **or** preserved foie gras 1 fresh or preserved truffle, weighing 20 g ($\frac{3}{4}$ oz), sliced

---

Water for cooking the vegetables	1·5 litres (2$\frac{1}{2}$ pints) water 30 g (1 oz) coarse salt

---

Vinaigrette Gourmande	Salt and pepper 1 teaspoon lemon juice 2 teaspoons arachide oil 2 teaspoons olive oil 1 teaspoon sherry vinegar 1 teaspoon chervil 1 teaspoon tarragon

---

Equipment	1 stainless-steel saucepan

Cooking the vegetables

1   Throw the French beans into a saucepan of boiling well-salted water and cook them uncovered and at a galloping boil for between 4 and 8 minutes according to their size. They should be 'al dente'. Take them quickly out of the water with a slotted spoon and plunge for 10 seconds in a basin of iced water. Then drain in a colander.

2   If you are using fresh asparagus, cook in the same water after the beans have been taken out (*for technique see page 55*).

Preparing the Vinaigrette Gourmande

3   Make the dressing like an ordinary vinaigrette, using a small wire whisk. Add the ingredients in the following order: salt, pepper and lemon juice, both kinds of oil, then the sherry vinegar, chervil and tarragon.

Finishing and serving the salad

4   In separate bowls, dress the French beans, asparagus and sliced truffle with the Vinaigrette Gourmande.

5   Wash and dry the chosen salad leaves and arrange them on two plates or in a salad-bowl. Pile the French beans on top in the form of a dome, scatter with chopped shallot and stud here and there with asparagus spears.

6   Dip a little knife in hot water and slice the foie gras in paper-thin escalopes. Arrange them prettily on the dome of French beans and decorate with slices of truffle.

Suggestions for the home cook

* If you can only obtain large French beans, cut them in half lengthways to make them 'slender'.
* If you have no truffles, use a large raw button mushroom cut in delicate slices and sprinkled with lemon juice.

25 Hot Salad from the Landes

Salade chaude des dames landaises 'A splendid mixture of flavours'

For four people

Main ingredients	100 g (3½ oz) duck fillets, eight in all Salt and freshly-ground pepper 3 tablespoons any cheap red wine 100 g (3½ oz) duck foie gras, fresh or preserved 100 g (3½ oz) lamb's lettuce 100 g (3½ oz) dandelion leaves 40 g (1½ oz) fresh or tinned truffle(s)
Ingredients for the dressing	1 tablespoon olive oil 2 tablespoons lemon juice salt and freshly-ground pepper

Suggestions for the home cook

* This salad is a lot of work, but taking this recipe as a starting point you can vary it by replacing the diced foie gras with diced ham fried in a tablespoon of olive oil, and the truffles with raw sliced button mushrooms, sprinkled with a little lemon juice.

* Duck fillets can make a dish on their own. In this case they should be marinated rather longer, then grilled or fried, allowing four to each person. They are good served with a nut of butter or Vintner's Butter (beurre vigneron) **(No 91),** a salad, or Onion Purée with Grenadine **(No 100).**

For a note on duck fillets and the 'magret' of which they form a part see **No 27.**

Preparing the meats

1 Using a small knife, cut out the nerve which runs through the duck fillets.

2 Put the fillets in a deep dish, season them with salt and freshly-ground pepper, moisten them with the red wine and allow to marinate while you prepare the other ingredients.

3 Cut the foie gras into small dice 1 cm ($\frac{1}{2}$ inch) square.

Preparing the salads

4 Pick over the lamb's lettuce and dandelions and wash them scrupulously in several waters. Drain them in a colander and dry them in a cloth.

5 With a small knife, cut the truffle(s) in paper-thin slices.

6 Mix the lamb's lettuce, dandelions and truffles carefully in a salad-bowl, season with salt and pepper, and set aside.

Finishing and serving the salad

7 Heat a frying-pan and then fry the foie-gras dice for 30–40 seconds without adding any extra fat, so that they brown on all sides and give up their own fat.

8 Pour the hot fat through a conical strainer on to the salad. Keep the foie-gras dice on one side.

9 Add the tablespoon of olive oil and the two tablespoons of lemon juice to the salad and mix thoroughly.

10 Dry the marinated duck fillets on kitchen paper and fry them in a little oil made very hot in the same frying pan, for 15 seconds on each side. Take them out, drain them quickly on kitchen paper and place them on the salad. Scatter the diced foie gras over the top and serve immediately.

26 Rectory-Garden Salad

Salade du jardin de curé 'A jumble of different salads and herbs with crisp bacon and quails' eggs'

For four people

Main ingredients	60 g (2 oz) carrots
	60 g (2 oz) celeriac
	1 clove garlic, crushed but not peeled
	8 peppercorns
	400 ml ($\frac{2}{3}$ pint) olive oil
	15 g ($\frac{1}{2}$ oz) watercress leaves
	8 leaves radicchio trevisano **or** red batavia
	15 g ($\frac{1}{2}$ oz) lamb's lettuce in six little bunches
	20 g ($\frac{3}{4}$ oz) curly endive **or** purslane
	100 g ($3\frac{1}{2}$ oz) bean sprouts
	40 g ($1\frac{1}{2}$ oz) fresh or frozen petits pois
	1 litre ($1\frac{3}{4}$ pints) water and 15 g ($\frac{1}{2}$ oz) coarse salt for cooking the bean sprouts and petits pois
	24 quails' eggs **or** 4 hens' eggs (see note)
	150 g ($5\frac{1}{4}$ oz) smoked streaky bacon in three slices, each cut into 12 little cubes
	2 tablespoons chives, freshly chopped
	2 tablespoons chervil sprigs
	500 ml (scant pint) each water and red wine for poaching the quails' eggs

Dressing	7 tablespoons Vinaigrette Gourmande **(No 24)**

Preparing the cooked vegetables

1 Clean and cut the carrots and celeriac into julienne strips, 3 cm (1¼ inches) long and ½ cm (¼ inch) wide. Put them in a sauté pan. Add the garlic and the peppercorns and cover with the olive oil. Bring to the boil and simmer for 10 minutes. Allow to cool, remove and drain the julienne strips, and keep the oil for further use.

Preparing the salad

2 Put a large saucepan on to boil with 1 litre (1¾ pints) water and 15 g (½ oz) coarse salt.

3 Pick over the various salads – cress, batavia, lamb's lettuce and curly endive – wash them carefully in cold water, drain them in the salad shaker and dry in a cloth.

4 Fill a bowl with cold water and ice-cubes. Plunge the bean sprouts into the boiling water in a large saucepan for 2 minutes, take out with a slotted spoon and immediately refresh in the iced water. Remove and drain in a colander.

5 Follow the same method with the petits pois, giving 15 minutes cooking for fresh peas and 6 minutes for frozen.

6 Mix the watercress, radicchio, lamb's lettuce and curly endive together in a large salad bowl. Add the bean sprouts, peas and julienne vegetables.

Preparing the poached eggs and smoked bacon

7 Heat the 500 ml (scant pint) each of water and red wine together in a large saucepan *without salt*, which would liquefy the albumen in the egg white. Meanwhile break the quails' eggs into a plate. When the liquid is simmering, slide the eggs in carefully and allow to poach very gently for 1 minute. Remove from the heat and keep them hot in the cooking liquid.

8 Heat a frying pan and brown the dice of smoked bacon. Don't add any extra fat; their own will be enough. Drain on kitchen paper.

(*continued on the next page*)

Finishing and serving the salad

9 Dress the mixed salads (6) with the Vinaigrette Gourmande **(No 24)** and add the smoked bacon dice.

10 Arrange this hotchpotch, either piled on four individual plates, or jumbled higgledy-piggledy in a salad bowl.

11 Carefully lift the quails' eggs out of their cooking liquid with a skimmer and place them on top of the salad. Finally, sprinkle over the chopped chives and chervil sprigs.

Suggestions for the home cook

* Quails' eggs can be replaced with one hen's egg per person, poached for 3 minutes.
* 50 g (1¾ oz) spaghetti, cut into 5 cm (2 inches) lengths and cooked 'al dente' – that is, just resistant to the bite – in boiling salted water, make an amusing alternative to bean sprouts, which are sometimes hard to find.
* A large slice of hot toast is the ideal partner for this salad.

27 Salad of Duck-breast Ham and Fresh Garden Peas

Salade de jambon d'aile de canard aux pois de jardin 'A delicate, well flavoured and previously undiscovered ham'

For two people

Main ingredients	1 'magret' or raw duck breast weighing 350 g (12½ oz) 15 g (½ oz) coarse salt 1 pinch of thyme A fragment of bayleaf 4 coriander seeds, crushed 4 peppercorns, crushed
Ingredients for the garnish	500 ml (scant pint) of water and 1½ teaspoons salt for cooking the onions 8 button onions, peeled 1 litre (1¾ pints) water and 15 g (½ oz) coarse salt for cooking the peas and lettuce 100 g (3½ oz) shelled petits pois ½ lettuce
Dressing	3 tablespoons Vinaigrette Gourmande (**No 24**)
Special equipment	1 straining cloth 1 flexible sharp knife

Preparing the duck-breast ham (The preparation takes about two weeks.)

1 Put the raw duck breast, skin side down, on a small oval plate. Cover it with the coarse salt, thyme, bayleaf, crushed coriander and coarsely crushed pepper. Put the plate in the refrigerator for 24 hours, during which time the salt will gradually be absorbed.

2 The next day, wrap the duck breast, exactly as it is, in a small piece of muslin and tie it up as if it were a small sausage. Hang it up in a draught, in a dry atmosphere, for 12 to 15 days. You can tell when your duck-breast ham is ready by pinching it; it should feel firm but supple.

Preparing the garnish

3 Bring the 500 ml (scant pint) of water and 1½ teaspoons coarse salt to the boil in a saucepan and cook the button onions in it, for 7 minutes if they are new, and for 15 minutes if they are dried. Remove with the slotted spoon and discard the cooking water.

4 In the same saucepan, bring the litre (1¾ pints) water and 15 g (½ oz) coarse salt to the boil and throw in the petits pois. Cook them for 15 minutes if they are fresh and tender, for 6 minutes if frozen. Drain them in a colander.

5 Meanwhile, wash the half lettuce. Remove two large curled leaves from the heart, to hold the petits pois. Cook the rest for 4 minutes in the same water that the petits pois have cooked in, then drain with the slotted spoon.

Finishing and serving the salad

6 Separate the leaves of the cooked lettuce and cut out the stalks. Mix the petits pois, onions, lettuce leaves and the Vinaigrette Gourmande together carefully in the salad bowl. Put one of the curved uncooked lettuce leaves on each plate, and fill with the salad.

7 Unwrap the duck-breast ham, and trim it with a sharp knife, leaving a paper-thin layer of fat. With a sharp flexible knife, cut it into very thin, almost transparent slices.

8 Arrange the duck-breast ham slices round the salad, arranging them so that they form undulating waves round the edge of the plate. Season with a few turns of the peppermill.

Suggestions for the home cook

* A last-minute dish can be made by replacing the duck-breast ham with Parma ham.
* The petits pois salad can be made with 100 g (3½ oz) of petits pois tinned 'à la Française'. You need only rinse them under the cold tap, season and proceed from step 6.
* In the summer, you can throw in a few thin slices of juicy melon, traditional partner of ham throughout the world.

The 'magret' or duck breast and its 'filet mignon' or fillet

The 'magret' is the white meat or breast of the fat ducks which are used for 'confits' in France, especially in the south-west. It appears on the table fairly often, usually grilled like a steak on an open fire, or cooked in a casserole (see **No 78**). Underneath the 'magret' there is another succulent morsel, the 'filet mignon de canard', a long narrow strip of tender meat which can be used in various ways (see **No 77**). This is also present in ordinary ducks, but is less well-developed.

Editor's note   Preserving or curing meat can be a potentially hazardous business and it is essential that the basic rules of food hygiene are scrupulously observed and that your refrigerator is operating reliably.

28 Smoked Fish Salad with Crudités

*Salade buissonière aux poissons fumés 'A
smoky salad'*

For four people

Main ingredients	120 g (5 oz) smoked salmon 120 g (5 oz) smoked sturgeon 1 teaspoon olive oil

Ingredients for the garnish	60 g (2 oz) carrots 60 g (2 oz) celeriac 1 clove garlic, crushed but not peeled 8 peppercorns 400 ml ($\frac{3}{4}$ pint) olive oil 4 little bunches of lamb's lettuce 8 leaves red batavia 1 small handful watercress leaves 20 g ($\frac{3}{4}$ oz) curly endive **or** purslane 2 small very ripe avocado pears 8 g ($\frac{1}{4}$ oz) fresh ginger **or** 1$\frac{1}{2}$ teaspoons finely grated lemon peel 1 tablespoon chopped shallot 48 green peppercorns 4 tablespoons chervil **or** parsley sprigs 24 redcurrants (optional)

Dressing	5 tablespoons Vinaigrette Gourmande **(No 24)**

Preparing the cooked vegetables

1   Clean and cut the carrots and celeriac into julienne strips 3 cm (1¼ inches) long and ½ cm (¼ inch) wide, and put them in a sauté pan. Add the garlic, and peppercorns and cover with the 400 ml (¾ pint) olive oil. Bring to the boil and allow to simmer gently for 10 minutes, cool, remove and drain the julienne strips, keeping the oil for further use.

Preparing the smoked fish

2   Using a sharp flexible knife, slice the smoked salmon and sturgeon very thinly, making 24 miniature escalopes out of each. Arrange them overlapping on a large plate and brush them very lightly with olive oil to make them shine.

Preparing the salads

3   Pick over the various salads – the lamb's lettuce, batavia, watercress and endive or purslane – and wash them carefully in running water. Shake them in a salad shaker and dry in a cloth.

4   Peel the avocados with a potato peeler, cut them in half, take out the stone, and cut each into eight crescent-shaped pieces. Put the pieces in a dish and dress them with one-third of the dressing (about 1½ tablespoons).

5   Peel the fresh ginger and cut it into very fine julienne strips. If you are using lemon peel it must be cut into tiny julienne strips, and then blanched in boiling water for 7–8 minutes.

6   Mix the various salads together in a salad bowl (3) and dress them with the remaining dressing – about 3½ tablespoons – and the chopped shallot.

Finishing and serving the salad

7   Arrange the slices of smoked fish round the inside rim of the chilled plates, and sprinkle the salmon (only) with the green peppercorns.

8   Place a ring of avocado pear crescents inside the circles of smoked fish.

(continued on the next page)

9 Pile the dressed salads in the middle of the plates, in little mounds. Decorate them by planting the little 'batons' of cooked carrot and celeriac here and there. Sprinkle with the ginger or lemon peel, sprigs of chervil or parsley and the red currants, whose cheerful colour will brighten the salad.

Suggestions for the home cook

* Preserved herrings of various kinds provide a good way of making this salad more economical.
* You can have fun smoking your own fish in one of the small fish-smokers now available from fishing-tackle shops and elsewhere. A good brand is the ABU Smoke Box, which comes from Sweden, and will quickly turn you into a competent amateur smoker.
* This salad is delicious eaten with a large slice of toasted wholemeal bread, spread with a mixture of whipped cream and horseradish.

29 Lobster Salad

Salade de homard 'A majestic seafood salad'

For two people

Main ingredients	1 litre (1¾ pints) court-bouillon (**No 2**) 1 live lobster weighing about 500 g (18 oz), preferably female so you have the eggs as well 160 g (6 oz) fine French beans, topped and tailed 12 asparagus tips, fresh **or** tinned 1·5 litres (2½ pints) water and 30 g (1 oz) coarse salt to cook the vegetables 1 teaspoon chopped shallot 4 nice salad leaves, batavia, radicchio trevisano etc. 1 tablespoon chervil sprigs

---

Ingredients for the dressing	1 egg yolk ½ teaspoon Dijon mustard 3 tablespoons arachide oil 3 tablespoons olive oil salt and white pepper 1 teaspoon lemon juice ½ teaspoon tomato purée ½ teaspoon freshly-chopped tarragon 1 heaped tablespoon of vegetables from the court-bouillon, chopped A few drops of armagnac (optional)

Cooking the lobster

1   Bring the court-bouillon to the boil in a saucepan. Kill the lobster in the way recommended on page 215 and plunge it into the boiling liquid. Let it cook for 10 minutes at a galloping boil, then take it out with a slotted spoon and allow to cool.

2   If the lobster is a female, remove the cluster of eggs from under the body and set them aside in a bowl. Detach the tail and, having cut the shell through on the underside with kitchen scissors, remove it. Cut the flesh into 8 rounds.

3   Crack the claws with the back of the heavy knife and remove the flesh. The head is not used in this recipe but can be used for Sauce Américaine (page 77).

Cooking the vegetables

4   Bring the 1·5 litres (2½ pints) water to the boil in a saucepan with the 30 g (1 oz) coarse salt, and throw in the French beans. Cook them 'al dente' at a galloping boil, uncovered, for 4 to 8 minutes, according to their size. Meanwhile, prepare a basin of iced water. When the beans are cooked take them quickly out of the pan with the slotted spoon and plunge them in the iced water for 10 seconds. Drain in a colander.

5   If you are using fresh asparagus, clean and peel it carefully and cook in the same water as the beans were cooked in, following the same method. If you are using tinned asparagus, rinse and drain.

Preparing the dressing

6   Make a thin mayonnaise (*for the technique see page 70*), whisking the oil and the other dressing ingredients into the egg yolk gradually in the following order: the ½ teaspoon Dijon mustard, the two types of oil, the salt and pepper, the lemon juice, then, when the mayonnaise is made, the ½ teaspoon of tomato purée, the ½ teaspoon tarragon, the tablespoon of vegetables, and the armagnac, if used.

Finishing and serving the salad

7   Put the asparagus and French beans in separate bowls, dress them with half the dressing, and sprinkle them with chopped shallot.

(*continued on the next page*)

8 Wash and dry the salad leaves and put them on two chilled serving plates or in a chilled salad bowl. Pile the French beans in the centre in the form of a dome and stud here and there with asparagus tips. Arrange the slices of lobster round the beans, cover them with the remaining sauce, and sprinkle with the red lobster eggs and the sprigs of chervil.

9 Place the flesh of the claws on top, pointing in the air.

Suggestions for the home cook

* Lobster is expensive – scampi are slightly less so and can be perfectly well used for this salad, while mussels are even cheaper.
* If you want a sauce with more substance than the one I have chosen, add a tablespoon of Sauce Américaine (page 77) to the dressing at the end of step 6.
* On the other hand, a simple vinaigrette dressing with a little chopped shallot will do very well, especially if you add some chopped tarragon.

30 Hot Scampi Salad, with Mangetout Peas

Salade tiède de langoustines aux pois gourmands 'A simple and refreshing salad'

For two people

Main ingredients

3 litres (5¼ pints) water and 60 g (2 oz) coarse salt
16 fresh scampi (Dublin Bay prawns)
1 litre (1¾ pints) water and 15 g (½ oz) course salt
100 g (3½ oz) mangetout peas, topped and tailed
12 asparagus tips, fresh **or** tinned
100 g (3½ oz) fresh morels (morilles) **or** 15 g (½ oz) dried morels soaked in water
7 tablespoons water
½ lemon
salt and pepper
80 g (2¾ oz) butter
1 teaspoon chopped chervil **or** ½ teaspoon chopped flat parsley

Cooking the scampi or Dublin Bay prawns

1   Put the 3 litres (5¼ pints) water and the 60 g (2 oz) salt in a large saucepan and bring to the boil. Throw in the scampi, cook for 1½ minutes, then remove from the heat and keep them warm in the cooking water.

Cooking the vegetables

2   Bring 1 litre (1¾ pints) water and 15 g (½ oz) salt to the boil in a second large saucepan, and put in the mangetout peas and prepared asparagus tips (if you are using fresh asparagus). Cook for 6 minutes at a galloping boil, remove from the heat and keep warm in the cooking water.

3   Wash the morels several times in running water in order to get rid of every trace of sand, and drain them on a cloth. Cut each one into 4 lengthwise slices, put them in a small sauté pan and cover with 7 tablespoons of water acidulated with a few drops of lemon juice. Season, cover, and simmer for 10 minutes over a medium heat. The liquid should reduce by half.

Finishing and presenting the salad

4   Take the scampi out of their cooking water and shell the tails (for the technique see **No 21**).

5   Drain the peas and asparagus in the colander and line two hot plates with a layer of peas.

6   Arrange the scampi tails on top of the peas and scatter the asparagus tips on top. Drain the morels, keeping the cooking water, and add them to the salad on the plates. Put the plates to keep warm in a very low oven with the door slightly open.

7   Return the sauté pan with the cooking liquid from the morels to the heat, add 80 g (2¾ oz) butter in small pieces and boil gently for 3 minutes. Now give the pan several swirling circular movements, to blend the butter sauce thoroughly. It will become thick and rich.

8   Taste the sauce for seasoning and stir in half the chervil or parsley. Then, pour it carefully over the hot salad. Sprinkle with the rest of the chervil or parsley and serve immediately.

(*continued on the next page*)

Suggestions for the home cook

* It is boiling the butter and liquid together which thickens the sauce, after a certain amount of water has evaporated, and gives it its rich texture.

* This simple sauce can be embellished with fines herbes, with spices such as green peppercorns, saffron etc., and can be served with all sorts of dishes, for instance poached or grilled fish, and boiled steamed vegetables.

* **Pastries with Scampi and Mangetout Peas.** This recipe makes a superb filling for a hot pastry, adding one more light leaf to the book I have given you on pages 169–184.

FIRST COURSES

31 Dame Tartine

A fried open sandwich
'A sandwich first course – crisp and succulent'

For four people

Main ingredients	200 g (7 oz) grated Gruyère 20 g ($\frac{3}{4}$ oz) flour 2 teaspoons salt 10 turns of the pepper-mill 2 eggs 1 tablespoon of kirsch 4 slices of bread, 16 cm ($6\frac{1}{2}$ inches) long, 10 cm (4 inches) wide and 1·5 cm ($\frac{3}{4}$ inch) thick oil for frying
Ingredients for the garnish	1 slice cooked ham weighing 100 g ($3\frac{1}{2}$ oz) 100 g ($3\frac{1}{2}$ oz) raw tomato pulp **(No 99)** 30 g (1 oz) chopped raw onion 1 tablespoon freshly-chopped parsley
Equipment	1 liquidiser, 1 chip pan with basket

1 Blend the grated Gruyère, flour and salt and pepper for 3 minutes in a food processor or liquidiser, adding the eggs one after the other, then the kirsch. Turn the resulting creamy mixture into a large bowl and put in the refrigerator for 10 minutes to thicken a little.

2 Chop the slice of ham into $\frac{1}{2}$ cm ($\frac{1}{4}$ inch) dice.

3 Add the diced ham and the tomato pulp, chopped onion and parsley to the mixture in the large bowl (1) and stir well with a wooden spatula.

4 Spread the mixture thickly on the slices of bread.

5 Heat the frying oil to 180°C/350°F and plunge in the slices, frying them for 1 minute with the coated side upwards and then for 30 seconds on the other side.

6 Take the slices out with the skimmer and place them on kitchen paper to absorb any excess oil. Serve as they are, on hot plates.

Suggestions for the home cook

* The open sandwiches can be prepared in advance to step 4 and stored in plastic bags in the refrigerator until they are needed.
* You can vary the mixture endlessly, replacing or adding different ingredients. Try, for instance, capers, pieces of anchovy, diced mushrooms – and so on.
* For those who don't care for deep-fried food, the slices can be cooked on a baking sheet in a very hot oven (250°C/480°F/Mark 9) for 6 minutes. Brush the underside of each slice with melted butter to prevent it burning.

32 Brioche of Bone Marrow with Beurre Rouge

Brioche à la moelle au beurre rouge 'A simple and savoury first course'

For four people

Main ingredients

350 g (12 oz) beef marrow
1 litre cold water and 15 g (½ oz) coarse salt
2 heaped tablespoons chopped shallots ⎫
250 ml (scant ¼ pint) red wine ⎪
250 g (8¾ oz) butter, taken out of the ⎬ for the
    refrigerator 15 minutes beforehand ⎪ sauce
salt and pepper ⎪
1 tablespoon freshly-chopped parsley ⎭
4 slices of brioche bread, 10 cm (4 inches)
    across, 2 cm (¾ inch) thick
coarse salt and freshly-ground pepper

Suggestions for the home cook

* The secret of success with beurre rouge and beurre blanc is simply this: they must be kept at a very low heat – on the edge of the hot-plate over a low gas flame or in a bain-marie – of not more than 60°C/140°F. The back of the finger dipped in the sauce should easily be able to bear the heat. At this temperature the sauce will remain creamy and will not separate.
* It is vital that marrow be served very hot. Cool, it becomes pasty and unattractive.

Preparing the marrow a day in advance

1   Put the marrow to soak overnight in a basin of cold water in the refrigerator.

2   The next day, cut up the marrow into 1 cm (½ inch) rounds, put them in a medium-sized saucepan with the water and salt and leave to soak.

Preparing the beurre rouge (red wine and butter sauce)

3   Put the chopped shallots and red wine in a thick-bottomed pan and reduce, uncovered, over a medium heat. The mixture should reduce by about three-quarters of its original volume until it becomes a moist purée. Turn the heat right down and let the mixture cool to a temperature of around 60°C/140°F.

4   Add the butter, in pieces, one or two at a time, whisking all the while. The sauce will become creamy. Whisk faster as the last pieces of butter go in and turn the heat up for a few seconds to compensate for the drop in temperature caused by the cool butter. Season with salt and pepper, add the chopped parsley and keep the sauce hot in a bain-marie.

Finishing and serving the dish

5   Put the saucepan containing the marrow on the heat. Bring it to the boil and immediately remove it from the heat; take out the marrow slices, which have become translucent, with a slotted spoon. Put the drained slices on a very hot plate and keep hot in a low oven with the door slightly open.

6   Grill the slices of brioche to a golden brown on each side.

7   Put a slice of grilled brioche in the middle of each of four hot plates, and garnish with the hot slices of marrow. Season with salt and pepper.

8   Pour the beurre rouge round, not over, the brioche toast, and serve immediately.

33 Caviar with Creamed Eggs

*Oeufs poule aux caviar 'Eggs
overflowing with caviar'*

For four people

Main *ingredients*	8 very fresh eggs 50 g (1¾ oz) finely-chopped onion ½ tablespoon finely-chopped fresh chives 2 teaspoons butter, softened to room temperature 2 teaspoons salt freshly-ground pepper 1 tablespoon double cream 4 × 30 g (1 oz) pots Iranian Sevruga caviar
'Soldiers' to *accompany the* *eggs*	12 'soldiers' of bread, toasted under the grill **or** 12 hot cooked asparagus spears
Equipment	1 special egg-opening gadget **or** 1 small serrated-edged knife 1 cast-iron saucepan 8 egg-cups

Preparing the eggshells

1 Slice the tops off the eggs with a fine saw-edged knife, cutting the shell about 1 cm ($\frac{1}{2}$ inch) above its widest part. Empty six of the eggs into one bowl, and two (to be used for another recipe) into another. Wash all eight shells and their 'hats' in hot water and put them on a cloth to dry.

Cooking the creamed eggs

2 Beat the six eggs lightly with a whisk and strain through a wire sieve to remove fragments of shell and the strings in the egg whites.

3 Cover the bottom of the pan with the softened butter and add the strained eggs. Cook over a gentle heat and gradually increase the temperature, whisking continuously as you do so. The temperature should not exceed 65°C/150°F, by which time the eggs will be of a light creamy consistency.

4 Remove from the heat and season with salt and pepper. Add the cream, chopped onion and chives, whisking all the time.

Finishing and serving the dish

5 Put the eight clean dry eggshells in the egg-cups and, using a tea-spoon, fill them four-fifths full with the creamed eggs. Complete each one with a little mound of 15 g ($\frac{1}{2}$ oz) caviar and top with an eggshell 'hat'. The caviar should be just visible.

Suggestions for the home cook

* The creamed eggs in this recipe are equally delicious served cold, and the dish can therefore be prepared in advance. The caviar, chilled, should be added at the last moment.
* Salmon or lumpfish roe can be used instead of caviar.
* The caviar can also be replaced very happily with fine shavings of smoked salmon or eel (120 g ($4\frac{1}{4}$ oz) of either) ... or, more simply, by a purée of tomatoes and chives (*see* **No 15**).

(For a non-fattening version of this recipe, see Michel Guérard's Cuisine Minceur **No 50**)

34 Snails in Pots with Croûtons

Escargots en pots aux croûtons 'Little tops of golden fried bread cover delicious snails'

For four people

Main ingredients	48 fresh snails
	1 handful of coarse salt
	1 handful of flour
	2 litres (3½ pints) water
	500 ml (scant pint) water
	500 ml (scant pint) dry white wine
	1 carrot, peeled and sliced
	1 onion, peeled and sliced
	1 bouquet garni
	2 teaspoons salt
	pepper
Ingredients for the snail butter	400 g (14 oz) butter
	40 g (1½ oz) peeled garlic
	100 g (3½ oz) fresh parsley
	1 teaspoon Dijon mustard
	20 g (¾ oz) ground almonds (optional)
	2 teaspoons salt
	2 turns of the peppermill
	1 pinch nutmeg
	40 g (1½ oz) button mushrooms, diced
	60 g (2 oz) ham, diced
Ingredients for the garnish	200 g (7 oz) cooked tomato pulp **(No 99)**
	50 g (1¾ oz) butter
	48 little rounds of white bread, 1·5 cm (¾ inch) across, 3 mm ($\frac{1}{10}$ inch) thick, cut with a pastry-cutter
Special equipment	48 earthenware snail-pots
	1 pastry-cutter 1·5 cm (¾ inch) across
	1 liquidiser

Preparing the snails

1   Remove the operculum or lid with a small knife.

2   Let the snails rest for 2 hours in a basin with the salt and flour, stirring them regularly.

3   Wash them several times.

4   Bring the 2 litres (3½ pints) of water to the boil in a large saucepan. Throw in the snails and cook for 5 minutes.

5   Remove them with a slotted spoon and extract the snails from their shells with the help of a large pin. Discard the shells.

6   Remove the black part (the digestive system) at the end of the snail.

7   Put the snails into a medium saucepan and add the 500 ml (scant pint) of water and the same quantity of dry white wine. Add the sliced carrot and onion, the bouquet garni and the pepper. Bring to the boil, skim and simmer gently for from 1½ to 2½ hours, according to the size of the snails. When they are done, a pin will pierce the flesh fairly easily. Let them cool in the cooking water.

Preparing the snail butter

8   In the liquidiser, blend the butter, garlic, parsley, mustard, ground almonds (if used) and the seasonings together. Put into a bowl and mix in the diced ham and mushrooms.

Finishing and preparing the snails

9   Drain the snails on a cloth. Preheat the oven to 220°C/425°F/Mark 7.

10   Put half a teaspoonful of cooked tomato pulp in the bottom of each snail-pot, place a snail in each and finish by filling up the pots with the snail butter.

11   Spread the little rounds of bread with the 50 g (1¾ oz) butter and place one on each filled pot, buttered side upwards.

12   Bake the snail-pots on a baking sheet for 8 minutes.

(continued on the next page)

13 Arrange the pots on each of four hot plates and serve at once.

Suggestions for the home cook

* The time in the oven must exactly correspond to the time needed to brown and crisp the croûtons and reheat the snails and their butter. Snail butter should never be oily, but should keep its thickness and creaminess. The mustard and powdered almonds help enormously.
* The best snails are those that have spent the winter hibernating, locked up in their shells behind a calcareous door, the operculum. Any other kind must be purged for several days before use.
* There are some excellent tinned snails – Bourgogne and Petits Gris – which can, if time is short, be used instead of fresh snails.

35 Terrine of Duck

Terrine fondante de canard sauvage 'A smooth game pâté which can be eaten with a spoon'

For eight people

Main ingredients	2 young mallards weighing about 1 kg (2¾ lb) apiece salt and pepper 1 tablespoon arachide oil
Ingredients for the forcemeat	190 g (6¾ oz) fat bacon (no lean) 320 g (11 oz) wild duck livers with threads removed 2 heaped teaspoons salt ¾ teaspoon pepper a pinch of 'quatre-épices' 250 ml (scant ½ pint) double cream 4 egg yolks 2½ tablespoons armagnac
Ingredients for the garnish	50 g (1¾ oz) sultanas
Special equipment	1 roasting-pan 1 liquidiser 1 earthenware oven-dish

161

A day in advance: cooking the ducks

1   As only the breasts or 'supremes' of the ducks are used in this recipe, ask your butcher to remove the thighs and drumsticks, or do it yourself before cooking the ducks. They can be cooked in other ways, for instance in **No 80.**

2   Preheat the oven to 250°C/480°F/Mark 9. Put the ducks, with legs removed, into an oval roasting pan, season with salt and pepper, sprinkle with the tablespoon of oil and roast in the very hot oven for 15 minutes. The flesh should still be rosy.

Preparing the forcemeat

3   Put the fat bacon, the duck livers, salt, pepper and 'quatre-épices' in the liquidiser and blend to a smooth creamy consistency. Add the cream, egg yolks and armagnac and continue to blend until the mixture becomes liquid, perhaps thirty seconds.

4   Push the mixture through a wire sieve into a bowl with the help of a spoon. Any small fibres from the bacon or livers will be caught in the mesh.

5   Rinse the sultanas in warm water and drain on a cloth.

6   Remove the four breasts or fillets from the cooked ducks by sliding a flexible knife along the breast bone on either side and lifting the flesh away. Skin the fillets and cut them into dice, ½ cm across.

7   Add the diced duck fillet and the raisins to the liver mixture (4) and mix thoroughly.

Cooking the terrine

8   Preheat the oven to 200°C/390°F/Mark 6. Pour the forcemeat into an earthenware oven-dish, cover with aluminium foil and cook in a bain-marie for 30 minutes in the medium oven. The pâté should be about 5 cm (2 inches) thick. Leave in a cool place overnight.

Serving the terrine

9   Serve it straight from the earthenware dish, with a spoon, and eat it with thick slices of toast.

(*continued on the next page*)

Suggestions for the home cook

* The age and quality of a duck, either wild or domestic, can be recognised by the following tests: the beak should be flexible, and bend easily when pinched between the thumb and index finger; the flesh of the wings and wing tips should be supple.
* Tease your friends by asking them to guess what this terrine is made of. Most of them will swear that it is foie gras!

Editor's note

Quatre-épices is a French spice blend used mainly in pork products. It can occasionally be found in shops outside France, but can easily be made up at home. The proportions are: pepper 125 g (4¼ oz), powdered cloves 4 teaspoons, ginger 30 g (1 oz) and nutmeg 35 g (1¼ oz).

Chicken livers can successfully be substituted for duck livers.

36 Homemade Chicken-Liver Pâté

Terrine ménagère aux foies de volaille 'A real old-fashioned pâté'

For eight people

Main ingredients	500 g (18 oz) chicken livers **or,** better, 350 g (12 oz) livers and 150 g (6 oz) hearts 200 g (7 oz) fresh belly of pork 200 g (7 oz) sausage meat 200 g (7 oz) pork back fat for lining the terrine, cut in thin slices 4 bayleaves 4 sprigs of thyme
Ingredients for the marinade	7 tablespoons armagnac 3 tablespoons port 3 tablespoons sherry 2 teaspoons peeled and chopped garlic 20 g ($\frac{3}{4}$ oz) freshly-chopped parsley 1 level teaspoon thyme 1 pinch freshly-grated nutmeg 1 level teaspoon caster sugar 2 heaped teaspoons salt 12 turns of the pepper-mill
Accompanying vegetable	Onion Purée with Grenadine **(No 100)**
Special equipment	1 ovenproof porcelain terrine with a lid, 16 cm (6$\frac{1}{2}$ inches) long, 11 cm (4 inches) wide and 7 cm (3 inches) deep 1 bain-marie

Two days in advance: preparing and marinating the meat

1 With a small knife, carefully remove all greenish patches from the chicken livers. Cut the livers and hearts (if used) in half.

2 Chop up the belly of pork into four slices, and cut each one into cubes 1 cm ($\frac{1}{2}$ inch) by 2 cm ($\frac{3}{4}$ inch).

3 Put livers, hearts and pork cubes in a large bowl, add the sausage meat and the ingredients for the marinade – armagnac, port, sherry, garlic, thyme, nutmeg, sugar, salt and pepper. Mix all the ingredients together thoroughly with a fork and put to marinate overnight in the refrigerator.

One day in advance: filling and cooking the terrine

4 Preheat the oven to 220°C/425°F/Mark 7. Line the terrine with fine slices of back fat, then fill it to the brim with the marinated meat and its juices (3). Cover the pâté with the remaining strips of back fat and top with alternate overlapping bayleaves and thyme sprigs.

5 Put the terrine to cook in a bain-marie in the hot oven for 1$\frac{3}{4}$ hours, uncovered. The top will be pleasantly browned.

6 Take the terrine out of the oven and out of the bain-marie, allow to cool for 3 hours at room temperature and then keep overnight in the refrigerator.

Serving the terrine

7 On the day it is to be eaten, present the terrine, uncut, to your guests and slice it at the table. Serve with gherkins, pickled onions and Onion Purée with Grenadine **(No 100)**.

37 Terrine of Eel with White Wine

*Terrine d'anguilles au vin de Tursan 'A
well-flavoured fish for a herb-scented terrine'*

For eight people

Main ingredient	2 large fresh eels, skinned and boned, or 450 g (16 oz) eel fillets

Ingredients for the marinade	Salt and freshly-ground pepper 200 ml ($\frac{1}{3}$ pint) dry white wine, preferably Tursan, a wine from the Landes district 3 tablespoons armagnac (optional) 1 level tablespoonful freshly-chopped tarragon 1 level tablespoonful freshly-chopped chervil 1 level tablespoonful freshly-chopped chives

Ingredients for the forcemeat	20 g ($\frac{3}{4}$ oz) butter 350 g (12$\frac{1}{4}$ oz) button mushrooms, peeled and cut into 5 mm ($\frac{1}{5}$ inch) dice 1 level tablespoonful chopped shallot 1 level tablespoonful freshly-chopped parsley salt and pepper 350 g (12$\frac{1}{4}$ oz) skinned and boned salmon **or,** failing this, whiting 2 heaped teaspoons salt freshly-ground pepper 2 eggs 200 g (7 oz) softened butter 1 teaspoon each of roughly-chopped parsley and chervil 1 level teaspoon each of roughly-chopped tarragon and chives A pinch of cayenne A pinch of saffron

Accompanying sauce	Watercress Sauce (**No 8**)

Special 1 ovenproof terrine in white porcelain, 15 cm
equipment (6 inches) long, 9 cm (3¾ inches) wide and
10 cm (4 inches) deep
1 liquidiser, chilled

Two days in advance: marinating the eels

1 Put the eel fillets into a deep earthenware dish, season them with
salt and freshly-ground pepper and add the ingredients for the
marinade: dry white wine, armagnac, tarragon, chervil, chives, and
leave to marinate overnight in the refrigerator.

One day in advance: cooking the eels

2 Put the earthenware dish containing the eels in their marinade
over a low heat until the liquid is bubbling gently. Cover with a piece
of foil and cook for 20 minutes.

3 Take the foil off and allow the eels to cool in the marinade. Their
flesh will have shrunk somewhat during the cooking.

Preparing the forcemeat

4 Heat the 20 g (¾ oz) butter in the frying-pan until it is golden and
throw in the diced mushrooms. Sauté them for 5 minutes.

5 Add the chopped shallot and chopped parsley, season and continue cooking for another 2 minutes. Put them on a plate to cool.

6 Put the salmon, two heaped teaspoons of salt and some freshly-
ground pepper into the liquidiser, previously chilled. Blend for from
30 to 40 seconds, in order to obtain a smooth purée. Add the eggs,
one after the other, and blend for a further 20 seconds.

7 Add the 200 g (7 oz) softened butter, chopped herbs, cayenne and
saffron and blend for a further 30 seconds, until the mixture is
smooth. If necessary, switch off the machine and scrape the mixture
away from the sides of the liquidiser into the middle, to make sure
it is evenly blended, then continue as before.

8 Decant the forcemeat into a bowl and mix in the cooled mushroom mixture (5).

(continued on the next page)

Filling and cooking the terrine

9   Take the eel fillets out of the marinade, drain them and cut each one in two lengthwise.

10   Preheat the oven to 140°C/275°F/Mark 1. Using a metal spatula spread the inside of the terrine with the forcemeat to a depth of 1 cm ($\frac{1}{2}$ inch). Then fill the terrine by laying alternating layers of eel fillets and the remaining forcemeat, ending with a layer of forcemeat. Cover with a piece of aluminium foil, which acts as a lid, and place the terrine in a bain-marie.

11   Bake for 3 hours in the slow oven. When it is cooked, let the terrine cool for several hours at room temperature and then place it, nearly cold, in the refrigerator overnight.

Serving the terrine

12   Serve the terrine as it is, without turning it out. Cut it in slices 1 cm ($\frac{1}{2}$ inch) thick, in the terrine, and eat it accompanied by a Watercress Sauce (**No 8**).

Suggestions for the home cook

* The admittedly long, slow cooking of this terrine is what gives it its melting richness.
* To make it even more melting and moist you can line the terrine with strips of pork back fat, covered with fine rounds of lemon peel, before coating it with the forcemeat.

* Carp or Red Mullet Terrine with Saint-Emilion (*Terrine de carpes ou rougets au Saint-Emilion*)
I only like fish terrines when they are made with really well-flavoured fish so I suggest you try making a terrine with carp or red mullet and red wine. Use this eel recipe as a basis, but substitute for the eel fillets the same weight of carp fillets or boned red mullet, and for the white wine, a red Bordeaux from Saint-Emilion. The tomato variation of Watercress Sauce (**No 9**) goes very well with this version of the dish.

HOT PASTRIES

for a light

first course

38 Asparagus-filled Pastries with Chervil Butter

Feuilleté d'asperges au beurre de cerfeuil
'Hot asparagus in a pastry cloud'

For four people

Main ingredients	40 medium-sized fresh **or** tinned asparagus spears 1 litre (1¾ pints) water and 15 g (½ oz) coarse salt 1 handful flour 180 g (6¼ oz) fresh **or** frozen Flaky Pastry (**No 118**) 1 beaten egg
Ingredients for the sauce	4 tablespoons of the water in which the asparagus has cooked 3 tablespoons chervil sprigs 4 tablespoons double cream 240 g (8½ oz) butter, at room temperature salt and pepper 1 tablespoon lemon juice
Equipment	1 medium-sized saucepan 1 rolling-pin 1 heavy knife 1 shallow sauté pan 2 baking-sheets

Preparing the asparagus, if fresh

1   Peel the spears with a potato-peeler, working from the head to the butt and holding the asparagus flat on the work-top. Wash them and cut each one 8 cm (3½ inches) below the tip. (The remainder of the spear can be used for soup.) Bring the salted water to the boil in the medium-sized saucepan and throw in the asparagus higgledy-piggledy. Cook for 7 minutes, then remove from the heat and keep hot in the cooking water.

Making the pastries

2   Preheat the oven to 220°C/425°F/Mark 7. Roll out the flaky pastry on a lightly-floured board, to form a rectangle 26 cm (10½ inches) by 16 cm (6½ inches) and about 4 mm (⅕ inch) thick.

3   Using a large sharp knife, trim the rectangle cleanly and neatly to measure 24 cm (9½ inches) by 14 cm (5½ inches). Cut it into four smaller rectangles, each 6 cm (just under 2½ inches) by 14 cm (5½ inches).

4   Prepare two clean baking-sheets by brushing them lightly with water. Turn the rectangles of pastry upside down and place them on the baking-sheets. Glaze the tops by brushing them very carefully with beaten egg, taking great care to see that none of it trickles down the sides, as this would prevent the pastries from rising properly.

5   Put the pastries in the oven and bake for 12–15 minutes. When they are done, turn the oven right down and leave them to keep hot with the oven door open.

Preparing the sauce

6   Remove the asparagus from their cooking water (or from the tin if you are not using fresh asparagus), keeping 4 tablespoons of the water. Drain, and arrange the spears in the bottom of the shallow sauté pan. Pour over the 4 tablespoons of water and add 2 tablespoons of chervil. Bring to the boil, and reduce by half.

7   Add the cream and the butter, cut in pieces, season with salt, pepper and lemon juice and boil for 1 minute, shaking the pan with a circular motion to blend the sauce, taking care not to break the asparagus spears. Remove from the heat.

(*continued on the next page*)

Finishing and serving the pastries

8 Using a serrated knife, carefully cut each pastry in half horizontally. Put the lower halves on hot plates or a serving-dish and arrange ten drained asparagus spears across each. Pour over the chervil sauce (5) and sprinkle with the remaining tablespoon of chervil sprigs. Top with the upper halves of pastry and serve immediately.

Suggestions for the home cook

* The fresh asparagus season is a short one, and if you want to make this dish at other times of the year you can use the same quantity of tinned asparagus.
* If you are feeling poor, you can replace the asparagus with the same quantity of cauliflower florets. The result is appetising and unusual.

For a more detailed description of flaky pastry, see **No 118.**

39 Truffle-filled Pastries with White Wine Sauce

Feuilleté de truffes au vin de Graves
'Truffles enriched with a layer of foie gras'

For four people

Main ingredients	1 handful flour
	180 g (6¼ oz) fresh **or** frozen Flaky Pastry **(No 118)**
	1 beaten egg
	120 g (4¼ oz) tinned truffles – about four whole truffles
	120 g (4¼ oz) fresh **or** tinned foie gras

Ingredients for the sauce	50 g (1¾ oz) butter
	1 heaped teaspoon salt
	4 turns of the pepper-mill
	4 tablespoons dry white Bordeaux wine
	4 tablespoons sherry
	4 tablespoons of juice from the truffle tin
	500 ml (scant pint) whipping cream
	1 tablespoon lemon juice

Equipment	1 rolling-pin
	1 heavy knife
	1 shallow sauté pan

Making the pastries

1   Preheat the oven to 220°C/425°F/Mark 7. Roll out the flaky pastry on a lightly-floured board, to form a rectangle 26 cm (10½ inches) by 16 cm (6½ inches) and about 4 mm (⅛ inch) thick.

2   Using a large sharp knife, trim the rectangle cleanly and neatly to measure 24 cm (9½ inches) by 14 cm (5½ inches). Cut it into four smaller rectangles, each 6 cm (just under 2½ inches) by 14 cm (5½ inches).

3   Prepare two clean baking-sheets by brushing them lightly with water. Turn the rectangles of pastry upside down and place them on the baking-sheets. Glaze the tops by brushing them very carefully with beaten egg, taking great care to see that none of it trickles down the sides, as this would prevent the pastries from rising properly.

4   Put the pastries in the oven and bake for 12–15 minutes. When they are done, turn the oven right down and leave them to keep hot with the oven door open.

Preparing the truffles

5   While the pastries are cooking, cut the truffles in paper-thin slices and season with salt and pepper. Heat the butter in the sauté pan and soften the truffles over a gentle heat for 3 minutes.

6   Add the white wine, sherry and truffle juice. Bring to the boil and reduce by one-third. Add the cream, bring to the boil again and simmer over a gentle heat for 15 minutes, until the mixture thickens. Test the consistency by dipping a wooden spatula into the sauce and tracing a channel with your finger through the sauce which clings to the spatula. If the channel holds its shape, the sauce is perfect.

Finishing and serving the pastries

7   Slice the foie gras into eight pieces with a hot knife.

8   Having first removed the truffle slices with a slotted spoon, check the seasoning of the sauce and add the tablespoon of lemon juice.

9   Using a serrated knife, carefully cut each pastry in half horizontally. Put the lower halves on hot plates or a hot serving-dish and cover with a slice of foie gras and a layer of truffle slices. Pour over the sauce (6), top with the upper halves of pastry and serve immediately.

40 Pastries with Frogs' Legs and Wood Mushrooms

Feuilleté de grenouilles au cresson et aux mousserons 'Frogs' legs in a watercress sauce'

For four people

Main ingredients	1 handful flour 180 g (6¼ oz) fresh **or** frozen Flaky Pastry (**No 118**) 1 beaten egg 800 g (1 lb 12 oz) frogs' legs – 20 pairs
Ingredients for the sauce	15 g (½ oz) butter 100 g (3½ oz) millers (mousserons), washed twice in running water and drained 1 level teaspoon fine salt 4 turns of the peppermill 500 ml (scant pint) whipping cream 1 level teaspoon Watercress Purée (**No 104**) 1 teaspoon lemon juice 2 tablespoons dry white wine 1 level tablespoon chopped shallot 15 g (½ oz) watercress leaves, with their little stalks
Equipment	1 rolling-pin 1 heavy knife 1 medium-sized saucepan with lid

Making the pastries

1 Preheat the oven to 220°C/425°F/Mark 7. Roll out the flaky pastry on a lightly-floured board, to form a rectangle 26 cm (10½ inches) by 16 cm (6½ inches) and about 4 mm (⅛ inch) thick.

2 Using a large sharp knife, trim the rectangle cleanly and neatly to measure 24 cm (9½ inches) by 14 cm (5½ inches). Cut it into four smaller rectangles, each 6 cm (just under 2½ inches) by 14 cm (5½ inches).

3 Prepare two clean baking-sheets by brushing them lightly with water. Turn the rectangles of pastry upside down and place them on the baking-sheets. Glaze the tops by brushing them very carefully with beaten egg, taking great care to see that none of it trickles down the sides, as this would prevent the pastries from rising properly.

4 Put the pastries in the oven and bake for 12–15 minutes. When they are done, turn the oven right down and leave them to keep hot with the oven door open.

Preparing the frogs' legs and the sauce

5 Heat the butter in the saucepan and soften the millers (mousserons) for 2 minutes without allowing them to brown. Season with a level teaspoon of salt and four turns of the pepper-mill.

6 Add the cream and bring to the boil. Put in the frogs' legs, cover and simmer for 5 minutes. Then remove the frogs' legs with a slotted spoon (be careful not to catch any of the millers at the same time) and put them on a plate to cool.

7 Simmer the cream for a further 8 minutes, uncovered, adding the watercress purée and lemon juice, and allow to reduce by half.

8 Meanwhile, bone the frogs' legs carefully and return the flesh to the pan (7). Remove from the heat and stir in the white wine and chopped raw shallot. Mix all together thoroughly, cover the pan and keep hot.

Finishing and serving the pastries

9 Using a serrated knife, carefully cut each pastry in half horizontally. Put the lower halves on hot plates or a hot serving-dish and arrange five frogs' legs on each, crossways. Pour over the sauce, sprinkle with the watercress leaves, top with the upper halves of pastry and serve immediately.

Suggestions for the home cook

* It is the combination of dry white wine, chopped raw shallot and crisp, slightly peppery watercress that gives the sauce its freshness.
* Frogs' legs, not always easy to obtain, can be replaced by small pieces of firm fresh fish, such as angler-fish, conger eel, etc. Allow 8 minutes cooking time in step 6.
* Millers (mousserons) can be replaced by an equal quantity of button mushrooms, chanterelles, morels or ceps, cut in fine slices or quartered according to their size.

For a note on frogs' legs see **No 19** and for a note on wild mushrooms page 17.

41 Scallop-filled Pastries with Truffle Sauce

Feuilleté de Saint-Jacques aux truffes 'The flavour of the sea with the aroma of truffles'

For four people

Main ingredients	24 fresh scallops
	1 handful flour
	180 g (6¼ oz) fresh **or** frozen Flaky Pastry (**No 118**)
	1 beaten egg

Ingredients for the sauce	15 g (½ oz) butter
	80 g (2¾ oz) tinned truffles, cut in julienne strips
	1 tablespoon of juice from the truffle tin
	300 ml (½ pint) whipping cream
	salt and pepper

Equipment	1 rolling-pin
	1 heavy knife
	1 shallow sauté pan
	1 small saucepan, with lid

Preparing the scallops (if the fishmonger hasn't already done so)

1   Open each shell with a strong knife and cut the scallop flesh away from the flat shell. Then scoop out the whole scallop from the concave shell with a tablespoon, catching the juices in a cloth-lined strainer placed over the small saucepan. Cut away the black intestinal tracts and tough membranes, wash the scallops in running water and dry them on kitchen paper.

Making the pastries

2   Preheat the oven to 220°C/425°F/Mark 7. Roll out the flaky pastry on a lightly-floured board, to form a rectangle 26 cm (10½ inches) by 16 cm (6½ inches) and about 4 mm (⅛ inch) thick.

3   Using a large sharp knife, trim the rectangle cleanly and neatly to measure 24 cm (9½ inches) by 14 cm (5½ inches). Cut it into four smaller rectangles, each 6 cm (just under 2½ inches) by 14 cm (5½ inches).

4   Prepare two clean baking-sheets by brushing them lightly with water. Turn the rectangles of pastry upside down and place them on the baking-sheets. Glaze the tops by brushing them very carefully with beaten egg, taking great care to see that none of it trickles down the sides, as this would prevent the pastries from rising properly.

5   Put the pastries in the oven and bake for 12–15 minutes. When they are done, turn the oven right down and leave them to keep hot with the oven door open.

Making the sauce

6   Heat the butter in the shallow sauté pan and cook the julienne strips of truffle gently for 2 minutes. Add the truffle juice and the cream, season, and boil for 3 or 4 minutes over a moderate heat. The sauce should reduce by half.

7   While the sauce is reducing, heat the scallop juices (1) in the small saucepan and poach the scallops for 1 minute in the simmering liquid, covered. Add the poaching liquid to the truffle sauce (6) and simmer for a minute or two.

(*continued on the next page*)

Finishing and serving the pastries

8   Using a serrated knife, carefully cut each pastry in half horizontally. Put the lower halves on hot plates or a hot serving-dish and arrange six drained scallops on each. Pour over the sauce (6), which has been enriched with the poaching liquid (7), cover with the upper halves of pastry and serve immediately.

Suggestions for the home cook

* You can intensify the sea-flavour of this dish by replacing 12 of the scallops with 12 plump oysters, poached in their own juices for 30 seconds. The oyster cooking liquid is added to the sauce in the same way.

* For an original finishing touch, strew the scallops with 4 tablespoons of braised vegetables (see **No 60**) after they have been sauced but before covering them with the upper halves of pastry.

* An amusing way to serve these pastries is to use four sets of scallop shells (1) carefully scraped and washed, and lightly buttered on the inside, as moulds for the flaky pastry. Line each shell with pastry and bake in the oven as indicated above (5). The pastries will take on the shape of the shells, and are then filled with the scallops and their sauce.

42 Freshwater Crayfish Pastries with Onion

Feuilleté d'écrevisses a l'oignon croquant 'A Russian flavour for freshwater crayfish'

For four people

Main ingredients	1 handful flour 180 g (6¼ oz) fresh **or** frozen Flaky Pastry (**No 118**) 1 beaten egg 32 freshwater crayfish **or** Dublin Bay prawns, shelled, and their sauce (*see* **No 7**)
Ingredients for the garnish	60 g (2 oz) freshly-chopped onions 1 teaspoon freshly-chopped chives
Equipment	1 rolling-pin 1 heavy knife 1 shallow sauté pan 1 bain-marie

Making the pastries

1   Preheat the oven to 220°C/425°F/Mark 7. Roll out the flaky pastry on a lightly-floured board, to form a rectangle 26 cm (10½ inches) by 16 cm (6½ inches) and about 4 mm (⅛ inch) thick.

2   Using a large sharp knife, trim the rectangle cleanly and neatly to measure 24 cm (9½ inches) by 14 cm (5½ inches). Cut it into four smaller rectangles, each 6 cm (just under 2½ inches) by 14 cm (5½ inches).

3   Prepare two clean baking-sheets by brushing them lightly with water. Turn the rectangles of pastry upside down and place them on the baking-sheets. Glaze the tops by brushing them very carefully with beaten egg, taking great care to see that none of it trickles down the sides, as this would prevent the pastries from rising properly.

4   Put the pastries in the oven and bake for 12–15 minutes. When they are done, turn the oven right down and leave them to keep hot with the oven door open.

Finishing and serving the pastries

5   Put the freshwater crayfish or Dublin Bay prawns and their sauce to warm through in a bain-marie.

6   Using a serrated knife, carefully cut each pastry in half horizontally. Put the lower halves on hot plates or a hot serving-dish, divide the crayfish and sauce equally between them, strew with chopped onion and chives, cap with the upper halves of pastry, and serve immediately.

Suggestion for the home cook

* The raw onion in this recipe is agreeably crunchy and surprising. It gives the dish a hint of freshness and sweetness. You can use the same idea in other recipes.

43 Chilled Freshwater Crayfish Mousse in Millefeuilles

Millefeuille d'écrevisses 'Crayfish in a creamy mousse for a summer lunch'

For four people

Main ingredients	1 handful flour 300 g (10½ oz) fresh **or** frozen Flaky Pastry (**No 118**) 32 freshwater crayfish **or** Dublin Bay prawns, shelled, with their sauce (*see* **No 7**) 8 crayfish or Dublin Bay prawn heads, for decoration (*see* **No 7**)
Ingredients for the crayfish cream	2 leaves of gelatine 200 ml (⅓ pint) whipping cream, chilled 1 teaspoon freshly-chopped tarragon 1 teaspoon freshly-chopped chervil salt and pepper
Equipment	1 bain-marie 1 rolling-pin 1 heavy knife

Suggestions for the home cook

* The pastry can be rolled out the night before and put in the refrigerator, on the baking-sheet, overnight. It will not shrink during cooking next morning, as sometimes happens.

* The dish can be made more easily if you modify the recipe for Crayfish Sauce **No 7** as follows. Incorporate 2 teaspoons of chopped fines herbes, 1 teaspoon lemon juice, 1 tablespoon tomato purée, salt, pepper and cayenne, with 300 ml (½ pint) whipped cream. 32 small Dublin Bay prawns are poached for 1½ minutes in boiling salted water, then shelled. The millefeuille and the final preparation remain the same.

(*continued on the next page*)

Preparing the crayfish cream

1   Heat the crayfish sauce through in the bain-marie and meanwhile soak the gelatine for 10 minutes in cold water to soften and swell it.

2   When the sauce is hot, add the drained gelatine and mix well. Cool either in the refrigerator or in a basin of ice cubes, stirring with a wooden spatula from time to time.

3   Whip the chilled cream until it is firm, light and clings to the whisk or beater.

4   Just as the sauce (2) is beginning to thicken and set, fold in the chopped herbs, the crayfish tails and the whipped cream (3) delicately with a wooden spatula. The result should be foamy and velvety. Taste for seasoning, and put in the refrigerator.

Preparing the millefeuille

5   Preheat the oven to 220°C/425°F/Mark 7. Lightly flour the work-top and roll out the flaky pastry into a large rectangle 20 cm (8 inches) by 45 cm (18 inches) and 2 mm ($\frac{1}{12}$ inch) thick.

6   Using the heavy knife, cut the pastry cleanly into three rectangular strips 15 cm (6 inches) by 20 cm (8 inches).

7   Brush the baking-sheet with water, lay the three strips of pastry on it and prick the surfaces all over with a fork. This stops the pastry 'ballooning' too much during the cooking.

8   Bake for 20 minutes in the hot oven (in two batches if your oven won't hold a baking-sheet large enough to take the three pieces of pastry).

9   Remove from the oven and allow to cool on a wire rack; the pastry should be an attractive nutty brown colour.

Finishing and serving the millefeuille

10   Using a metal spatula, spread the first layer of pastry with half the cream (4) and garnish with sixteen crayfish tails. Cover with the second layer of pastry and repeat the same process. Cap with the third layer of pastry, brushed on the upper side with a fine coating of the cream left in the bowl. Decorate with the eight crayfish heads, and serve on a long dish.

FOIE GRAS and FRESH CALVES' LAMBS' AND CHICKEN LIVERS

44 Fresh Foie Gras Terrine

Terrine de foie gras frais des Landes 'The best pâté in the world!'

For ten people

Main ingredients	2 raw fresh duck livers, weighing 600 g (1 lb 5 oz) each
Ingredients for the marinade	16 g ($\frac{1}{2}$ oz) fine salt $\frac{1}{2}$ teaspoon black pepper 1 pinch grated nutmeg 1 pinch quatre-épices (see page 163) 1 level teaspoon caster sugar 1$\frac{1}{2}$ tablespoons port 1$\frac{1}{2}$ tablespoons sherry 1$\frac{1}{2}$ tablespoons armagnac
Equipment	1 oval earthenware dish 1 oblong fireproof porcelain terrine with a lid, 16 cm (6$\frac{1}{2}$ inches) long, 11 cm (4$\frac{1}{2}$ inches) wide and 7 cm (2$\frac{3}{4}$ inches) deep

Editor's Note

The recipes in this section were originally intended to be made with foie gras, the rich, fattened livers of ducks rather than geese in this case, since they are a famous product of the farms round Eugénie-les-Bains in the Landes. However, Michel Guérard is aware that not everybody can readily buy these expensive and exquisite livers, and he therefore recommends substituting other sorts of liver, calves', lambs' or chicken, in most of the recipes. The first recipe, included for interest's sake and for those who are sometimes able to cook in France, is the classic method of preparing foie gras, and is not really suitable for other livers, although good-quality fresh chicken livers prepared in this way have a lovely flavour reminiscent of the real thing.

Two days in advance: preparing the foie gras and the marinade

1 Put the livers to soak for 1 hour in a basin of water at blood-heat (37°C/98·4°F). This cleans them as well as making them soft and easier to deal with.

2 Drain the livers and, with your hands, separate the larger from the smaller lobe of each liver. Cut each lobe open, using a small sharp knife, to reveal the network of veins inside. With the point of the knife, loosen each vein from the liver, working progressively towards the base of the lobe. Detach them by pulling them carefully away from the lobe, loosening them further with a small knife if necessary.

3 Very carefully, scrape away the greenish part which may be left by the gall-bladder.

4 Arrange the four opened lobes in the earthenware dish, season with salt, pepper, nutmeg, quatre-épices and sugar and moisten with the port, sherry and armagnac. Let the livers marinate for 12 hours in the refrigerator, turning them once or twice.

One day in advance: cooking the livers

5 Take the livers out of the refrigerator 1 hour before you want to start cooking them, and arrange the lobes as nearly in their original shape as you can. In the terrine, place first a large lobe, then the two small ones, and lastly the second large one, pressing them all down firmly.

6 Preheat the oven to 150°C/300°F/Mark 2. The oval earthenware dish in which the livers were marinated can be used as a bain-marie; wash it thoroughly and put in 2 cm (¾ inch) water. Bring it to 70°C/158°F in the low oven. Keeping the oven at the same temperature, place the terrine, without its lid, in the bain-marie. Cook for 40 minutes, during which time the temperature of the water in the bain-marie must on no account fall below or rise above 70°C/158°F. Keep checking with a thermometer.

Finishing and serving the terrine

7 Take the bain-marie and terrine out of the oven, remove the terrine, cover it with its lid and allow to cool slowly, at room temperature, for 2–3 hours. It should then be kept in the refrigerator overnight, before serving. (*continued on the next page*)

8   The terrine is served just as it is, with thick slices of 'pain de campagne'.

Suggestions for the home cook

* Depending on the quality of the livers and the fidelity with which you have been able to follow the cooking instructions in (5) the livers will have produced a layer of between $\frac{1}{2}$ cm ($\frac{1}{4}$ inch) and 1 cm ($\frac{1}{2}$ inch) of fat on top of the terrine.

* Liver terrines are the better and more succulent for being kept in the refrigerator for 3–4 days before serving, and they can be kept for up to a week.

* You can recognise the quality of a raw foie gras by taking it in your two hands, one lobe in each, and gently separating them. If the liver breaks up like a piece of suet it is very fat and will melt copiously during the cooking. If the flesh stretches like elastic before it tears it is full of fibres and will not melt in the cooking, but remain dry and flavourless. If the flesh stretches gently and without resistance, rather like chewing-gum, before falling cleanly apart, you can be sure that you have a perfect liver for this beautiful terrine.

45 Fresh Foie Gras or Calves' Liver with Pepper Jelly

Foie gras frais en gelée de poivre 'Foie gras cooked whole'

For four people

Main ingredients	1 raw foie gras, weighing 600 g (1 lb 5 oz) **or** 600 g (1 lb 5 oz) calves' liver in a piece larded all the way through and all over with strips of smoked streaky bacon fat 1½ teaspoons fine salt ⅓ teaspoon white pepper 600 g (1 lb 5 oz) duck or goose fat **or** 600 g (1 lb 5 oz) fresh lard, flavoured by heating with a small sprig of thyme
Ingredients for finishing the dish	15 g (½ oz) aspic powder dissolved in 250 ml (scant ½ pint) cold water 1 teaspoon caster sugar 4 tablespoons wine vinegar 1 teaspoon armagnac 1 teaspoon very coarsely crushed peppercorns ('poivre mignonette')
Equipment	1 oblong porcelain terrine 16 cm (6½ inches) long, 11 cm (4½ inches) wide and 7 cm (2¾ inches) deep 1 basin containing crushed ice 1 long serving-dish

Suggestions for the home cook

* You can keep liver prepared in this way for up to a month in the refrigerator. The morning after it has been cooked (4) drain it well and wrap tightly in aluminium foil, pressing it to the shape of the liver. Return it to the terrine and cover with the cooking fat. Store in the refrigerator. The fat will keep it moist and the foil preserve its shape, and you will be able to offer your guests a perfect whole foie gras at short notice, either served in the pepper jelly suggested in this recipe, or just as it is. *(continued on the next page)*

Two days in advance: macerating the liver

1   Keep the liver whole. (If using foie gras do *not* separate the lobes or remove the veins as instructed in the previous recipe **(No 44)**, but merely carefully scrape away all traces of the gall bladder from between the lobes.) Season the liver all over with salt and the white pepper and allow to stand, in a deep dish, overnight in the refrigerator.

One day in advance: cooking the liver

2   Take the liver out of the refrigerator 1 hour before you want to cook it. Preheat the oven to 160°C/320°F/Mark 2½ and melt the duck or goose fat or lard in the terrine, bringing it up to simmering point, either in the oven or on the top of the stove.

3   Place the liver carefully in the terrine and cook at a very slow simmer, in the oven for 15 minutes (duck liver) or 35 minutes (calves' liver), turning it over half-way through the cooking.

4   Take the liver out of the terrine with a slotted spoon and place it carefully on a flat dish. Cover liver and dish with an airtight layer of aluminium foil and, when the liver has cooled, put it in the refrigerator overnight.

Finishing and serving the dish

5   Bring the dissolved aspic to the boil in a small saucepan.

6   In a second saucepan, boil the sugar and wine vinegar together for 2 minutes or until the liquid is syrupy and golden-brown. Add this syrup to the aspic in the first saucepan (5) and add the teaspoon of armagnac.

7   Put the saucepan into the bowl of crushed ice and stir the liquid until it is nearly set.

8   Take the liver out of the refrigerator, put it in the oval serving-dish, and coat it carefully with half the almost-set jelly. Sprinkle it evenly all over with the crushed peppercorns, and coat with the remainder of the jelly. Return the liver to the refrigerator for at least 1 hour before serving.

9   Present the whole liver to your guests, and slice it at the table into 1 cm (½ inch) slices. Serve with its jelly and with large slices of toasted 'pain de campagne'.

46 Foie Gras or Chicken Livers in a Green Waistcoat

Foie gras en habit vert aux blancs de poireaux 'Rosy foie gras in a lettuce wrapping'

For four people

Main ingredients	1 fresh duck liver weighing 600 g (1 lb 5 oz) or chicken livers 1 litre (1¾ pints) water and 2 teaspoons coarse salt salt and freshly-ground pepper
Ingredients for the garnish	1 litre (1¾ pints) water and 2 teaspoons coarse salt 12 handsome lettuce leaves, washed 200 g (7 oz) – about 16 – very young leeks, white parts only ⎱ cut in 4 cm 200 g (7 oz) very fine French beans ⎰ (1¾ inch) lengths 25 g (1 oz) butter
Ingredients for the sauce	150 ml (¼ pint) stock made with ¼ chicken stock cube dissolved in 150 ml (¼ pint) water 3 tablespoons port 1½ tablespoons truffle juice (optional) 50 g (1¾ oz) butter
Equipment	2 medium-sized saucepans 1 oven-dish 1 frying-pan 1 small saucepan

A day in advance: preparing the foie gras

1 If using foie gras, scrape away all green traces of the gall bladder from the liver, using a small knife. Bring the litre (1¾ pints) of salted water to the boil in a saucepan and plunge in the liver for 1 minute so that it can give off some of its fat. When the minute is up, take the pan off the heat, let the liver cool in the cooking water and put it in the refrigerator overnight. (If you are using chicken livers see method at the end of the recipe.)

Preparing the vegetables and foie gras

2 Bring 1 litre (1¼ pints) salted water to the boil in a medium saucepan and blanch the lettuce leaves for 1 minute. Remove carefully with a slotted spoon, refresh in cold water and lay out on a clean cloth, with the central rib of each leaf towards you.

3 Tie the leeks in a bundle and cook for 10 minutes in the same water. After 4 minutes add the French beans. Drain them as soon as they are cooked, and untie the leeks.

4 With a slotted spoon, take the foie gras carefully out of its cooking liquid and drain carefully on a cloth or kitchen paper. Separate the two lobes and then, using a sharp knife dipped in hot water, slice the liver, as if it were a fillet of beef, into 12 slices 1·5 cm (½ inch) thick. Season with salt and freshly-ground pepper.

5 Place a slice of liver in the middle of each lettuce leaf (2) and wrap it up into a little parcel. Cut away about a third of the leaf on either side of the central rib so that the rib will act as a kind of stalk for the leaf bundle.

6 Preheat the oven to 180°C/355°F/Mark 4. Arrange the bundles in the oven-dish 'seam' side down. Add the chicken stock, port and (if used) truffle juice. Cook gently for 10 minutes in the oven.

Finishing and presenting the dish

7 While the liver is cooking (6), gently toss the leeks and beans (3) in the 25 g (1 oz) butter in the frying-pan to heat through.

8 Arrange the leeks in a semi-circle round each plate or round a serving-dish, alternating them with little piles of beans. Place three lettuce bundles in the shape of a trefoil on each individual plate, or arrange all twelve prettily on the serving-dish. Keep the plates or dish warm in the oven with the door open.

9   Pour the liquid from the oven-dish (6) into a small saucepan, bring to the boil and reduce by half. Gradually incorporate 50 g (1¾ oz) butter, in pieces, shaking the pan with a circular motion to blend the sauce thoroughly. Taste for seasoning and pour the sauce around the lettuce bundles and vegetables.

Suggestions for the home cook

* If you are using chicken livers you will need one per bundle (12 in all). Instead of poaching them (1), sauté them briskly in a little butter and season with salt, pepper, finely-chopped shallot and a pinch of thyme. The insides should be rare, so that the livers will still be rosy after the little lettuce bundles have been cooked in the oven.

47 Hot Duck Foie Gras or Calves' Liver on a Bed of Corn and Pulses

Foie gras chaud de canard aux petites céréales 'Fried crisp and made piquant with sharp vinegar'

For four people

Main ingredients	1 fresh duck liver, weighing 600 g (1 lb 5 oz) **or** best calves' liver **or** a very young lamb's liver, in a piece weighing 600 g (1 lb 5 oz) salt and pepper 20 g ($\frac{3}{4}$ oz) flour 1$\frac{1}{2}$ tablespoons arachide oil

Ingredients for the vegetable garnish	1 litre (1$\frac{3}{4}$ pints) water and 15 g ($\frac{1}{2}$ oz) salt 20 g ($\frac{3}{4}$ oz) fresh **or** frozen **or** tinned sweetcorn kernels 20 g ($\frac{3}{4}$ oz) extra small dried red haricot beans, soaked overnight 20 g ($\frac{3}{4}$ oz) fresh **or** frozen peas 8 handsome lettuce leaves $\frac{1}{2}$ lemon 500 ml (scant pint) water 2 tablespoons cold water 40 g (1$\frac{1}{2}$ oz) butter

Ingredients for the accompanying sauce	2 tablespoons chopped shallot 4 tablespoons sherry vinegar 4 tablespoons walnut oil 2 teaspoons of freshly-chopped parsley 2 teaspoons freshly-chopped chervil salt and pepper

Equipment	1 large saucepan 1 small saucepan 1 shallow sauté pan 1 large heavy-bottomed frying-pan

Cooking the sweetcorn, pulses and vegetables

1   Bring the litre (1¾ pints) salted water to the boil in a large sauce-pan and cook everything as follows; the sweetcorn, if fresh, for 20 minutes, the red beans for at least 10 minutes, the peas, if fresh, for 6 minutes (if frozen peas or sweetcorn are used cook them for 3 minutes), and the lettuce leaves for 2 minutes.

2   Meanwhile, peel the half lemon with a vegetable peeler and cut the zest into tiny julienne strips the size of pine needles. Blanch them for 2 minutes in the 500 ml (scant pint) unsalted water in a small saucepan.

3   When the vegetables are cooked, put them (except the lettuce leaves) in the shallow sauté pan, together with the lemon peel, and moisten with 2 tablespoons of cold water. Bring to the boil and add the 40 g (1½ oz) butter, in pieces, gradually, shaking the pan in a regu-lar circular motion to thicken the sauce and coat the vegetables lav-ishly. Keep hot over a very low heat.

Preparing and cooking the foie gras

4   If using duck's liver scrape away all green parts left by the gall bladder from between the lobes of the liver, using a small knife. If using calves' or lamb's liver carefully cut out any large veins. Dip the knife in hot water and slice the liver across into 4 slices of about 150 g (5¼ oz) each. Season with salt and pepper and coat each slice with flour, tapping it to shake off any surplus.

5   Heat the oil in the frying-pan, and just as it begins to smoke, put in the slices of liver. Fry them for 2–3 minutes on each side.

Finishing and serving the dish

6   Lay the blanched lettuce leaves (1) on individual plates or a hot serving-dish and place a slice of liver on each. Scatter the little pulses and grains (3) round and keep hot. Soften the chopped shallot for 10 seconds in the frying-pan (5), pour in the sherry vinegar, bring to the boil and reduce by half. Away from the heat, add the walnut oil, herbs, salt and pepper. Pour this sauce over the liver and serve at once.

Suggestion for the home cook

* Liver tends to be rather damp, and coating the slices with flour enables the hot fat to seal the surfaces and make them crusty. But it must be done immediately before cooking, or the flour will turn into a soggy blanket.

48 Duck Foie Gras or Calves' Liver with Glazed Turnips

Foie gras de canard aux navets confits 'A combination of foie gras and a simple vegetable'

For four people

Main ingredients	1 fresh duck liver weighing 600 g (1 lb 5 oz) **or** fresh calves' liver, cut in small escalopes 20 g (¾ oz) flour 1½ tablespoons arachide oil
Ingredients for the vegetable garnish and the accompanying sauce	1 litre (1¾ pints) water and 15 g (½ oz) coarse salt 48 miniature turnips made by peeling, cleaning and 'turning' 500 g (1 lb 2 oz) of ordinary turnips 25 g (1 oz) butter 1 tablespoon caster sugar 1 tablespoon wine vinegar 4 tablespoons sherry vinegar 4 tablespoons port 2 tablespoons water 30 g (1 oz) truffles, cut in tiny julienne strips (optional) 40 g (1½ oz) butter
Equipment	1 stainless-steel saucepan with lid 1 shallow sauté pan 1 large heavy-bottomed frying-pan

Preparing the turnips and the sauce

1 Bring the 1 litre (1¾ pints) salted water to the boil in the stainless-steel saucepan, throw in the baby turnips and cook, uncovered for 15 minutes. Drain in a colander.

2 Heat the 25 g (1 oz) butter in the sauté pan until it becomes golden 'beurre noisette'. Put in the drained turnips and brown lightly all over. Sprinkle them with the caster sugar and shake gently over the heat for 3 minutes until they turn the colour of amber.

3 Add the wine vinegar to the pan and boil for 10 seconds or until the liquid has almost completely evaporated. Then, add the sherry vinegar, port and water and simmer gently for 1 minute.

4 Sprinkle on the julienne of truffles (if used) and add the 40 g (1½ oz) butter in pieces. It will melt in the simmering liquid and give the sauce the desired silkiness. Leave the pan on a low heat, covered, until needed.

Preparing and cooking the liver

5 If using duck liver scrape away all green traces left by the gall-bladder from between the lobes using a sharp knife. Dip the knife in hot water and slice the cleaned duck liver or calves' liver across into four even slices each weighing 150 g (5¼ oz). Season with salt and pepper and roll each slice in flour, tapping it to shake off any surplus.

6 Heat the arachide oil in the frying-pan, and just as it begins to smoke put in the slices of liver. Fry them for 2–3 minutes on each side.

Finishing and serving the dish

7 Arrange the slices on individual hot plates or a hot serving-dish and cover completely with the turnip sauce.

49 Foie Gras Pot-au-Feu

Pot-au-feu de foie gras 'Sumptuous rusticity'

For four people

Main ingredients	1 large onion, unpeeled 1·5 litres (2½ pints) stock made from 3 chicken stock cubes and 1·5 litres (2½ pints) water 1 fresh duck liver weighing 600 g (1 lb 5 oz) **or** 600 g (1 lb 5 oz) calves' liver in a piece 8 tablespoons port 8 tablespoons madeira coarse salt and freshly-ground pepper
Ingredients for the vegetable garnish and accompanying sauce	16 miniature carrots ⎫ 16 miniature turnips ⎬ Made from 200 g (7 oz) each of normal-sized vegetables peeled and 'turned' into miniature vegetables 16 miniature cucumbers ⎭ 8 tiny onions 4 small leeks 24 asparagus spears, fresh or tinned 1·5 litres (2½ pints) water and 20 g (¾ oz) coarse salt 4 waxy potatoes 8 tender cabbage leaves 120 g (4¼ oz) noodles (tagliatelle) 200 ml (⅓ pint) Butter Sauce with Truffles **(No 5) or** 200 ml (⅓ pint) Fresh Tomato Sauce **(No 4)**
Equipment	3 large saucepans 1 cloth

Cooking the vegetables

1 Cut the large unpeeled onion in two, cross-ways, and put the two halves to toast to a golden colour and caramelise under a hot grill, cut side up.

2 In a large saucepan, boil up the 1·5 litres (2½ pints) stock with the golden onion halves and cook the carrots, turnips, tiny onions and leeks for 10 minutes and the cucumbers and asparagus (if fresh) for 5 minutes. Remove from the heat and keep hot in the cooking stock. (If you are using tinned asparagus, drain it and add to the pan to heat through.)

3 Bring 1·5 litres (2½ pints) of salted water to the boil in a second saucepan and cook the small potatoes for 20 minutes and the cabbage leaves for 10 minutes.

Cooking the liver

4 If using duck liver, scrape away all green traces left by the gall bladder from between the lobes of the liver, using a sharp knife.

5 Leaving just enough stock – about one-third – to cover the vegetables and keep them hot, transfer the rest of the cooking stock from the first saucepan (2) to a third saucepan. Add the port and madeira, bring to the boil and reduce by one-third.

6 Lower the heat so that the liquid is barely simmering and poach the liver for 15 minutes if using foie gras, up to 35 minutes for calves' liver. Take it out carefully with a slotted spoon, wrap it in a cloth and put it between two soup-plates in a low oven with the door open to keep hot.

7 Turn up the heat a little under the saucepan and throw the noodles into the boiling stock. Cook them for 6 minutes from the time the stock returns to the boil or until they are just cooked. Take them out with a slotted spoon and drain in a colander.

Finishing and serving the pot-au-feu

8 Carpet the serving-dish with the drained cabbage leaves.

9 Unwrap the liver and cut into 8 escalopes with a thin sharp knife and season them with salt and pepper. Rearrange the liver in its original shape and lay on the cabbage-leaf bed.

(*continued on the next page*)

10   Place the vegetables and noodles all round the liver in little bunches and mounds, using their shapes and colours to make a pretty arrangement. Sprinkle the vegetables with 4 tablespoons of the cooking stock in which they were cooked (5).

11   Serve the dish as it is, and pass the hot Butter Sauce with Truffles **No 5** in a sauceboat, so that the guests can moisten their noodles with it as they choose.

Suggestions for the home cook

* Cooking times for foie gras vary according to its shape – round or elongated – and quality. I have given the average time, but you may find you need 2–3 minutes more or less. The same thing applies to calves' liver in a piece.
* Keep the cooking stock; it is delicious and, if thoroughly skimmed with a small ladle to remove the fat, can be served piping hot in soup-bowls, with an egg poached in each one.
* In spring, the 'turned' miniature vegetables can be replaced with proper baby vegetables – carrots, turnips, onions – each with a little top-knot of leaves or fronds about 2 cm ($\frac{1}{2}$ inch) long.

FISH, SHELLFISH AND CRUSTACEANS

50 Poached Oysters in Green Waistcoats

Huîtres chaudes en feuilles vertes
'Oysters wrapped in lettuce with hot butter
sauce'

For four people

Main ingredients	24 plump oysters – native or Portuguese
Ingredients for the accompanying sauce	150 g (5¼ oz) butter, softened to room temperature pepper 1 tablespoon lemon juice
Ingredients for the garnish of vegetables	70 g (2½ oz) carrots 80 g (2¾ oz) white part of leeks 20 g (¾ oz) butter 1 litre (1¾ pints) water and 2 teaspoons coarse salt 24 lettuce leaves salt and pepper
Equipment	4 oyster plates **or** 4 plates covered with coarse salt 1 shallow saucepan 1 large saucepan 1 small saucepan

Preparation of the vegetables

1 Clean and wash the carrots and leeks, and cut them into fine julienne strips.

2 Heat the butter in a shallow pan and cook the julienne briskly, seasoned with salt and pepper, for 2 minutes. Keep hot.

3 Bring the water and salt to the boil in a large pan. Blanch the lettuce leaves in it for 1 minute and drain them on a cloth.

Preparing the oysters

4 If the oysters have not been opened by the fishmonger, open them with an oyster knife. Using a teaspoon, remove the oysters from their shells and put them in a sieve, placed over a small saucepan so that the juice is caught.

5 Wash the concave halves of the shells and place them in the hollows of the oyster plates or on the salt-covered plates, making sure they are firm and won't tip over. Keep them hot in a low oven with the door open.

6 Heat the oyster juices to simmering point in the small saucepan and poach the oysters for 30 seconds in the simmering liquid. Remove the oysters with a slotted spoon. Reserve the cooking liquid.

7 Wrap the oysters in the lettuce leaves, making them into little parcels. Put them back in the shells and keep hot.

Preparing the sauce

8 Bring the oyster cooking liquid to the boil and reduce by half, (*don't* add salt!). Add the 150 g (5¼ oz) butter in pieces over a lowered heat, shaking the pan with a swirling circular motion to blend the butter sauce. It will become thick and rich. (You can whisk the sauce instead of shaking the pan.) Season with two turns of the peppermill and add the tablespoon of lemon juice.

Finishing and serving the dish

9 Cover each individual oyster with a tablespoon of butter sauce and strew with a few of the julienne vegetables. Serve immediately.

(*continued on the next page*)

Suggestions for the home cook

* The oysters can be cooked, wrapped in their lettuce leaves and replaced in their shells the day beforehand, and stored in the refrigerator overnight. When you need them, let them return to room temperature then give them 1 minute in a very hot oven (240°C/470°F/ Mark 9). Take them out of the oven, and pour over the butter sauce, which *must* be made the same day.
* For a special dinner, Christmas for instance, the vegetable julienne could be replaced with half a teaspoon of chilled caviar per oyster.

51 Scallops with Shredded Endives

*Coquilles Saint-Jacques à l'effilochée
d'endives 'The sweet, light flavour of scallops
with subtly bitter endives'*

For four people

Main ingredients	24 fresh scallops salt and pepper 2 heaped tablespoons flour 60 g (2 oz) butter
Ingredients for the endive sauce	250 g (8¾ oz) endives, trimmed and washed 40 g (1½ oz) butter salt and pepper 1 teaspoon caster sugar 500 ml (scant pint) whipping cream
Ingredients for finishing the dish	1 heaped tablespoon chervil sprigs **or** parsley
Equipment	1 large heavy-bottomed saucepan with lid 1 frying-pan

Suggestions for the home cook

* To save time in making the endive sauce, you can simply cut the endive into the thinnest possible rounds, instead of julienne strips.
* The sauce also goes well with veal escalopes or poached chicken.

(*continued on the next page*)

Preparing the scallops

1 If the scallops have not been opened for you by the fishmonger, open them by inserting a stiff-bladed knife between the two shells. Detach the scallop with its orange coral from the lower shell with a knife, remove it with a teaspoon, and pull away and discard the membrane or frill and the black stomach. Wash the scallops thoroughly and dry on a cloth or kitchen paper.

Preparing the shredded endive sauce

2 Cut the endives into pieces 4 cm (1½ inches) long and then slice them vertically into julienne strips.

3 Heat the 40 g (1½ oz) butter in the saucepan until it browns and stops 'singing' or sputtering, when all the water has evaporated from it (beurre noisette). Throw in the julienne of endives, season with salt and pepper and sprinkle with the teaspoon of sugar. Allow to brown lightly, stirring with the fork.

4 Cover the saucepan and cook on a low heat for 15 minutes.

5 Add the cream and simmer, uncovered, for 10 minutes. At the end of this time the mixture will be rather thicker and richer.

Cooking the scallops

6 Prick the orange 'corals' of the scallops with a fork to prevent them bursting while cooking. Season the scallops with salt and pepper, roll them in flour and tap them with the fingers to remove the surplus.

7 Heat the 60 g (2 oz) butter in a frying-pan until it becomes 'beurre noisette'. Throw in the scallops and let them cook on a brisk heat for 1–1½ minutes on each side, according to their size. They should be lightly browned at the end of cooking.

Serving the scallops

8 Coat the bottoms of four individual dishes, or a large serving-dish, with the endive sauce.

9 Using a slotted spoon, take out and drain the scallops and place on the plates or dish. Sprinkle the sprigs of chervil over the scallops and serve at once.

52 Didier Oudill's Braised Scallops in their Shells

Les coquilles à la coque de Didier Oudill
'simple and subtle'

For four people

Main ingredients	12 fresh scallops in their shells 2 kg (4 lb 6½ oz) coarse salt salt and pepper 80 g (2¾ oz) butter 120 g (4¼ oz) flaky pastry **(No 118)** ½ beaten egg
Ingredients for the vegetable garnish	100 g (3½ oz) carrots 100 g (3½ oz) onions 100 g (3½ oz) button mushrooms 50 g (1¾ oz) butter salt and pepper 1 level teaspoon freshly-chopped tarragon 1 tablespoon chopped shallot
Equipment	1 mouli-julienne 1 heavy-bottomed saucepan with lid 1 baking-sheet

Preparing the scallops

1 Open the scallops with a strong knife and detach the scallop from the lower shell. Scoop out the scallops with a spoon, catching all their juice in a strainer lined with a fine cloth and placed over a bowl. Pull away and discard the membrane or frill and the black stomach parts, wash the scallops thoroughly in running water, dry them on a cloth, separate the 'corals' and cut the white parts in two across the middle to obtain 24 rounds.

2 Scrub eight of the shells (tops and bottoms) under running water and keep them on one side.

Preparing the vegetable garnish

3 Shred the scraped and washed carrots on the julienne blade of the mouli-julienne. Cut the washed and peeled onions and the button mushrooms, which have a springy texture, into julienne strips by hand.

4 Heat the 50 g (1¾ oz) butter in the saucepan and cook the onions and carrots for 5 minutes. Then, add the button mushrooms and cook for a further 3 minutes. Salt, pepper, add the teaspoon of chopped tarragon, cover and simmer for 2 minutes.

Preparing the flaky pastry

5 Roll out the flaky pastry (**No 118**) with a rolling pin and cut it into 8 strips 25 cm (10 inches) long by 3 cm (1¼ inches) wide.

Cooking the scallops

6 Preheat the oven to 250°C/480°F/Mark 9. Spread the coarse salt on the baking-sheet and arrange the eight deep scallop shells on it, making sure they are firmly based and won't tip.

7 Divide half the vegetables (4) among the eight shells and sprinkle them with the chopped shallot.

8 Put the coral and three rounds of the white part of the scallop on each shell, and season with salt and pepper.

9 Cover the scallops with the rest of the vegetables, sprinkle them with the strained scallop juice (1) and put an eighth of the butter on each.

Foie gras (or Calves' Liver) with Sweetcorn and Pulses **(No 47)** Foie gras (or Calves' Liver) in Pepper Jelly **(No 45)**

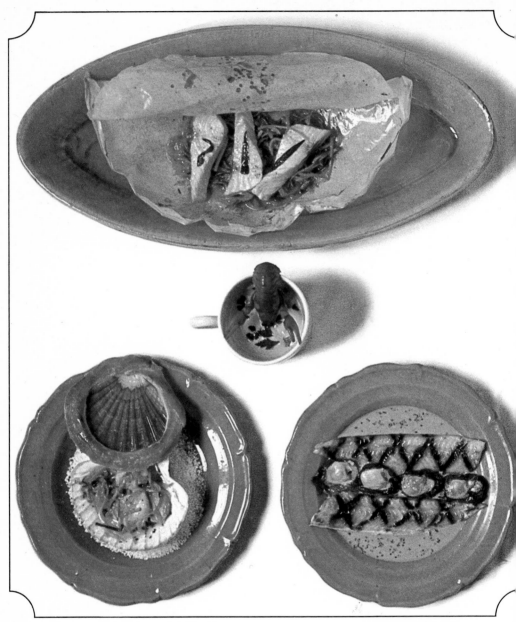

Salmon 'en papillote' **(No 60)** Freshwater Crayfish Soup **(No 21)** Didier Oudill's Braised
Scallops **(No 52)** Grilled Sole with Oysters and Chives **(No 67)**

Truffled Lobster with Tomato and Basil **(No 54)** 'Fish-Market in a Casserole' **(No 68)**
Sea-Bream in a Salt Crust **(No 62)**

Fish, shellfish and crustaceans

10 Put a flat scallop shell on top of each filled hollow shell and edge them with a strip of flaky pastry, brushed with beaten egg, to seal the shells completely.

11 Bake in the very hot oven for 10–12 minutes according to the size of the scallops.

Serving the scallops

12 Crush the salt, which will have hardened during the cooking, on the baking-sheet, and redistribute it between the plates. Put two scallops on each, just as they are, and let the guests have the pleasure of opening them.

Suggestions for the home cook

* For the bands of flaky pastry you could, of course, use commercial frozen flaky pastry... or even simpler, wooden clothes-pegs!

53 Scallop Mousse with Crayfish Sauce

Mousseline de Saint-Jacques au coulis d'écrevisses 'The secret of fish mousses'

For six people

Main ingredients	375 g (13¼ oz) fresh scallops, without shells 2 teaspoons salt 10 turns of the peppermill 1 whole egg 1 egg white 50 ml (scant pint) double cream 50 g (1¾ oz) melted butter 6 whole freshwater crayfish or Dublin Bay prawns removed from their shells, plus 6 tails and 6 emptied head shells kept back from making the Freshwater Crayfish Sauce **(No 7)** 6 slices of fresh or preserved truffle (optional)
Accompanying sauce	400 ml (¾ pint) Freshwater Crayfish Sauce **(No 7)**
Equipment	1 liquidiser **or** food processor 6 white porcelain ovenproof cocottes 9 cm (3½ inches) across and 4 cm (1½ inches) deep

Preparing the mousse

1 Blend the scallops, seasoned with salt and pepper in the liquidiser or food processor for 3–4 minutes.

2 When the scallops have become a smooth purée add the whole egg and the egg white. Blend for a further minute. Put the container in the refrigerator for 30 minutes to firm the mixture.

3 Then return the container to the mixer, add the 500 ml (scant pint) of cream and blend for several seconds. The mousse should have become very rich and creamy.

Preparing the moulds and cooking the mousse

4 Preheat the oven to 220°C/425°F/Mark 7. Brush the interior of the six cocottes with melted butter. Fill them to the brim with the scallop purée and cook, in a bain-marie, for 30 minutes in the oven. To make sure that a hard skin does not build up, cover the cocottes with a sheet of foil.

Finishing and serving the scallop mousse

5 When the cocottes have been in the oven for 15 minutes, gently heat the previously prepared Crayfish Sauce **(No 7)**. Add the six shelled crayfish tails, but not until 2 minutes before serving, as they will otherwise shrink and toughen.

6 When the mousses are cooked, turn them out on six hot plates or a hot serving dish.

7 Pour hot crayfish sauce generously over each mousse and decorate with a truffle slice (if used) and a 'crayfish' made up of a tail from the sauce and one of the empty head shells.

Suggestions for the home cook

* These mousses can be made with many fish, but you will need to modify the quantities according to the kind used. For 500 ml (scant pint) cream, 1 whole egg and 1 egg white, you will need 375 g (13¼ oz) of lobster or Dublin Bay prawn flesh, but only 250 g (8¾ oz) of pike, turbot, John Dory, whiting, sole, hake or squid.

(*continued on the next page*)

* A simpler method is to take 200 g (7 oz) of boned and skinned fish, purée it in the liquidiser and blend it briefly with 500 ml (scant pint) milk, 4 egg yolks and 2 whole eggs. Season the mixture and cook in cocottes in a bain-marie as you would a crême caramel. The result is delicious and melts in the mouth.

* If you have more crayfish tails left over from making the crayfish sauce, try burying one in the mousse in each cocotte before cooking, to surprise your guests.

* The truffle slice can be replaced with half a stoned black olive.

* The Freshwater Crayfish Sauce can be replaced with a light Hollandaise Sauce (page 74) or simply with a Tomato Sauce (**No 4**) flavoured with basil and tarragon.

54 Truffled Lobster with Tomato and Basil

Homard aux truffes à la tomate fraîche et au basilic 'Truffles and basil – an unusual and delicious combination with lobster'

For four people

Main ingredients	4 small live lobsters weighing 400 g (14 oz) each 2 litres (3½ pints) water and 50 g (1¾ oz) coarse salt 150 ml (¼ pint) wine vinegar 1 bouquet garni 1 teaspoon crushed peppercorns
Ingredients for the accompanying sauce	2 teaspoons butter 20 g (¾ oz) truffles, fresh or preserved, cut in julienne strips salt and pepper 400 ml (¾ pint) whipping cream 2 heaped tablespoons raw tomato pulp **(No 99)** ¼ teaspoon fresh basil pounded or liquidised with ½ teaspoon olive oil
Equipment	1 large saucepan 1 heavy cleaver 1 small saucepan 1 pair kitchen scissors

Cooking the lobsters

1   Bring the ingredients for the court-bouillon (water, salt, vinegar, bouquet garni and peppercorns) to the boil in the large saucepan.

2   Kill the lobsters as recommended on page 215. Crack the claws carefully with the back of the heavy cleaver to make it easier to extract the flesh after cooking.

3   Plunge the lobsters into the boiling court-bouillon for 5 minutes.

4   Remove the pan from the heat and let the lobsters finish cooking in the hot court-bouillon as you make the sauce.

Preparing the sauce

5   Heat the butter in the small saucepan and sauté the truffle julienne quickly for 30 seconds. Season lightly with salt and pepper and stir in the cream. Bring to the boil and reduce over a moderate heat for 10 minutes, until the mixture has thickened slightly and become smooth and velvety.

6   Add the 2 tablespoons tomato pulp and the pounded basil. Taste for seasoning and let the sauce mellow on a very low heat or in a bain-marie, for 15 minutes, without boiling.

Finishing and serving the dish

7   Take the lobsters out of the court-bouillon. Remove the tails and take out the flesh, cutting through the underside of the tail shell with scissors. Slice the shelled tails in $\frac{1}{2}$ cm ($\frac{1}{4}$ inch) medallions. Remove the flesh in one piece from the cracked claws.

8   Empty the heads completely, discarding the gravel sac and putting the succulent coral and intestines (tomali) on one side for another use (Sauce Américaine page 77 for instance, or soups).

9   With a pair of sharp scissors cut a rectangular opening in the top of the lobsters' head-shells and plant a pair of shelled claws in each.

10   On the hot plates or a hot serving dish, arrange the heads decorated with their claws, followed by the medallions of tail-flesh arranged as far as possible in the original shape of the lobster. Cover the medallions *only* with the accompanying truffle and basil sauce (6).

Suggestions for the home cook

* Leaving the sauce to mellow (6) allows the three flavours of truffle, basil and tomato to enrich and permeate each other thoroughly. This sauce can therefore be prepared a day ahead.

* The dish can be embellished with 12 oysters, poached for 20 seconds in their own filtered juices. This cooking liquid is added to the sauce at the same time as the cream (5) and the oysters arranged around the lobsters on the serving dish.

* If you haven't any truffles they can be replaced pleasantly by 30 g (1 oz) button mushrooms cut in julienne strips.

Editor's note

Dealing with a live lobster at home is a problem – if possible ask your fishmonger to kill it for you and then hurry home and cook it. On a hot day take a cold insulated bag to carry it in. Remember that raw shellfish should be kept for a minimum of time as it deteriorates very rapidly. If you *are* stuck with doing the job yourself, however, the following method is probably the kindest. Take a cleaver or heavy knife and bang it down sharply where the shell of the head meets the body. This will kill the creature instantly.

55   Freshwater Crayfish Paupiettes with Thyme

Paupiettes d'écrevisses au thym et aux choux de Bruxelles 'Little parcels of shellfish redolent of river and garden'

For four people

Main ingredients	750 g (1 lb 10½ oz) live freshwater crayfish **or** about 20 Dublin Bay prawns 500 ml (scant pint) water and 2 teaspoons coarse salt 24 fine green leaves from the outside of Brussels sprouts 1 bass fillet weighing 500 g (1 lb 2 oz), skinned and boned by the fishmonger 75 g (2½ oz) softened butter
Ingredients for cooking the crayfish	2 tablespoons olive oil ½ carrot ⎫ ¼ onion ⎬ peeled and cut in tiny mirepoix dice 1 shallot ⎭ 1 small bouquet garni 1 unpeeled, crushed clove of garlic salt and pepper a pinch of cayenne 1½ tablespoons armagnac 2 tablespoons port 200 ml (⅓ pint) dry white wine 2 deseeded tomatoes, cut in quarters 1 teaspoon tomato purée
Ingredients for the stuffing	4 heaped tablespoons cooked tomato pulp **(No 99)** 1 small sprig of thyme ½ teaspoon fresh tarragon, chopped

Equipment 1 sauté pan with lid
1 liquidiser **or** mortar and pestle
1 oval ovenproof dish
2 small saucepans

Cooking the crayfish

1 Heat the oil in the sauté pan. Throw in the crayfish or Dublin Bay prawns and let them fry and colour, covered, for 6 minutes.

2 Remove the pan from the heat and remove the crayfish with a slotted spoon. Put them on a plate. Remove and shell the tails and keep them until needed.

Making the sauce

3 Reserve four cleaned and washed head-shells for decorating the finished dish and put the rest of the head-shells and tail-shells into the liquidiser or mortar. Pound them coarsely. Return to the pan and add the finely-diced carrot, onion and shallot, the bouquet garni, garlic, salt, pepper and cayenne and cook without browning, uncovered, for 5 minutes.

4 Then, add the armagnac and port and half-cover the saucepan. Bring the armagnac and port to the boil and allow to reduce by half of their volume, impregnating the crayfish debris with their flavours.

5 Add the dry white wine, the deseeded tomatoes and the tomato purée. Allow to boil, uncovered, for 15 minutes, until the liquid has reduced by half.

6 Strain this sauce into the oval ovenproof dish in which the paupiettes are to be cooked, pressing the crayfish debris and the vegetables with the back of a ladle to extract the last drops of juice.

Making and cooking the paupiettes

7 In the small saucepan, heat the tomato pulp, thyme and tarragon over a gentle heat. Add the shelled crayfish tails and mix them in gently. Keep until needed in a warm place.

(*continued on the next page*)

8 In the second small saucepan bring the 500 ml (scant pint) water and 2 teaspoons salt to the boil and blanch the Brussels sprout leaves for 15 seconds. Take the pan off the heat and keep them hot in their cooking water until needed.

9 Slice the fillet of bass against the grain with a long flexible knife into four good slices about 12 cm (4¾ inches) square. If you don't find it easy to cut the fillet evenly and finely, slide the slices between two sheets of foil and flatten them with a steak-beater.

10 In the centre of each of the bass slices put a generous tablespoon of tomato pulp and five hot crayfish tails (7). Fold up the slices into little parcels or paupiettes, turning the edges inwards to make them airtight. Place the parcels with the seams downwards in the crayfish sauce (6) in the oval ovenproof dish.

Cooking and finishing the dish

11 Preheat the oven to 250°C/480°F/Mark 9. Bake the paupiettes in their dish for 4 minutes. Remove them from the dish with a slotted spoon and place on hot plates or a hot serving dish.

12 Put the cooking dish on a brisk heat and bring the sauce to the boil. Add the 75 g (2½ oz) butter, in little pieces; these will melt in the boiling liquid and make it into a rich and velvety sauce.

13 Coat the paupiettes with the sauce, decorate them with the four reserved crayfish heads (3) and arrange the hot Brussels sprout leaves round the edge of the dish like a diadem of petals. Serve immediately.

Suggestions for the home cook

* The crayfish sauce can be replaced with the equivalent quantity of Sauce Américaine (page 77), made in advance. Use 250 ml (scant ½ pint) double cream instead of butter to thicken the sauce.
* The paupiettes can be stuffed, more simply, with mussels cooked with shallots in white wine and cream, then taken out of their shells. The cooking liquid, slightly reduced and nicely flavoured with chopped herbs, is a pleasant substitute for the crayfish sauce.

56 Roast Lobster

*Homard rôti au four 'Succulent lobster
in its shell, drenched with herb butter'*

For two people

*Main
ingredients*

1 live lobster weighing 900 g (2 lbs)
250 ml (scant ½ pint) court-bouillon **(No 2)**
  or 250 ml (scant ½ pint) water and $1\frac{1}{4}$
  teaspoons salt
2 tablespoons olive oil

*Ingredients for
cooking and
accompanying
sauce*

150 ml ($\frac{1}{4}$ pint) dry white wine
1 pinch thyme
1 teaspoon freshly-chopped flat parsley **or**
  chervil for the herb butter
1 pinch tarragon
250 g ($8\frac{3}{4}$ oz) well-softened butter
salt and pepper
1 anchovy fillet   ⎱ for the
15 g ($\frac{1}{2}$ oz) well-softened butter ⎰ anchovy butter

Equipment

1 oval enamel cast-iron dish
2 stainless-steel saucepans, one with lid
1 large nail
1 heavy cleaver

Preparation of the herb butter

1   Bring the white wine and herbs to the boil in the first small saucepan. Reduce until only about 3 tablespoons of liquid remain. Allow to cool somewhat, then add the 250 g (8¾ oz) softened butter and salt and pepper. Mix with a fork, or better a small wire whisk, until you have a smooth thick cream; keep in the saucepan until needed.

Preparation of the anchovy

2   Chop the anchovy fillet finely and beat it into the 15 g (½ oz) softened butter with a fork or whisk, until you have a smooth thick cream.

Cooking the lobster

3   Preheat the oven to 250°C/480°F/Mark 9. Kill the lobster by plunging it briefly into boiling water. Break off the claws with a clean jerk, then crack them gently with the flat side of the cleaver to make extracting the flesh after cooking easier.

4   Bring the 250 ml (scant ½ pint) court-bouillon or salted water to the boil in the second small saucepan and throw in the claws. Cook covered, for 8 minutes, then take off the heat and keep in a warm place until needed.

5   Take 100 g (3½ oz), or about a third of the herb butter (1) and mix thoroughly with the anchovy butter (2).

6   Heat the olive oil in the oval ovenproof dish over a brisk heat and put in the lobster from which the claws have been removed. Turn it over several times in the hot oil to coat the shell thoroughly all over.

7   Put the dish in the very hot oven and cook for 8 minutes. Turn the oven down to 220°C/425°F/Mark 7 for the second stage of the cooking.

8   Take the dish out of the oven. Make a hole the size of your little finger in the lobster's head, using a large nail or the point of a knife, and insert a third of the herb and anchovy butter mixture (5) with a teaspoon, to drench the meat inside.

9   Return the dish to the slightly cooled oven and cook for a further 15 minutes, removing it after 5 and 10 minutes to insert more butter.

Finishing and serving the lobster

10   When it is cooked, place the lobster on the work-top and split it lengthwise with a cleaver.

11   Remove the sac from the top of the head.

12   Arrange the open lobster in the hot cooking dish. Shell the claws and plant them in the head cavities.

13   Serve immediately, accompanied by the rest of the hot herb butter in a sauceboat.

Suggestions for the home cook

* The lobster, like all crustaceans, consists of three parts: the head, the claws and the tail. The head contains the sac, which must always be discarded: the intestines and stomach, called coral or tomali, turn red when cooked and can be used for binding Sauce Américaine (page 77). The claws and the tail contain the meat. In female lobsters the eggs are found in bunches adhering to the tail; like the coral, they turn red when cooked and are sometimes used for binding sauces.
* Live lobsters split in half and grilled often become dry during cooking; their flesh shrinks and becomes tough. In this recipe, the flesh is well protected by the shell, and, 'nourished' with flavoured butter, remains exceptionally moist. The crawfish or langouste benefits from the same treatment.
* With this dish I like to serve a hot salad, consisting of 50 g ($1\frac{3}{4}$ oz) carrots, 25 g (1 oz) celery, 25 g (1 oz) white part of leek and 50 g ($1\frac{3}{4}$ oz) button mushrooms cut in julienne strips, seasoned with salt, pepper and lemon juice and cooked gently in butter so that the vegetables are still crunchy.

57 Poached Lobster, Crawfish or Freshwater Crayfish

Homard, langouste ou écrevisses à la nage
'Designed to conserve the natural flavours'

Serve hot or cold
For two people

Main ingredients

1 live lobster weighing 800 g (1 lb 12¼ oz),
   preferably female **or** 1 live crawfish or
   langouste weighing 800 g (1 lb 12¼ oz),
   preferably female **or** 20 freshwater crayfish
   or Dublin Bay prawns of about 60 g (2 oz) each
1 tablespoon of freshly-chopped parsley
court-bouillon **(No 2)** according to the size
   of the crustaceans

Cooking the crustaceans

1 Kill the lobster or crawfish in the way recommended in **No 56,** and crack the claw shells with a cleaver to make extracting the cooked flesh easier.

2 Bring the court-bouillon to the boil in a large saucepan and plunge in the chosen shellfish. Cook a lobster or crawfish of 800 g (1 lb 12¼ oz) for 14 minutes and freshwater crayfish or Dublin Bay prawns for 2 minutes.

Dressing lobsters and crawfish

3 Split the crustacean in two lengthways with the cleaver. Remove and shell the claws. Remove the gravelly sand sac from top of the head.

Serving the crustaceans

4 Arrange lobster or crawfish halves on a deep oval dish and strew them with the vegetables from the court-bouillon. Moisten with 250 ml (scant ½ pint) court-bouillon and sprinkle with chopped parsley. Freshwater crayfish or Dublin Bay prawns should be arranged in a pyramid in a vegetable dish and sprinkled with chopped parsley.

5 You can serve shellfish à la nage with either: Sauce Vierge **(No 3)**, Rouille **(No 1)**, or Beurre Blanc **(page 75)**.

Suggestions for the home cook

* If you are worried about the blackish intestinal tract which runs along the upper side of a freshwater crayfish, put them live, twelve hours before cooking them, in a bucket of water to which some dried milk powder has been added. This cleanses the intestine. When the shelled tails only are to be used, you simply extract the black thread, pulling towards the tail, after the crayfish have been cooked and shelled.
* Over-cooking crustaceans toughens their flesh unappetisingly.
* Leaving them very slightly undercooked keeps them moist.
* Letting them stand for a few minutes after the end of the cooking, and before serving, allows the flesh to relax and become more tender.

58 Lobster Cakes with Glazed Carrots

Gâteau de homard soufflé aux carottes fondantes 'An airy lobster mousse with fine slices of carrot'

For five people

The lobster and its garnish	1 live lobster weighing 350 g (12¼ oz) 1 litre (1¾ pints) water and 25 g (1 oz) coarse salt ½ teaspoon freshly-chopped chervil ½ teaspoon freshly-chopped tarragon 25 g (1 oz) truffle, fresh or preserved, cut in julienne strips
Ingredients for the mousse	160 g (5½ oz) raw lobster meat from 1 live lobster weighing 350 g (12¼ oz), preferably female ½ teaspoon salt 2 turns of the pepper-mill ½ a beaten egg ½ an extra egg white 150 g (5¼ oz) chilled double cream 1 tablespoon of lobster eggs (from female lobster only, see page 227) 250 ml (scant ½ pint) water
Ingredients for the sauce	250 ml (scant ½ pint) water 15 g (½ oz) butter pinch of sugar salt and pepper 250 g (8¾ oz) carrots, peeled and very finely sliced 1½ tablespoons port 1½ tablespoons Sauce Américaine (page 77) **or** Crayfish Sauce (**No 7**) 250 ml (scant ½ pint) double cream 1 pinch freshly-chopped tarragon

Final garnish	6 slices of truffle, fresh or preserved

Equipment	10 squares of aluminium foil 10 cm (4 inches) across
	1 large fish-kettle 37 cm (15 inches) across, with a rack

Preparing the lobster

1   Kill the first lobster in the way recommended on page 215. Pull off the claws with a rapid jerk and then crack them carefully with the back of a heavy knife blade to make extraction of the flesh easier after cooking.

2   Bring the 1 litre (1¾ pints) water and 25 g (1 oz) salt to the boil and plunge in the lobster and the claws. Boil for 5 minutes and refresh under cold running water for 1 minute.

3   Shell the lobster and claws and cut the meat in dice 1 cm (¾ inch) square. Put into a bowl, add the chopped chervil and tarragon and the truffle julienne, and keep on one side till needed.

Preparing the mixture for the lobster cakes

4   If you are starting with fresh lobsters, kill the second in the same way as the first. Detach the tail and cut through the underside of the shell with scissors so that you can remove it. Detach and shell the claws, cracking them with a sharp blow from the back of a heavy knife blade. Finally, extract the intestines and coral (tomali) from the head.

5   Blend the flesh of tail and claws, the tomali, intestines and coral together with salt and pepper in the liquidiser for 2 minutes. When the mixture is smooth, add the ½ beaten egg and ½ egg white and blend for a further minute. Put the container and its contents in the refrigerator for 30 minutes to become firm.

6   Return the container to the liquidiser and add the 150 g (5¼ oz) chilled cream. Blend for about 20 seconds, or until the mixture has become smooth and velvety, and replace in the refrigerator for 15 minutes.

(*continued on the next page*)

7   Pour the mixture into the large bowl containing the lobster and its garnish (3), and mix lightly and carefully with a wooden spatula. If you have used a female lobster lightly fold in a tablespoon of the cooked eggs.

Making the cakes

8   Divide the lobster mixture (7) equally between 5 squares of aluminium foil laid flat on the work-top. Using a spoon and a metal spatula make the piles of mixture into little cakes 10 cm (4 inches) across and $1\frac{1}{2}$ cm ($\frac{3}{4}$ inch) high. Place the remaining foil squares on top of the cakes.

Making the sauce

9   Bring the 250 ml (scant $\frac{1}{2}$ pint) water, 15 g ($\frac{1}{2}$ oz) butter, sugar, salt and pepper to boil in the second saucepan, and throw in the thin rounds of carrot. Half cover and cook over a moderate heat for 20 minutes. The water should almost completely evaporate and the carrots be bathed in a coating of glossy syrup.

10   Remove the lid, add the $1\frac{1}{2}$ tablespoons port and reduce by half. Add the Sauce Américaine, the 250 ml (scant $\frac{1}{2}$ pint) cream and the tarragon, and reduce by one-third. Taste for seasoning and keep hot in a bain-marie.

11   Put 250 ml (scant $\frac{1}{2}$ pint) of water in the bottom of the fish kettle, put in a rack with feet long enough to hold it above the water, and put the kettle on a brisk heat.

12   When the water boils, place the lobster-cakes on the rack, cover and cook for 6 minutes turning the cakes over after 3 minutes. They will rise, becoming light and tender 'soufflés'.

Serving the lobster-cakes

13   Coat the bottom of individual plates or a serving dish with the hot sauce with its slices of carrot (10). Take the cooked lobster-cakes off their protective foil, place them delicately on the sauce, and decorate each with a slice of truffle.

Suggestions for the home cook

* I always try to buy female lobsters, because their flesh is particularly tender and for the iodiney richness of their eggs, which improve stuffings and sauces for lobster and other crustaceans.
* This recipe can be prepared more economically by replacing the cubed lobster with shelled Dublin Bay prawns, prepared the same way and the meat of the second lobster (4–7) with 160 g (5½ oz) raw salmon.
* You can also serve the lobster-cakes with the more easily prepared Beurre Blanc (page 75), having first added the glazed carrots (9).

59 Sardines Marinated in Red Wine

Sardines glacées au vin rouge 'A refreshing dish for a hot summer's night'

For four people

Main ingredients	650 g (1 lb 8 oz) fresh sardines, 16 in all salt and freshly-ground pepper
Ingredients for the marinade	1 litre (1¾ pints) Algerian red wine 200 ml (⅓ pint) red wine vinegar 2 medium carrots, about 90 g (3 oz), peeled and very finely sliced 1 medium onion, about 80 g (2¾ oz), peeled and very finely sliced 1 very small bouquet garni 3 cloves
Ingredients for the garnish	2 peeled lemons cut into thin slices 2 tablespoons lemon juice 1 tablespoon chervil sprigs
Accompanying sauce	Light Tomato Purée (No 9)

One day in advance: preparing the marinade and the sardines

1 Put all the ingredients for the marinade in a saucepan. Bring to the boil and simmer, uncovered, over a gentle heat for 25 minutes, reducing the marinade by a quarter of its original volume.

2 Pour into a flat oval enamelled iron dish and allow to cool.

3 Scale and clean the sardines and cut off their heads. Wash them quickly in cold water and dry them carefully on kitchen paper. Season them with salt and pepper, immerse in the marinade and leave overnight in the refrigerator.

Cooking and serving the sardines

4 Take the dish of sardines from the refrigerator, cover them with the lemon slices and sprinkle with the lemon juice.

5 Put the dish on a low heat, bring the marinade to a gentle simmer and cook for 30 seconds. Remove, and pour the marinade into a saucepan. Put the saucepan on a low heat, uncovered, and simmer for 15 minutes reducing the liquid further by one-third of its volume.

6 Pour the reduced marinade back over the sardines, and allow to cool, turning the sardines over from time to time.

7 Put the dish in the refrigerator and serve chilled, a day or two later. Before bringing them to the table, sprinkle with sprigs of chervil, and serve with a cold tomato purée (**No 9**) in a sauceboat.

Suggestions for the home cook

*Instead of a first course, this summer recipe can become a main course on its own. To do this, replace the sliced onion with 20 little new onions, which must be added to the marinade at the first cooking (1) and add 125 g (4½ oz) lean bacon, cut in little sticks 1 cm (½ inch) across, and blanched for 1 minute in unsalted boiling water, to the second cooking of the marinade (5).

60 Salmon 'en papillote' with braised vegetables

Papillotes de saumon à l'étuvée de légumes
'The flavours of river and garden'

For four people

Main ingredients	4 tablespoons arachide oil 600 g (1 lb 5 oz) skinned and boned salmon salt and pepper 1 teaspoon chopped shallot 12 tarragon leaves 80 g (2¾ oz) softened butter 8 tablespoons dry white wine 5 tablespoons stock made from ¼ chicken stock cube dissolved in 5 tablespoons water

---

Ingredients for the vegetable garnish	100 g (3½ oz) carrots, peeled 100 g (3½ oz) button mushrooms, peeled 100 g (3½ oz) onions, peeled 50 g (1¾ oz) butter salt and pepper 1 level teaspoon freshly-chopped tarragon

---

Equipment	1 mouli-julienne 4 sheets of greaseproof paper or aluminium foil cut into 4 rounds, each 35 cm (14 inches) across 1 pair tweezers 1 oval roasting-dish large enough to hold the 4 papillotes

---

Preparing the vegetable garnish

1 Put the carrots through the julienne blade of the mouli-julienne.

2 Cut the mushrooms and onions, which have rather more resilient flesh, into julienne strips by hand.

3 Heat the 50 g (1¾ oz) butter in a saucepan and put the vegetables in to soften without browning, in the following order: carrots and onions, then after 5 minutes the mushrooms. Cook together for a further 3 minutes. Stir carefully during cooking to prevent the vegetables sticking.

4 Season, add the level teaspoon of tarragon, cover and soften for 2 minutes. Take the saucepan off the heat and allow to cool.

Preparing and cooking the papillotes

5 Preheat the oven to 250°C/480°F/Mark 9. Brush the paper rounds with oil, and fold them in two with the oil inside. Open them up sufficiently to enable you to pile a quarter of the vegetable julienne on the lower half-moon of each.

6 With the tweezers, remove any little bones which may be sticking out of the salmon. You can find them by running your fingers over the surface of the fish. Then carve the raw salmon into twelve 1 cm (½ inch) slices with a flexible knife.

7 Lay three slices of salmon per papillote on top of the vegetable julienne and season with salt, pepper and chopped shallot. Then add to each papillote 3 tarragon leaves, 20 g (¾ oz) butter in pieces, 2 tablespoons of white wine and 1 tablespoon of stock.

8 Make and seal each papillote by turning over the edges twice and pinching them together, so that it looks like an apple turnover, and makes an airtight seal.

9 Brush the roasting-dish with oil and heat it in the hot oven for 5 minutes. Take it out of the oven and put in the papillotes, taking care that they do not touch one another. Put the dish back in the oven and cook for 2 minutes for greaseproof parcels and 3–4 minutes for aluminium foil.

(continued on the next page)

10 Present them to your guests just as they come out of the oven, in the dish, all puffed up and enticing, and serve them immediately on hot plates, just as they are, so that your guests can have the pleasure of unwrapping them.

Suggestions for the home cook

* A Beurre Blanc made with limes (page 75) will make these papillotes a richer dish.

* If you do not have fresh tarragon, you can use half the quantity of tarragon preserved in vinegar.

* Frozen salmon can be successfully used for this dish, the papillotes being cooked for $\frac{1}{2}$ minute less. Alternatively, try cod or hake slices cut to the same thickness.

61 Bass cooked in Seaweed

Bar aux algues
'Permeated with the flavour of the sea'

For two people

Main ingredients	1 sea-bass weighing 800 g (1¾ lb) 2 large handfuls of seaweed 7 tablespoons water salt, black pepper
Ingredients for accompanying sauce	200 ml (⅓ pint) Sauce Vierge **(No 3)**
Other ingredients	2 whole freshwater crayfish **or** Dublin Bay prawns (optional) 6 tablespoons Watercress Purée **(No 104)**

Preparing the fish

1   Clean the fish and cut away its sharp dorsal fin. Do not scale it; the scales contain a salty deposit which intensifies the fish's savour of the sea as it cooks underneath its seaweed blanket, and also makes it easier to skin once it is cooked.

2   Put a layer of half the seaweed in the bottom of the casserole and pour in the water; season the bass inside and lay it on top, together with the two freshwater crayfish or Dublin Bay prawns, if used. Blanket with the remaining seaweed. Cover the casserole and cook it over a fast heat for 20 minutes.

Finishing and serving the fish

3   Meanwhile heat the Sauce Vierge and the watercress purée separately in the bain-marie.

4   When the cooking time is up, serve the fish in the casserole and lift the lid in front of your guests so that they can inhale the smell of the sea. Then, remove the skin, complete with scales, in one piece. Lift off the fillets, season them with salt and pepper and place them on the hot plates, on to which you have poured the Sauce Vierge. On either side of the fillets put a spoonful or two of the watercress purée, the deep green of which can be heightened by placing a cooked crayfish or Dublin Bay prawn on each plate.

Suggestions for the home cook

* I find this a thoroughly satisfactory way of cooking salt-water fish; it gives an incomparable depth and richness to the flavour. To increase the savour and give an added freshness, you can replace the black pepper with freeze-dried green peppercorns crushed in a peppermill.
* If you cannot get seaweed, use a couple of large bunches of parsley, in which case the cooking liquid must be salted.
* Bass can be replaced by other fish, for instance sole, John Dory, sea bream, angler-fish, pollack.
* If you are in the country you can use this method for river and lake fish – trout, perch, pike, etc. – using wild plants for the 'bed' – sorrel, trefoil, thyme, nettles, etc.

62 Sea-Bream in a Salt Crust

*Daurade en croûte de sel 'Fish
cooked in a shell of sea-salt'*

For two people

Main ingredients	1 grey, pink or, better, royal, sea-bream weighing 800 g (1 lb 12¼ oz) 1 kg (2¼ lb) sea salt
Accompanying sauces	8 tablespoons Sauce Vierge **(No 3)** *or* 8 tablespoons Cream Chive Sauce **(No 6)**
Accompanying vegetable	Watercress Purée **(No 104)**
Equipment	1 oval enamelled cast-iron dish large enough to take the fish

Preparing and cooking the fish

1 Preheat the oven to 220°C/425°F/Mark 7. Gut the fish and cut off the dorsal fin with kitchen scissors if this has not already been done by the fishmonger. Do not scale it: the scales are covered with a salty deposit which intensifies the fish's savour of the sea and also makes it easier to skin once it is cooked.

2 Spread one-third of the salt evenly in the bottom of the cast-iron dish, lay the bream on this bed and spread the rest of the salt round and over it. It should be completely covered.

3 Bake in the oven for 18 minutes.

Finishing and presenting the dish

4 When it is cooked, show the dish to your guest, then break and remove the slightly hard salt crust, remove the fish and peel off the skin complete with its scales. It should come away easily, in one piece. Lift off the fillets, salt very very lightly if necessary, season with pepper and arrange in the serving dish.

5 Pour over the chosen sauce, and accompany the fish with Watercress Purée **(No 104)**. Serve immediately.

Suggestions for the home cook

* During cooling the salt crystallises and forms a second, airtight oven.
* This is a splendid method of serving a fish and can be used for many kinds – hake, pollack and cod, for instance. It is also the perfect way of cooking sardines, because it avoids filling the kitchen with their pervasive aroma. . . .

63 John Dory in a Pepper Sabayon Sauce

Saint-Pierre en sabayon de poivre
'A foamy fish sauce, with the taste of pepper'

For two people

Main ingredients	1 John Dory weighing 800 g (1 lb 12¼ oz)
	2 teaspoons butter
	1 teaspoon chopped shallot
	salt and pepper
	7 tablespoons stock made by dissolving ⅓ chicken stock cube in 7 tablespoons water
	1 tablespoon dry white wine
	7 tablespoons double cream
	1 teaspoon white peppercorns
Ingredients for the sabayon sauce	1 egg yolk
	1½ tablespoons cold water
Equipment	1 baking-dish

Suggestions for the home cook

* The recipe can be used for many other kinds of fish; for instance, sole, bream, rascasse, whiting, gurnard.
* The pepper can be replaced with an infusion of some other flavour, for instance, tarragon, basil, dill or saffron.

Preparing and cooking the fish

1 Preheat the oven to 220°C/425°F/Mark 7. Scale the fish, cut off the spines and gut it.

2 Brush the baking dish with the butter and strew the chopped shallot over the bottom. Place the John Dory on top, season it with salt and pepper and moisten it with the stock.

3 Cover the dish with a sheet of aluminium foil, and braise the fish in the oven for 20 minutes, basting it frequently with the cooking liquid and juices while it cooks. Add the cream and cook for a further 5 minutes.

Preparing the sauce

5 Crush the peppercorns coarsely to make 'mignonette' pepper (you can also sometimes buy it ready prepared).

6 Take the John Dory out of the pan and put it to keep hot between two hot plates.

7 Strain the cooking juices through a conical strainer into a small saucepan, add the 'mignonette' pepper and reduce over a brisk fire by one-third of its original volume.

8 Meanwhile, skin the fish carefully and lift off the flesh in four unbroken fillets with a flexible knife. Arrange them on a hot serving-dish and keep hot in the oven with the door open.

9 Beat the egg yolk and the cold water with a whisk for 45 seconds until the mixture has increased in volume and become frothy. Pour into the boiling cooking-juices, whisking all the time. The egg yolk will coagulate in the heat and give the sauce yet more body and lightness.

10 Immediately coat the fillets of John Dory with the sauce, and serve straight away.

64 Skate with Sea-Urchins

*Aile de raie aux oursins 'A simple dish
with a silky cream sauce'*

For four people

Main ingredients	1 piece of skate weighing 800 g (1 lb 12¼ oz) 1 litre (1¾ pints) court-bouillon **(No 2)** and its vegetables
Ingredients for the sauce	200 ml (⅓ pint) double cream 4 egg yolks 3 tablespoons cold water
Equipment	1 large saucepan with lid 1 small saucepan
Ingredients for the garnish	4 large sea-urchins

Preliminary preparation

Open the sea urchins. With kitchen scissors, trim a border 2 cm ($\frac{1}{2}$ inch) wide from the outer edge of the skate's fin, and cut the fish into 4 slices.

Preparing and cooking the fish

1   Wash the pieces of skate carefully under the cold tap in order to remove any of the viscous coating which covers the skin.

2   Put the skate in the bottom of the large saucepan, cover with the court-bouillon and bring to the boil. Cover, reduce the heat so that the liquid is barely simmering and cook for 15 minutes.

3   Meanwhile, remove the rosy corals of the urchins with a teaspoon and place them on a serving-dish. Put to heat through.

4   Carefully lift out the pieces of skate with a slotted spoon and place them on a cloth or kitchen paper, to finish draining.

5   Skin the pieces of skate carefully with a small knife and keep them hot on the serving-dish beside the urchins.

Preparing the sauce

6   Bring 7 tablespoons of the court-bouillon and some of the vegetables (2) to the boil in the small saucepan and simmer, uncovered, until it has reduced by half. Add the cream and again reduce by half.

7   Whip the egg yolks and the cold water together for 1 minute, until the mixture increases in volume and becomes frothy. Pour this mixture into the reduction (6), whisking continually. The egg yolks will coagulate on coming into contact with the hot liquid and will give the sauce a beautiful lightness. Take the saucepan off the heat immediately.

Finishing and serving the dish

8   Arrange the pieces of skate attractively on the serving-dish and decorate each with pieces of sea-urchin in the shape of a flower. Pour over the sauce (7) and serve immediately.

Suggestions for the home cook

* Skate is perhaps the only fish which is actually *better* eaten two or three days after it has been caught.

* The sea-urchins can be replaced with either 20 fresh or frozen asparagus spears or 1 tablespoon of green peppercorns, rinsed three times in cold running water. Add $\frac{1}{2}$ teaspoon Dijon mustard to the sauce after it has reduced (7). It should not boil.

* Steamed broccoli is the perfect vegetable to accompany skate.

Editor's note   To open sea-urchins, cut a round hole in the domed top with a small pair of scissors.

65 Whiting with Julienne Vegetables

Merlan à la julienne de légumes 'A sublime recipe for delicate flaky whiting'

For four people

Main ingredient	4 whiting weighing 220 g (7¾ oz) each

Ingredients for the stuffing	100 g (3½ oz) carrots, peeled 50 g (1¾ oz) celeriac, peeled 100 g (3½ oz) button mushrooms 50 g (1¾ oz) butter salt and pepper 4 tablespoons white port 200 ml (⅓ pint) double cream ½ teaspoon freshly-chopped tarragon 1 egg yolk

Ingredients for cooking the whiting	salt and pepper 20 g (¾ oz) softened butter 1 tablespoon chopped shallot 2 tablespoons dry white wine 7 tablespoons double cream 2 tablespoons white port 1½ tablespoons dry vermouth 1 teaspoon freshly-chopped parsley

Suggestions for the home cook

* The vegetable stuffing (7) can be prepared in advance and the whiting stuffed then and there, so that the following day the cook has only to put the dish into the oven just before the meal.
* This recipe is pleasant for freshwater fish such as trout, perch, etc.
* The julienne sauce goes remarkably well with poached chicken and sautéd veal, chicken poached in bouillon, blanquette de veau etc.

Preparing the whiting

1 Cut off the fins and clean the whiting, removing their guts through the gills.

2 Bone them whole; make two incisions along the spine and ease the fillets on either side away from the bone. Cut through the now-free backbone with scissors, just by the tail, and remove it. The whiting can now be opened and shut like a book.

Preparing the stuffing

3 Peel and slice the carrot and celeriac into julienne strips, either by hand (see illustration on page 98) or on the appropriate blade of a mouli-julienne or mandoline. The mushrooms, with their more resilient flesh, should be cut into julienne strips by hand with a small sharp knife.

4 Heat the butter in a saucepan and cook the vegetables, without browning, adding them in the following order, at 3-minute intervals: carrots, celery, mushrooms. The carrots will cook for 9 minutes, the celery for 6 and the mushrooms for 3. Stir well throughout this operation, to prevent the vegetables sticking to the pan.

5 Season with salt and pepper, add the port, cream, chopped tarragon and bring to the boil. Simmer, half covered, on a moderate heat for 5 minutes.

6 Meanwhile, beat the egg yolk with a fork.

7 Remove the saucepan from the heat and mix the beaten egg yolk (6) in carefully. Allow to cool.

8 Preheat the oven to 250°C/480°F/Mark 9. Season the whiting inside with salt and pepper and, using a spoon, stuff them with two-thirds of the vegetable julienne (7). Butter an oval gratin dish, sprinkle with the chopped shallot and lay the whiting on it. Strew the remaining one-third of the vegetable julienne over and round the fish and add the white wine and cream. Cook in the very hot oven for 6–8 minutes.

9 Remove from the oven and add the vermouth and the port. Return to the oven for 2–3 minutes; fish and sauce will now become a pretty golden colour.

10 Serve the whiting in their cooking dish, or remove with a slotted spoon and place on heated plates, covering them generously with their cooking juices. In either case, sprinkle lightly with freshly chopped parsley.

66 Salt Cod Bouillabaisse

Bouillabaisse de morue 'Salt cod cooked in the way I like it'

For four to six people

Main ingredients	750 g (1 lb 10½ oz) fillet of very white salt cod 7 tablespoons olive oil 100 g (3½ oz) onion, peeled and finely chopped 80 g (2¾ oz) white part of leeks, cleaned and finely chopped 1 clove garlic, peeled and finely chopped 2 tomatoes 300 g (10½ oz) waxy potatoes, peeled and cut into slices 1 cm (¼ inch) thick 1 teaspoon saffron freshly-ground pepper 1 bouquet garni 1 litre (1¾ pints) water 7 tablespoons dry white wine
Ingredients for finishing the dish	½ a long loaf of French bread cut into 20 thin slices 7 tablespoons olive oil 1 teaspoon freshly-chopped parsley
Accompanying sauce	Rouille **(No 1)**
Equipment	1 heavy casserole 40 cm (16 inches) across

The day before: soaking the salt cod

1   Cut the fillet of salt cod into 4 pieces and put to soak for 24 hours in a bowl placed under a dribbling cold tap so that the water changes continually.

On the day: preparing the vegetables

2   Heat the oil in the casserole over a moderate heat and throw in the finely chopped onions, leeks and garlic. Let them soften, without browning, for 15 minutes, stirring from time to time with a wooden spatula to prevent them from sticking.

3   Meanwhile, peel the tomatoes, cut them in half and squeeze them gently in the hollow of your palm to expel the juice and seeds, then chop them coarsely with a knife and add to the casserole and cook for a further 5 minutes.

4   Place a layer of peeled and sliced potatoes on top of the vegetables.

Cooking the salt cod

5   Drain the de-salted cod carefully on a cloth and cut into squares 3 cm (1¼ inches) across. Lay them on the bed of potatoes in the casserole and sprinkle with the saffron and four turns of the peppermill. On no account add salt! Finally, add the bouquet garni and moisten with the water and white wine.

6   Cook uncovered on a brisk fire for 25 minutes, then taste for seasoning. The galloping boil will cause the oil and water/wine mixture to emulsify, helped by the starch in the potatoes. At the end the liquid will be syrupy, almost velvety, and permeated with the flavours of the vegetables, herbs, spices and fish.

7   Brush the 20 rounds of bread with olive oil and grill to a golden brown on both sides.

Serving the bouillabaisse

8   Remove the bouquet garni, sprinkle with chopped parsley and put the casserole just as it is in the middle of the table. Serve the Rouille separately in a sauceboat and arrange the grilled bread on a hot plate.

Suggestions for the home cook

* This dish can be got ready up to step 6 in the morning or the previous day (if you have remembered to put the salt cod to soak the day before *that*), and simply put on to boil when your guests are sipping their drinks.
* You can embellish the dish by serving large slices of bread, rubbed with garlic and oil and grilled on both sides, then spread with fresh tomato pulp and anchovies or with Rouille.

67 Charcoal-Grilled Sole with Oysters and Chives

Sole grillée aux huîtres et à la ciboulette
'Mingled scents of saltwater, chives and
woodsmoke'

For two people

Main ingredients	1 large sole weighing 600 g (1 lb 5 oz) salt and pepper 1 tablespoon arachide oil 8 plump oysters 8 lettuce leaves, washed 1 litre (1¾ pints) water 2 teaspoons coarse salt
Accompanying sauce	7 tablespoons Cream Chive Sauce **(No 6)** 1 level teaspoon chopped chives

Preparing the sole

1   Remove the head, cutting across the fish diagonally with a sharp knife. Remove the grey skin from the back of the fish; leave the white underskin but scale it. Then score the skin in a lozenge pattern with a sharp knife.

2   Using the scissors, remove the fins from round the fish, cut open the stomach cavity to remove the insides and wash it out under the cold tap.

3   Season the sole with salt and pepper, brush it with arachide oil and leave it aside until needed.

4   Prepare the accompanying sauce **(No 6)**.

5   Place the spotlessly clean grill rack over the fire to become really hot.

Preparing the oysters

6   Open the oysters with an oyster knife if it has not been done for you at the fishmonger's. Hold each oyster shell above a sieve lined with a damp cloth so that the juices can drip through into a small saucepan placed underneath, and remove the oysters delicately with a teaspoon.

7   When all the oysters have been dealt with, poach them for 30 seconds in their simmering juices in the small saucepan. Drain them on a towel.

8   Bring the 1 litre (1¾ pints) water and 2 teaspoons salt to the boil in a medium saucepan and blanch the lettuce leaves for 1 minute. Drain on a towel.

9   Wrap the oysters in the lettuce leaves, folding them into little bundles. Keep them warm between two plates in a low oven with the door open while you are grilling the sole.

(continued on the next page)

Cooking the sole

10 Brush the grill rack with oil. Put the sole on it white skin side down, lying diagonally across the ridges and grill for 2 minutes. Detach it with the metal spatula and without reversing it place it diagonally across the ridges in the opposite direction. Grill for a further 2 minutes. Then turn the fish over and grill for 4 minutes on the other side, in the same way.

Finishing and serving the sole

11 Lift the fillets from the sole in four unbroken pieces, cutting along the length of the backbone with a thin flexible knife, and sliding the blade between flesh and bones to loosen the fillets.

12 Coat the bottom of the serving dish with the Creamy Chive Sauce and lay the four fillets upon it, with their criss-cross patterned side upwards. Arrange the eight little oyster bundles around them and strew the whole dish with chopped chives.

Suggestions for the home cook

* The Cream Chive Sauce can be pleasantly replaced with a Sauce Beurre Blanc (page 75) flavoured with a tablespoon of finely-sliced lemon peel blanched for 10 minutes in boiling water, and made lighter at the last minute by the addition of 2 egg yolks and 3 tablespoons water whisked up into a sabayon (see **No 63**).
* For me, the only method of cooking fillets of sole is on the bone. That way their flesh has no chance of shrinking into corkscrews with that particularly disagreeable rubbery texture.
* Breadcrumbed and grilled fish are good to eat and easy to succeed with. Before grilling them, roll them, not in beaten egg and flour, but in melted butter and fresh breadcrumbs. The butter will help keep the fish moist as well as preventing it sticking to the pan.

68 A Fish-market in a Casserole, steamed over seaweed

Le marché du pêcheur en cocotte à la vapeur d'algues 'A beautifully coloured and lighthearted dish'

For four people

Main ingredients	1 bass weighing 400 g (14 oz) filleted, but not skinned (after weighing) 4 scallops 4 small red mullet weighing 60 g (2 oz) each 24 winkles 500 ml (scant pint) water and 2 teaspoons coarse salt 4 lettuce leaves 4 Portuguese oysters 4 large mussels 1 fillet of sole weighing 100 g (3½ oz) 4 large Dublin Bay prawns 4 handfuls of fine seaweed used for the packing of oysters or lobsters 160 ml (¼ pint) water
Ingredients for the garnish	25 g (1 oz) each carrot, onion, leek and chives, cut into julienne strips salt and pepper
Accompanying sauces	5 tablespoons Sauce Beurre Blanc (Page 75) **and/or** 5 tablespoons Sauce Vierge (**No 3**)
Equipment	4 small cast-iron cocottes with lids and 4 round cake-racks 20 cm (8 inches) across 4 large hot plates 1 or 2 hot saucers

Preparing the fish

1 If the fishmonger has not filleted the bass and opened the scallops for you, follow the methods described on page 97 and **No 51**.

2 Wash the mullet and remove the gills, but do not gut them, their insides are largely succulent liver – hence their nickname 'woodcock of the sea'.

3 Wash the winkles, then poach them for 2 minutes in a small saucepan filled with boiling salted water. Take them out with a slotted spoon, drain them on a cloth and extract the flesh with a pin. Nip off the black corkscrew part at the end.

4 Blanch the lettuce leaves for 1 minute in the boiling water in which the winkles have been cooked.

5 Open the oysters. Hold them over a sieve lined with a damp cloth so that their juices can collect in a bowl placed underneath and remove them carefully with a teaspoon. Wash the oyster shells and line the concave ones with the lettuce leaves (4). Then, replace the oysters, sprinkle them with their juices and scatter the winkles round them.

6 Wash the exteriors of the mussels carefully, and make sure that they are closed.

7 With a flexible knife, cut the bass fillets in two, leaving on their silver skin, and cut the fillet of sole into four pieces.

Cooking the fish

8 Make a bed of seaweed at the bottom of each cocotte, sprinkle with 3 tablespoons of water and place the cake-rack, or a round of foil pierced all over with a skewer, on top. Then divide all the fish and crustaceans between the four cocottes, taking care to put the bass fillets skin side up.

9 Strew the julienne vegetables on top, season with salt and freshly-ground pepper, put the lids on the cocottes and cook over a brisk fire, allow exactly 3 minutes cooking after the liquid has reached the boil.

Finishing and serving the dish

10   Present the cocottes to your guests, lifting the lids so they may inhale the fragrant aromas of the sea.

11   Take them back to the kitchen. Split the Dublin Bay prawns in half lengthwise, detach and remove the upper shells of the mussels. Then, arrange the fish and crustaceans in a circle on the 4 hot plates in the same way as they were arranged in the cocottes.

12   Serve one or both of the accompanying sauces separately.

Suggestion for the home cook

* Some rounds of French bread grilled on both sides and spread with Rouille **(No 1)** are a good addition.

69 Seafood Pot-au-feu

Le pot-au-feu de la mer 'Closely related to the familiar pot-au-feu with beef'

For four people

Main ingredients	2 bass weighing 300 g (10½ oz) each 4 small red mullet weighing 100 g (3½ oz) each 16 medium-sized mussels 4 oysters 4 fillets of sole 8 Dublin Bay prawns 4 scallops, out of their shells
Ingredients for cooking the bass	1 tablespoon chopped shallot 1 bunch parsley 8 tablespoons water
Ingredients for cooking the sole	200 ml (⅓ pint) red wine 1 bouquet garni 1 sprig tarragon 6 peppercorns 1 level teaspoon sugar
Ingredients for cooking the prawns and the mullet	8 tablespoons dry white wine 1 teaspoon chopped shallot
Ingredients for the vegetable garnish	1 litre (1¾ pints) water and 15 g (½ oz) coarse salt 100 g (3½ oz) each of leeks, carrots, cucumbers and turnips, turned into miniature vegetables in the shape of large olives 12 fresh asparagus tips **or** 100 g (3½ oz) topped and tailed French beans

Ingredients for	250 g (8¾ oz) softened butter	
finishing the	4 slices French bread	
dish	1 tablespoon olive oil	1 teaspoon butter
	4 anchovy fillets	juice of ½ lemon

Equipment	3 oval enamelled cast-iron dishes and 2 lids

Preparing the vegetables

1 Bring the 1 litre (1¾ pints) water and 15 g (½ oz) coarse salt to the boil in a large saucepan and put the leeks, carrots and turnips into cook for 10 minutes. After 5 minutes, put in the cucumbers, and asparagus or beans. Remove from the heat and keep hot in their cooking water.

Preparing and cooking the fish

2 Preheat the oven to 220°C/425°F/Mark 7.

3 Scale, gut and wash the bass and cut the fins off with scissors. Scale and gut the mullet, carefully keeping their livers on one side.

4 Scrape and wash the mussels meticulously.

5 Open the oysters with an oyster-knife.

6 Strew the bottom of one of the three oval gratin dishes with chopped shallot and make a bed of half the parsley. Lay the bass on it, season, and cover with the rest of the parsley. Moisten with 8 tablespoons water, cover and cook for 8 minutes in the oven.

7 In the second oval dish, bring the red wine, bouquet garni, tarragon, pepper, and sugar to the boil and reduce for 5 minutes. Then poach the sole fillets gently in the simmering liquid for 3 minutes. Remove from the heat and keep hot in the cooking liquid.

8 In the third oval dish, bring the court-bouillon to the boil, poach the Dublin Bay prawns for 1½ minutes, and take them out with the slotted spoon. Bring the liquid back to simmering point and poach the mullet for 2 minutes. Reserve the cooking liquid.

9 Bring the white wine and chopped shallot to the boil in a small saucepan. Throw in the mussels, grind some pepper over them and cook, covered, for 6 minutes or until the shells have opened. Take

(*continued on the next page*)

immediately off the heat and remove the mussels from their shells. Reserve the cooking liquid.

10 Using a teaspoon, remove the oysters from their shells over a sieve lined with a damp cloth so that the juices can drip into a small saucepan underneath. Poach the oysters and scallops for 1 minute over a very gentle heat in the juices: you should be able to dip the back of your finger in the liquid without burning. Remove them with a slotted spoon and keep hot on a plate.

Preparation of the sauce

11 Add to the saucepan containing the oyster juices the cooking liquids from the mussels (9), the mullet (8) and the sole (7). Bring to the boil and reduce by three-quarters of the original volume. There should be about 7 tablespoons of liquid left.

12 Incorporate the 250 g (8¾ oz) butter, in pieces, into the boiling liquid, whisking all the while. Shake the pan in a circular swirling motion to blend the sauce and make it smooth and velvety.

Serving the pot-au-feu

13 Brush the slices of bread with oil and grill on both sides. Quickly fry the livers of the mullets (3) and spread them on the bread. Decorate each slice with an anchovy fillet seasoned with a few drops of lemon juice.

14 Coat the hot plates with half the sauce, and put the rest in a sauceboat to hand separately. Arrange the fish and shellfish on the plates in the following order, leaving a gap between each to be filled with the different coloured vegetables, prettily arranged: 1 mullet, 1 fillet of sole, 4 mussels, 1 fillet of bass, 2 Dublin Bay prawns, 1 oyster, 1 scallop.

15 Add the garnished slices of bread and serve at once.

Suggestions for the home cook

* If you do not have the time to make the sauce replace it with 250 ml (scant ½ pint) of hot Sauce Vierge (**No 3**) which you can make a day in advance.
* You can also make the sauce more quickly by blending together in the liquidiser the reduction (11) and the 250 g (8¾ oz) butter. The vegetables from the court-bouillon will add the required creaminess.
* You can adapt this recipe to more modest but nonetheless tasty fish – conger eel, mackerel, whiting, and so on.

POULTRY AND GAME

70 Chicken Winglets with White Wine and Cucumbers

Ailerons de volaille au Meursault et aux concombres 'Succulent mouthfuls of meat'

For four people

Main ingredients	48 chicken wings (*see note*) 1 litre (1¾ pints) water 30 g (1 oz) butter salt and pepper
Ingredients for the vegetable garnish	300 g (10½ oz) peeled cucumber 1 litre (1¾ pints) water and 15 g (½ oz) coarse salt 25 g (¾ oz) butter 1 teaspoon caster sugar 1 teaspoon chervil sprigs
Ingredients for the sauce	80 g (2¾ oz) button mushrooms, cut into tiny mirepoix dice 1 teaspoon chopped shallot 4 tablespoons dry vermouth 150 ml (¼ pint) white Meursault **or** other dry white wine 300 ml (½ pint) whipping cream 2 tablespoons raw tomato pulp **(No 99)** ½ teaspoon freshly-chopped tarragon 1 teaspoon chervil sprigs salt and pepper
Equipment	1 medium-sized saucepan 1 heavy-bottomed saucepan 1 frying-pan

* The 'winglets' used in this recipe are not the triangular extremities of the wing, but the plump little joint immediately next to it.

Boning the wings

1 First, using a large heavy knife, cut off the tips of the bones at either end of each wing to make them easier to bone.

2 Bring the 1 litre (1¾ pints) water to the boil in a saucepan and blanch the wings for 2–3 minutes. Take them out with a slotted spoon, drain them on a cloth and allow to cool.

3 Then, extract the two little bones by pressing the thumb hard down on one end of the wings so that they can be drawn out at the other end.

Preparing the cucumbers

4 Cut the cucumber into 3 cm (1¼ inch) lengths, chop each piece lengthwise into four, deseed them and 'turn' and cut them into the shape of large olives with a small sharp knife.

5 Bring 1 litre (1¾ pints) water and 15 g (½ oz) salt to the boil, in the cleaned saucepan, and blanch the cucumber pieces for 3 minutes. Drain and keep on one side on a plate.

Preparing the wings and their sauce

6 Heat the butter in a heavy-bottomed saucepan and throw in the blanched wings. Season with salt and pepper and let them cook gently on both sides for 10 minutes. Remove from the saucepan with the slotted spoon and keep on one side.

7 Put the diced mushroom and chopped shallot in the saucepan and sauté for 3 minutes.

8 Pour the fat from the saucepan into a bowl. Pour the vermouth and white wine into the saucepan, bring to the boil and reduce by three-quarters.

9 Add the cream, tomato pulp, chopped tarragon and chervil, season with salt and pepper and allow to reduce by half.

10 Lower the heat and add the wings to the sauce to heat through, but don't boil.

(*continued on the next page*)

Finishing and serving the dish

11 Heat the butter to golden brown in the frying-pan and throw in the miniature cucumbers. Let them brown all over, sprinkle with a teaspoon of caster sugar and sauté them briskly for 2 minutes.

12 Arrange the wings in their sauce on the serving dish or plates, scatter the little cucumbers and chervil sprigs over the top, and serve immediately.

71 Chicken Breasts with Leek Sabayon Sauce

Blancs de volaille au sabayon de poireau
'Chicken breasts stuffed, and perfumed with
leeks'

For four people

Main ingredients	4 chicken breasts salt and pepper 10 g (⅓ oz) butter 60 g (2 oz) white part of leeks, cleaned and sliced into rounds 1 level teaspoon chopped shallot ¼ bunch watercress, picked over and washed 2 tablespoons port 250 ml (scant ½ pint) stock made by dissolving ½ chicken stock cube in 250 ml (scant ½ pint) water 8 tablespoons double cream
Ingredients for the vegetable garnish	40 g (1½ oz) butter 60 g (2 oz) each of carrots, onions and button mushrooms cut into tiny mirepoix dice 20 g (¾ oz) diced truffle (optional) salt and pepper 1 pinch thyme
Ingredients for the sabayon sauce	2 egg yolks 3 tablespoons cold water
Equipment	1 small saucepan 1 cast-iron casserole 1 liquidiser

Preparing the vegetables

1 Heat the 40 g (1½ oz) butter in the small saucepan and add the vegetables in the following order, letting them soften without browning. Add the carrots first, then after three minutes the onions; after another three minutes add the mushrooms and truffles (if used), and cook for a further three minutes. The carrot will therefore cook for 9 minutes, the onion for 6 and the mushrooms and truffles for 3. Stir the vegetables frequently during the cooking to prevent them sticking. Season with salt and pepper and thyme and allow to cool.

Preparation and cooking of the chicken breasts

2 Skin the breasts. With a sharp knife, make an incision in the thickest part so that the breast opens up like a pocket. Season the inside of the pocket lightly and stuff with the vegetables.

3 Heat the 10 g (⅓ oz) butter in the cast-iron casserole and allow the leek and shallot to soften without browning for 10 minutes, stirring with a wooden spatula.

4 Add the watercress leaves, pour in the port, stock and cream, and simmer for 10 minutes.

5 Put in the stuffed chicken breasts and simmer for 10–12 minutes. Take them out with a slotted spoon and keep hot between two heated plates.

Preparing the leek sabayon sauce

6 Purée the entire contents of the casserole (5) in the liquidiser for 20 seconds or until the mixture is smooth. Pour the mixture into a small saucepan and keep hot over a gentle heat. Put the egg yolks and water into a large bowl and beat with a small wire whisk for 40 seconds or until the mixture increases in volume and becomes foamy. Incorporate it gradually into the hot but not boiling leek sauce, whisking all the time.

Serving the dish

7 Arrange the stuffed chicken breasts on the hot serving dish and pour the leek sabayon sauce over them.

Suggestions for the home cook

* The green part of leeks is not used for this recipe because of its strong flavour. Instead, watercress is used to give a tender green colour.

* A truffle weighing 30 g (1 oz) cut in julienne strips and added to the sauce at step 7 adds a very special note to this dish.

* Don't throw away the skin from the chicken breasts. You can cut it into little squares which, when fried till crisp in a little oil, will enliven a salad.

* The chicken legs can be used for the next recipe.

72 Jellied Chicken with Peppercorns

Volaille en gelée aux grains de poivre 'For country picnics'

For four people

Main ingredients	4 chicken legs (drumstick and thigh) weighing 220 g (7¾ oz) each, possibly left over from the previous recipe, **No 71** Salt 4 slices of smoked streaky bacon weighing 30 g (1 oz) each
Ingredients for the marinade and the cooking liquid	12 white peppercorns 1 tablespoon chervil sprigs 1 teaspoon tarragon leaves 200 ml (⅓ pint) dry vermouth 2 leaves of gelatine (about 1 oz) or 2 level teaspoons powdered gelatine ½ litre (scant pint) stock made by dissolving 1 chicken stock cube in ½ litre (scant pint) water
Equipment	1 wide-mouthed glass preserving jar and lid holding 1 kg (2¼ lb) 1 large tall saucepan for sterilising the jar

One day in advance: preparing the chicken legs

1 Salt the chicken legs all over lightly, rubbing the salt in with your hand, and roll each leg carefully in a slice of bacon. Arrange them in a dish, seasoned with the peppercorns, chervil and tarragon. Cover with the vermouth and put to marinate overnight in the refrigerator.

Finishing and sterilising the jellied chicken

2 Put the gelatine leaves to soak and swell in cold water, then dissolve them in the heated stock.

3 Take the chicken legs out of the marinade with a slotted spoon and pack them in the preserving jar. Pour in the marinade and the hot stock in which the gelatine has been dissolved.

4 Seal the jar hermetically, and sterilise for 2 hours in the large covered pan of boiling water. Cool in the water and store in the coldest part of the refrigerator.

Rules for preserving

1 Scald the jar and its lid and new rubber washer very thoroughly with boiling water and let them dry in the air.

2 Do not fill above the level recommended by the makers.

3 Put a perforated wooden board or a folded cloth on the bottom of the sterilising pan to prevent the jars cracking.

4 The level of the water in the sterilising pan must be the same level as the contents of the jars.

5 Do not remove the jars from the sterilising pan until the water has become cold.

Editor's note Preserving or curing meat can be a potentially hazardous business and it is essential that the basic rules of food hygiene are scrupulously observed and that your refrigerator is operating reliably.

73 Chicken with Wine Vinegar

Poulet au vinaigre de vin
'Wine vinegar in a light sauce'

For four people

Main ingredients	1 chicken weighing 1 kg 400 g (3 lb 1½ oz), drawn but not trussed salt and pepper 30 g (1 oz) butter 6 unpeeled cloves garlic
Ingredients for the sauce	5 tablespoons wine vinegar 250 ml (scant ½ pint) dry white wine 2¼ tablespoons armagnac 2 teaspoons pale Dijon mustard 1 teaspoon tomato purée 150 ml (¼ pint) double cream 30 g (1 oz) softened butter
Ingredients for the garnish	2 peeled, deseeded and chopped tomatoes (see **No 99**) 1 teaspoon chervil sprigs
Equipment	1 oval casserole with lid

Cutting up the chicken

1 Cut the breast and wing away in one piece from each side and remove the legs of the chicken. When detaching the latter, make sure you include the 'oysters' – succulent nuggets of flesh tucked into cavities on either side of the backbone about 6 cm (2¼ inches) up from the parson's nose. Lay the breasts and legs on the table and season them well with salt and pepper on both sides.

Cooking the chicken

2   Heat the butter in the casserole and brown the skin side of the chicken pieces for 5 minutes, then turn over and brown the other side for 5 minutes.

3   Add the unpeeled cloves of garlic and allow to cook covered for 20 minutes on a low heat. Remove the breasts and give the legs a further 5 minutes. Don't overcook the breasts; they will become dry and lose their succulence.

4   If the chicken has given out a lot of fat pour off four-fifths.

Preparing the sauce

5   Return the casserole to the heat, pour in the vinegar and mix in all the caramelised juices which have accumulated on the bottom of the pan, scraping them up carefully with a fork.

6   Half-cover the casserole and reduce the liquid by three-quarters of its original volume; the evaporating vinegar will permeate the chicken with its flavour. Then, remove the chicken and keep hot in a warm place between two heated plates.

7   Mix the white wine, armagnac, mustard and tomato purée together with a wire whisk. Pour this mixture into the pan and reduce for 5 minutes at a galloping boil stirring regularly.

8   Whisk in the cream, remove from the heat and beat in the 30 g (1 oz) butter in pieces, whisking all the time to obtain a well-blended and coherent sauce. Taste for seasoning.

9   Strain the sauce through a wire sieve, pressing the garlic cloves with the back of a ladle to extract their last drop of juice and pulp, which will help to make the sauce smooth and velvety.

Serving the dish

10   Arrange the chicken pieces on a heated serving dish or on individual plates and cover lightly with the sauce. Then scatter a few little pieces of raw tomato pulp and the sprigs of chervil over the top.

74 Parslied Chicken with Sherry Vinegar Sauce

Le poulet 'truffé' au persil et sa sauce au malvoisie 'A layer of moist parsley purée placed under the skin'

For four people

Main ingredients	1 chicken weighing 1 kg 400 g (3 lb 1½ oz), cleaned salt and freshly-ground pepper

Ingredients for the stuffing	50 g (1¾ oz) butter 1 tablespoon flat parsley, with stalks removed juice of 1 lemon 1 tablespoon water 1½ teaspoons salt ¼ teaspoon pepper or 4 turns of the pepper-mill 50 g (1¾ oz) fromage blanc (0% matière grasse or fat content cheese)

Ingredients for the mirepoix	3 tablespoons flat parsley ⎫ 1 tablespoon chives ⎪ 1 teaspoon tarragon ⎬ very finely 2 tablespoons shallot ⎪ chopped 50 g (1¾ oz) button mushrooms ⎪ 50 g (1¾ oz) streaky bacon ⎭

Ingredients for the sauce	½ oz butter 1 tablespoon chopped shallot 2 tablespoons sherry vinegar 3 tablespoons stock made by diluting $\frac{1}{10}$ chicken stock cube in 3 tablespoons water 2 tablespoons double cream 20 g (¾ oz) softened butter 15 g (½ oz) tomato pulp **(No 99)** diced 1 teaspoon chervil sprigs

Equipment 1 liquidiser
1 oval roasting pan

Preparing the stuffing

1 Blend together in the liquidiser the butter, tablespoon of parsley (which gives the stuffing its green colour), lemon juice, tablespoon of water, salt and pepper.

2 Put the butter mixture (1) into a large bowl. Mix in the finely-chopped herbs, shallot, mushrooms, bacon and fromage blanc and beat together with a fork to obtain a smooth stuffing.

Stuffing the chicken

3 Lift the skin away from the breast and legs of the chicken (by sliding your fingers between the skin and the flesh) working carefully and slowly to avoid tearing the skin. Insert the stuffing, again with your fingers, patting it in an even layer all over the breast and thighs.

Cooking the chicken

4 Preheat the oven to 240°C/470°F/Mark 9. Season the inside of the chicken with salt and pepper and put it to roast breast upwards in the hot oven, for 45 minutes, basting frequently with the fat and juices which the stuffing will produce.

5 When it is cooked, take the chicken out of the oven, transfer it to a dish and keep it hot, covered with a sheet of foil.

Preparing the sauce

6 Pour the fat from the roasting tin into a bowl, and replace it with 10 g ($\frac{1}{2}$ oz) butter. In this soften the tablespoon of chopped shallot without browning for 2 minutes, then add the vinegar, scraping up all the caramelised roasting juices. Reduce the vinegar by three-quarters of its volume. Add the chicken stock and cream, and let the mixture boil, reducing the liquid by one-third. Finally beat in the 20 g ($\frac{3}{4}$ oz) butter in pieces.

7 Strain this sauce through the wire sieve and add the diced tomato and chervil sprigs. If it is not to be served immediately, the sauce can keep hot in a sauceboat standing in a bain-marie.

(*continued on the next page*)

Serving the chicken

8 Put the chicken on a board and cut it into four pieces with a large sharp knife. Cover the plates or serving dish generously with the sauce and arrange the pieces of chicken on top.

Suggestions for the home cook

* As a general rule, chickens should be turned during roasting so that they will brown evenly. Start them lying on one side, then after one-third of the roasting time has elapsed, turn them over on to the other side. After two-thirds roasting time is up, turn them breast upwards. The cooking time is calculated according to the weight of the bird; around 15–18 minutes per pound. However, in this recipe the chicken is cooked entirely upright, in order to avoid tearing the skin.
* The chicken is done when a needle inserted in the joint between the drumstick and thigh produces clear juice, without any rosy tinge.
* A simple roast chicken can be enlivened by putting four little rounds of fried bread rubbed with garlic inside it, just before it goes into the oven.

Editor's note

Fromage blanc is a fresh cheese made from skimmed milk and containing no fat solids. It is now popular throughout France, packed and marketed like yoghurt, where it is eaten with sugar and fresh fruit. It can be replaced in this recipe with yoghurt, strained in a fine-meshed sieve for an hour or two or with petits suisses.

75 Guinea Fowl with Red Wine and Smoked Bacon

Pintade au vin de Margaux et au lard fumé
'An interesting variation of coq au vin'

For four people

Main ingredients	1 guinea fowl weighing 1 kg 200 g (2 lb 10½ oz) drawn, but not trussed freshly-ground pepper 180 g (6¼ oz) smoked streaky bacon in a piece 3 tablespoons arachide oil 30 g (1 oz) butter
Ingredients for the marinade	1 litre (1¾ pints) red Bordeaux or Spanish Rioja wine 2 medium carrots and ½ onion peeled and cut into mirepoix dice 1 cm across 1 small bouquet garni 1 clove 1 unpeeled clove garlic
Ingredients for the sauce and garnish	1 tablespoon flour 1 litre (1¾ pints) stock made by dissolving 2 chicken stock cubes in 1 litre (1¾ pints) water 80 g (2¾ oz) little pickling onions, peeled 5 tablespoons double cream 2 tablespoons crème de cassis (blackcurrant cordial)
Equipment	8 wooden cocktail sticks 1 frying pan 1 oval cast-iron casserole

One day in advance: marinating the guinea fowl

1 Using the large knife, cut each guinea fowl into 8 pieces – each breast (including the wing) and each leg being divided into two. Season them with several turns of the pepper-mill. The salt will be provided by the bacon.

2 Slice the bacon into 8 thin slices and wrap one round each piece of guinea fowl, fastening it with a wooden cocktail stick.

3 Put the pieces in a large bowl, cover with all the ingredients for the marinade – wine, mirepoix vegetables, bouquet garni, clove and garlic – and let them marinate overnight in the refrigerator.

Cooking the guinea fowl

4 Drain the marinated guinea fowl and pat dry with kitchen paper.

5 Heat the oil in the frying-pan and when it begins to smoke put in the pieces of guinea fowl, still wrapped in their bacon. Brown them with the skin side downwards for 4 minutes and then on the other side for a further 4 minutes.

6 Heat the butter in the casserole and transfer the drained pieces of guinea fowl to it. Add the strained vegetables from the marinade and continue to cook gently. Sprinkle with the table-spoon of flour and cook for 4 minutes, uncovered, stirring with a wooden spatula.

7 Add the wine marinade, together with the bouquet garni and garlic clove, the stock and the little onions. Bring to the boil and simmer, uncovered, for 20 minutes.

Finishing and serving the dish

8 Remove the pieces of guinea fowl and the onions with a slotted spoon, and put to keep hot between two plates having pulled out the cocktail sticks.

9 Add the cream and cassis to the liquid in the casserole, bring to the boil for ten minutes uncovered, reducing the aromatic liquid with its scents of wine and smoke, to half its volume. Strain through a wire sieve.

10 Arrange the pieces of guinea fowl on a serving-dish or individual plates, pour over the sauce, scatter the small onions over the top and serve as soon as possible.

Suggestions for the home cook

* This recipe can also be adapted to pheasant or chicken.
* The blackcurrant cordial has two purposes in this recipe, first to intensify the flavour of the wine and, second, to improve the colour of the sauce.
* Rather than cook the little onions in the sauce you can cook them separately as glazed onions (see **No 101**).

76 Squab Cooked like Woodcock

Pigeonneau en bécasse 'Young pigeons with a gamey flavour'

For four people

Main ingredients	4 domestic squabs weighing 450 g (15¾ oz) each, drawn but with heads left on (be sure to reserve the livers) 40 g (1½ oz) butter salt and pepper 2 tablespoons port
Ingredients for the stuffing-liaison	2 teaspoons butter 1 level tablespoon chopped shallot the livers of the 4 squabs 40 g (1½ oz) foie gras, fresh or preserved 30 g (1 oz) softened butter 1 level tablespoon double cream salt and pepper 4 thin rounds of French bread
Ingredients for the sauce	1 tablespoon chopped shallot 2 tablespoons armagnac 2 tablespoons port 500 ml (scant pint) rough red wine
Equipment	1 oval oven-dish 1 small saucepan 1 liquidiser

Preparing and cooking the squabs

1   If the butcher has not done so, draw the squabs, reserving the livers carefully. Leave the heads on but remove the eyes. Truss the birds with their heads tucked under one wing. Season inside and out.

2   Preheat the oven to 240°C/470°F/Mark 9. Heat the butter in the oval oven-dish in the hot oven and roast the squabs for 12 minutes, basting them two or three times with their juices.

3   When they are done, remove them from the oven and, with a sharp pointed knife, cut away the breasts together with the wings and the legs, sprinkle them with port and keep them hot between two heated plates in a very low oven (110°C/230°F/Mark ¼) where they will continue to cook very slowly, their flesh becoming tender and rosy. Reserve the carcases.

Preparing the purée liaison

4   While the birds are cooking, heat 2 teaspoons butter in the small saucepan, add the chopped shallot and squab livers and sauté briskly for 30 seconds. It should be done very quickly so that the livers remain rosy. Remove them from the pan and allow to cool a little.

5   Put the livers in the liquidiser with the foie gras (if used), 15 g (½ oz) butter and the cream. Season with salt and pepper, blend to a purée and transfer to a bowl.

6   Spread the slices of bread with the remaining 15 g (½ oz) butter and grill on both sides. Then spread them generously with half the purée and put them to keep hot with the squabs.

Preparing the sauce

7   Chop each of the squab carcases into six pieces with a cleaver, keeping the heads on one side. Pile into the oven-dish, add the tablespoon of chopped shallot and brown for 4 minutes.

8   Add the armagnac and port and scrape up all the caramelised juices from the sides and bottom of the pan. Bring to the boil and simmer for 15 minutes, letting it reduce by three-quarters. Add the red wine and reduce by three-quarters once again.

(*continued on the next page*)

9   Strain the reduction through the wire sieve into the (cleaned) small saucepan. Heat gently without boiling and gradually whisk in the rest of the pureé liaison (5) which will thicken and enrich the sauce. Keep hot.

Finishing and serving the squabs

10   Skin the breasts and legs of the squabs carefully and arrange them on the plates in the manner of an Aztec or Egyptian bas-relief, that is with the four pieces arranged symmetrically, as if the pigeon was being viewed from the air, with the heads split in two and opened up. Pour the sauce around them and put one of the little croûtons spread with the liver mixture on the side of each.

Suggestions for the home cook

* You can surround the squabs in the roasting dish with 24 cloves of garlic peeled and blanched for 1 minute in 3 separate lots of boiling water to soften their flavour and make them more digestible. They will brown in the hot butter and take on a delicious nutty flavour, serving also as a vegetable.

* To accentuate the shape of the squabs on the plate you can place them on a few spinach leaves blanched for 30 seconds in boiling water, giving them a pretty green background.

77 Fillets of Duck Breast with Green Peppercorns

Aiguillettes de caneton au poivre vert
'A fresh seasoning for duckling'

For four people

Main ingredients	2 ducks each weighing 2 kg 400 g (5 lb 4¾ oz), plucked and cleaned salt and pepper 1 tablespoon arachide oil
Ingredients for the sauce	8 tablespoons dry white wine 2½ tablespoons armagnac 2½ tablespoons of the water used to rinse out the empty green-peppercorn tin for the third time (the actual liquid in the tin and the first two rinsings are too fiery) 4 tablespoons stock made by dissolving $\frac{1}{10}$ chicken stock cube in 4 tablespoons water 300 ml (½ pint) double cream 1 tablespoon wine vinegar and ½ teaspoon caster sugar to make the caramel 1½ tablespoons port 20 g (¾ oz) green peppercorns 20 g (¾ oz) red pimentoes cut into tiny dice salt
Ingredients for the garnish	3 apples weighing 180 g (6¼ oz) each; use Golden Delicious or any eating apple which will stay firm during cooking 30 g (1 oz) butter
Equipment	1 oval enamelled cast-iron roasting-dish 2 small saucepans 1 frying pan with lid

Preparing the ducks

1   Remove the legs and thighs of the ducks. Lie one of the ducks on one side with the tail end to the left and sliding a knife between the leg and the body as near to the carcase as you can, at the same time, with the left hand, pulling the leg away from the carcase. Repeat the process, lying the duck on its other side. Do the same with the second duck. Keep the legs for Preserved Duck Legs **(No 80),** as only the two breasts with their fillets are used in this recipe.

Cooking the ducks

2   Preheat the oven to 250°C/490°F/Mark 9. Season the ducks, inside and out with salt and pepper and put them in the oven-dish, breasts downwards. Sprinkle them with the oil and cook for 20 minutes in the very hot oven.

3   Remove the dish from the oven and turn the heat down to 180°C/350°F/Mark 4. Cover the oven-dish with a sheet of foil and keep the oven door open. The ducks will slowly finish cooking, relax and become a uniformly rosy colour, while you prepare the sauce.

Preparing the green-peppercorn sauce

4   Bring the white wine and armagnac to the boil in the first small saucepan and simmer, uncovered, for about 6 minutes or until the mixture has reduced by two-thirds of its volume.

5   Add the water used for rinsing the peppercorn tin, and the stock and boil for 5 minutes. Add the cream, season lightly and simmer for 15 minutes or until the sauce has again reduced by one-third of its volume.

6   Meanwhile, bring the wine vinegar and sugar to the boil in the second small saucepan. Boil for 30 seconds, or until the mixture has become syrupy and brown, like a caramel.

7   Add the caramel (6) to the reduced sauce (5) and pour in the port, mixing the resulting sauce thoroughly with a wooden spatula, and adding the green peppercorns and the diced pimentoes. Taste for seasoning and keep hot in a bain-marie.

Preparing the apples

8 Peel the three apples with a potato-peeler, cut them in half, core them and cut each into 8 pieces. Heat the 30 g (1 oz) butter in the frying-pan and brown the apples gently for 10 minutes on each side. Remove from the heat and keep hot in the covered frying-pan.

Finishing and serving the dish

9 Delicately peel the skin off the duck breasts, and lift them away from the breastbone with the aid of a sharp flexible knife. Carve them in very thin slivers across the grain.

10 Arrange the slices in a fan on a serving-dish or on four heated plates. Cover generously with the sauce and decorate with the apples, arranged all round like a halo.

Suggestions for the home cook

* If you want to present the duck breasts still on the ducks to your guests and then to carve them into slices at the table, you should first remove the wishbone by cutting round it with a sharp knife and pulling it cleanly away by its point.

* The green-peppercorn sauce is excellent served with all white meats, poultry or veal, and also with red meat and with grilled or braised fish.

Editor's note

For this dish Michel Guérard recommends Challans or Rouennais ducks, which are killed in a special way – by smothering – to conserve their blood. Most cooks outside France, however, will have to be content with ordinary ducks.

78 Grilled Duck with Herb Butter Sauce

Grillade de canard de Chalosse au beurre d'herbes fines

For four people

Main ingredients	2 duck breasts or 'magrets' (*see* **No 27**) weighing 350 g (12¼ oz) each
Ingredients for the marinade	3 tablespoons olive oil 3 tablespoons arachide oil 3 tablespoons red Algerian or Spanish wine
Ingredients for the sauce	150 g (5¼ oz) peeled and chopped shallot 250 ml (scant ½ pint) wine vinegar 1 tablespoon sherry vinegar 60 g (2 oz) softened butter 1 teaspoon each of freshly-chopped chives, chervil, flat parsley and tarragon salt and freshly-ground pepper
Accompanying vegetables	Potatoes with Gros Sel (**No 111**)
Equipment	1 oval earthenware oven dish 1 casserole

One day in advance: marinating the duck breasts

1 With a small sharp knife, remove any nerve fibres from the duck breasts and incise with a crisscross lozenge pattern on the skin side. Put the breasts skin-side up in an earthenware dish with the ingredients for the marinade, and marinate for at least 24 hours in the refrigerator, turning after 12 hours.

Cooking the duck breasts

2 Grill the breasts over an open fire (see pages 34–9) or in the following way: heat a casserole over a moderate heat and put the breasts in, skin-side down, without any fat. Let them cook for 10 minutes. Their fat will flow and prevent them from sticking and burning. Turn them over and cook for 3 minutes only on the flesh side. Lift them out with a slotted spoon and keep them hot in a warm place between two heated plates. The meat will rest and relax. The melted fat from this operation can then be used for cooking Potatoes with Gros Sel **(No 111)** instead of the goose fat specified in the recipe.

Preparing the sauce

3 Put the chopped shallot and the wine vinegar to heat in the small saucepan over a moderate heat and allow to evaporate until the mixture is the consistency of a moist purée. There should be about 5 tablespoons.

4 Add the sherry vinegar and bring to the boil again. Then reduce the heat and add the 60 g (2 oz) butter in pieces, whisking all the time and giving the pan a few circular swirling movements to blend the sauce, which thickens and becomes smooth and velvety.

5 Season with salt and freshly-ground pepper and add the chives, chervil, parsley and tarragon. Keep hot in a bain-marie if the sauce is not to be served at once.

Serving the dish

6 Slice the duck breasts across, as you would a joint of roast beef, into paper-thin slices. Arrange them in a fan on a serving dish or on four heated plates, put the fried potatoes in the middle and coat the duck with the herb butter sauce (5).

Suggestions for the home cook

* The duck breasts can stay for a maximum of a week in their marinade in the refrigerator; their flesh will 'ripen' and become even more tasty.

79 Stuffed Geese Feet

Patte d'oie farcie 'A little earthy humour'

For four people

Main ingredients	8 geese feet 2 pig's trotters, bought ready-prepared 3 litres (5¼ pints) water 250 ml (scant half-pint) dry white wine 1 small bouquet garni 10 peppercorns 20 g (¾ oz) coarse salt

Ingredients for the stuffing	2 heaped teaspoons dried morels or morilles 1 teaspoon butter 100 g (3½ oz) peeled and finely-chopped onions 400 g (14 oz) raw prepared sweetbreads 60 g (2 oz) raw skinned chicken breast 1 sprig of thyme, crumbled salt and pepper 7 tablespoons white wine 7 tablespoons port 60 g (2 oz) fresh foie gras 50 g (1¾ oz) raw smoked ham 30 g (1 oz) truffles

Ingredients for the breadcrumb stuffing	1 egg 3 tablespoons olive oil 1 tablespoon mustard 80 g (2¾ oz) fresh breadcrumbs 80 g (2¾ oz) melted butter

Ingredients for the sauce	100 g (3½ oz) softened butter 50 g (1¾ oz) each of carrots and button mushrooms, diced 20 g (¾ oz) each of celeriac and truffles (optional), diced 2 tablespoons port 150 ml (¼ pint) stock made by dissolving ⅓ chicken stock cube in 150 ml (¼ pint) water salt and pepper
Accompanying vegetables	Fried Potatoes with Gros Sel **(No 111)** or Potatoes Cooked in their Skins **(No 109)**
Equipment	1 large saucepan 2 × 1 kg (2¼ lb) weights 1 large shallow saucepan or sautoir, with lid 1 deep gratin dish 2 chopping-boards 1 small saucepan

(continued on the next page)

Cooking and preparing the feet and trotters

1   Wash the geese feet and pig's trotters in cold water, and put them in a large saucepan. Cover with water, wine and add the bouquet garni, peppercorns and coarse salt. Bring to the boil, skimming regularly, and simmer for 3 hours, uncovered, over a low heat.

2   When they are cooked, remove the geese feet and press them flat under the weighted chopping-boards for 30 minutes. This operation will spread the feet, making them ready to receive the stuffing.

3   Skin the pig's trotters, extract the flesh and cut it into tiny dice.

Preparing the stuffing

4   Wash the dried morels in several waters, then soak them in warm water and when they have swelled, cut them in two.

5   In the large shallow saucepan heat the teaspoon of butter and soften the morels and chopped onion, without colouring, for 2 minutes. Add the sweetbreads, the chicken breast, thyme, salt and pepper, and bubble for 2 minutes. Then add the white wine, bring to the boil and reduce until half the liquid has evaporated. Add the port, cover and simmer for 30 minutes. Allow to cool.

6   Cut the cooked morels, sweetbreads and chicken breast into tiny dice. Repeat the process for the foie gras, ham and truffles.

7   Add to the diced ingredients (6) in a bowl, 3 tablespoons of the cooking liquid from step 5, and the diced pig's trotters. Mix it all together with a fork.

8   Make a little domed heap of this stuffing on each goose foot, and put them on a tray in the refrigerator for about 30 minutes to set firmly.

Preparing the breadcrumbs

9   Whisk together the egg, olive oil, and mustard, and brush the domes of stuffing with this mixture. Line up the feet in the gratin dish and strew them with the breadcrumbs. Grill for 15 minutes, or give them 15 minutes in a hot oven (220°C/425°F/Mark 7), sprinkling constantly with melted butter.

Preparing the sauce

10   While the stuffed feet are cooking, heat 20 g (¾ oz) of the butter in the small saucepan and soften the vegetables without browning. Put them in at 3-minute intervals in the following order: carrots, celery, button mushrooms, and truffles. Stir from time to time with a wooden spatula to prevent the vegetables sticking. Season with salt and pepper.

11   Add the port, mix well and allow to reduce by half. Add the stock, boil for 10 minutes and then add the 80 g (2¾ oz) remaining butter in pieces, giving the saucepan a swirling circular movement to blend the sauce thoroughly. If it is not to be served at once, keep hot in a bain-marie.

Finishing and serving the stuffed goose feet

12   Coat the hot plates or hot serving dish with the sauce and put a pair of feet on each plate. Serve with Fried Potatoes with Coarse Salt (**No 111**) or with Potatoes Cooked in their Skins (**No 109**).

Suggestions for the home cook

* It is the gelatinous texture of the pig's trotters which acts as binding agent for this country stuffing and makes it especially juicy.

80 Preserved Duck Legs

Cuisses de canard confites 'The way to make perfect preserved meat'

For four people

Main ingredients	4 duck legs left over from making Fillets of Duck Breast with Green Peppercorns (**No 77**) ½ clove garlic, peeled 2 teaspoons fine salt 8 turns of the peppermill 1 pinch grated nutmeg ½ bayleaf, chopped 1 small sprig thyme 1 × 750 g (1 lb 10 oz) jar preserved goose fat **or** pure fresh lard which has been heated with a little thyme
Equipment	1 cast-iron casserole 1 stainless-steel saucepan 1 frying-pan 1 large stoneware pot or 1 large wide-mouthed glass preserving-jar holding about 1 kg, with lid

Marinating the duck legs

1   Lay the duck legs on the work-top and rub them all over with garlic. Season them with fine salt and freshly-ground pepper and add the pinch of grated nutmeg. Put them in a deep plate, strew with the chopped bayleaf and crumbled thyme and leave overnight in the refrigerator.

Cooking the duck legs

2   Put the legs, with the herbs and spices, in the casserole. Pour in the melted goose fat or lard. Bring the fat to the boil and reduce the heat. Simmer, uncovered, for 1 hour 15 minutes if they are to be served at once and 45 minutes if they are to be preserved (4). When the meat is cooked, a straw will pierce it easily.

Finishing and potting the duck legs

3   If they are to be used at once, drain the legs and colour them in the frying-pan, skin-side down, in a little of their cooking fat. Let them cool in the refrigerator, but do not chill. They make a pleasant summer meal or an agreeable emergency standby. Serve them with a simple green salad dressed with walnut oil.

4   If you want to preserve the duck legs for future use, pack them in a stoneware or glass preserving-jar and pour over the goose fat or lard to cover them completely. Sterilise the jar, following the method given in **No 72,** for 1 hour. The sealed jar can be kept in the refrigerator for several months.

Suggestions for the home cook

* This 'confit' is used in Pot-au-Feu **(No 98)**.
* The same method can be used for preserving chicken and guinea-fowl. The result is unusual and savoury.

Editor's note   Preserving or curing meat can be a potentially hazardous business and it is essential that the basic rules of food hygiene are scrupulously observed and that your refrigerator is operating reliably.

81 Rabbit cooked with spinach and turnips

Baron de lapereau mangetout 'A rabbit cooked in its favourite bed'

For two people

Main ingredients	The back legs and saddle of a young rabbit, weighing 1 kg 200 g (2 lb 10½ oz) 20 g (¾ oz) butter salt and pepper
Ingredients for the garnish	1 litre (1¾ pints) water and 15 g (½ oz) coarse salt 12 small turnips with their leaves 40 g (1½ oz) spinach leaves 5 tablespoons water 45 g (1½ oz) softened butter salt and pepper 2 teaspoons caster sugar
Ingredients for cooking and the accompanying gravy	7 tablespoons stock, made by dissolving ⅕ chicken stock cube in 7 tablespoons water salt and pepper 30 g (1 oz) softened butter
Equipment	1 medium-sized saucepan 1 enamelled cast-iron casserole with lid

Preparing the vegetables

1   Cut off the turnip leaves, leaving a green topknot 3 cm (1¼ inches) high.

2   Bring the water and salt to the boil in the saucepan and blanch the turnip leaves and the spinach for 1 minute.

3   Peel the turnips with a potato-peeler, still preserving their top-knots, wash them in cold water and put in the casserole. Cover with 750 ml (1¼ pints) water and add the 45 g (1¾ oz) butter in pieces and the salt, pepper and sugar. Put to cook on a low heat for 18 minutes, uncovered, until the liquid has evaporated. Give the pan a shake from time to time to give the turnips a good coating of the lustrous syrup made by the butter and sugar.

Cooking the rabbit

4   Preheat the oven to 160°C/325°F/Mark 3. Heat the 20 g (¾ oz) butter in the casserole, and colour the rabbit all over for 4 minutes.

5   Season with salt and pepper, put the turnip and spinach leaves round the rabbit, cover and cook for 5 minutes over a moderate heat.

6   Remove the saddle, cutting it away from the legs at the joints and keep hot between two soup-plates in the low oven.

7   Add the hot stock to the casserole with the legs and greenery and cook, covered, for a further 5 minutes.

8   Remove the legs and greenery with a slotted spoon and put them to keep hot, between two other soup-plates, next to the saddle.

Preparing the sauce

9   Reduce the liquid in the casserole to two-thirds of its original volume. Add the 30 g (1 oz) butter in pieces, giving the pan a swirling circular movement to blend the sauce thoroughly. Lower the heat and keep the sauce hot but not boiling.

Finishing and serving the dish

10   Make a bed of turnip tops and spinach on two hot plates or on a serving dish and put the legs, boned with a sharp knife, on top. Remove the meat from the saddle and slice it finely lengthways.

(continued on the next page)

Arrange neatly around the legs. Re-season the meat and strew the turnips round the edge. Cover the meat with the sauce.

Suggestions for the home cook

* The cooking time for the rabbit may appear short, but it is really quite enough. Overcooking always causes meat to shrink and toughen. Doing it this way, you will obtain a yielding, juicy and melting result.

* The turnip-tops used in this recipe provide a vegetable worthy of respect in its own right, which goes well with white meats, poultry and grilled fish.

* The small new turnips can be replaced with the same weight of larger ones, peeled, but not washed, and cut into fine slices. Pepper them and sauté them in a tablespoon of olive oil, with a garlic clove and 150 g (5¼ oz) diced smoked bacon. Cook for 10 minutes uncovered, turning with a spatula to prevent them sticking. Do not salt, the salt in the bacon will be enough. The result has rare delicacy of flavour.

* You can use the same sliced turnips to make deep-fried turnip chips – delicious and unusual.

82 Woodcock in Red Wine

Bécasse au fumet de pomerol 'The king of gamebirds'

For four people

Main ingredients	4 woodcock, plucked but not drawn salt and pepper 4 good slices of lean streaky bacon for barding 50 g (1¾ oz) butter
Ingredients for the croûtons and liaison	4 thin slices of white bread cut into 5 cm (2 inches) diameter rounds with a pastry-cutter 50 g (1¾ oz) fresh or preserved foie gras 2 generous tablespoons double cream 1 tablespoon armagnac The entrails or trail of the woodcock removed after cooking salt and pepper
Ingredients for the sauce	1 level tablespoon chopped shallot 4 tablespoons armagnac 4 tablespoons port 320 ml (½ pint) red Bordeaux from the Pomerol district **or** Algerian or Spanish red wine 1 teaspoon lemon juice
Equipment	kitchen string 1 large oval roasting dish 1 pastry-cutter 5 cm (2 inches) in diameter 1 liquidiser 1 small saucepan

Preparing and cooking the woodcock

1   Pluck the woodcock just before cooking; it is not necessary to singe them, it's a waste of time. Above all, do not draw them. The heads should be left on but the eyes must be removed. A woodcock is not trussed, its claws are entangled together, and the thighs held close to its sides by transfixing the bird with its own long beak, like a skewer.

2   Preheat the oven to 240°C/470°F/Mark 9. Season the birds with salt and freshly-ground pepper. Roll each one in a slice of bacon, tied over the breast with string. This keeps the flesh succulent and prevents the skin browning too much and drying out.

3   Heat the 50 g (1¾ oz) butter in the roasting dish and turn the woodcock in it until they are golden on all sides. Then put the dish in the hot oven and roast for 18 minutes, basting them frequently with the cooking juices. When they leave the oven the flesh of the woodcock should still be rosy.

4   Remove the bacon slices and cut away the breasts and legs with a sharp knife. Put them between two heated soup plates and keep hot in a low oven with the door open.

5   Take the entrails out of the carcases with a teaspoon, discarding the gizzards. Reserve the trails and carcases in two different covered soup plates in the warm oven.

Preparing the garnished croûtons

6   Fry the little rounds of bread in the woodcock cooking juices (3), browning them on both sides.

7   Blend the foie gras, cream, 1 teaspoon of armagnac and the reserved entrails (5) in the liquidiser until smooth. Season with salt and freshly-ground pepper.

8   Take a third of this mixture and spread it on the 4 croûtons. Put them to keep hot.

Preparing the sauce

9   Remove the heads and chop the woodcock carcases into large pieces with the heavy knife. Put them in a roasting dish with the tablespoon of chopped shallot and cook for 4 minutes.

10 Pour in the remaining armagnac and the port and bring to the boil, scraping up all the caramelised juices from the bottom of the pan with a fork. Add the red wine and allow the mixture to reduce by three-quarters of its volume. Finally, add the lemon juice.

11 Sieve this sauce through the strainer into the small saucepan and reheat *without boiling*. Whisk in the rest of the foie gras mixture with a wire whisk (7), to give the mixture richness and body. Keep hot in a bain-marie.

Finishing and serving the woodcock

12 Take the breasts and legs of the woodcock and arrange them on four heated plates in the style of an Aztec or Ancient Egyptian bas-relief – a complete bird on each plate, laid out symmetrically as if seen from above. Include the heads, split neatly in half and placed skin side up. Nap lightly with the sauce and put a garnished croûton on each plate.

Suggestions for the home cook

* I am completely against the usual slices of fried bread placed underneath roast game-birds, which soak up the juices and sauce and quickly become pieces of soggy blotting paper. A croûton, whether spread with a stuffing or not, should remain crisp, and should therefore be placed away from the sauce and not in it.
* Heaven be praised, nobody has yet found a successful method of farming woodcock. It should be eaten at the most one week after it has been shot – and kept in a cool place meanwhile. Unlike pheasant, any hint of 'highness' will destroy its delicate flavour.
* Because the woodcock excretes during every flight, its intestines are white and delicate, with a marvellous flavour.

83 Pheasant Casseroled with Pig's Trotters

Navarin de faisan aux pieds de cochon 'A strange and sophisticated combination'

For four people

Main ingredients	1 hen pheasant weighing about 800 g (1 lb 12 oz) salt and freshly-ground pepper 1 large cooked pig's trotter 125 g (4½ oz) lean streaky bacon, cut in 5 slices, each one cut into 8 little 'lardons'
Ingredients for the vegetable garnish	12 small 'grelot' onions, peeled 12 white button mushrooms, peeled 8 miniature carrots, turnips, potatoes (made from 150 g (5¼ oz) of each vegetable) 60 g (2 oz) shelled fresh, or frozen peas 1 litre (1¾ pints) water and 15 g (½ oz) coarse salt
Ingredients for the sauce	7 tablespoons armagnac 250 ml (scant ½ pint) of stock made by dissolving ½ chicken stock cube in 250 ml (scant ½ pint) of water 250 ml (scant ½ pint) red wine 1 bouquet garni including a sprig of tarragon salt and pepper 2 large ripe tomatoes 1 clove garlic 2 tablespoons olive oil
Equipment	1 cast-iron casserole and lid 1 liquidiser

Preparing the pheasant and the pig's trotter

1   Pluck, singe and draw the pheasant, if the game-dealer has not already done so. Place the bird on its back on the table, hold it firmly with your left hand and, with a large sharp knife, inserted into the cavity, cut through the bone along each side of the backbone and remove it completely. Discard the backbone and cut the bird into four, whole legs and wings plus breasts, leaving the bones in the latter to prevent the flesh shrinking during cooking. Season with salt and freshly-ground pepper.

2   Plunge the pig's trotter into very hot water to soften it slightly. Remove and discard the large central bone. Slice each piece in two, lengthwise.

Cooking the meats and vegetables

3   Preheat the oven to 200°C/390°F/Mark 5. Heat the casserole and fry the diced bacon and the onions. Remove them with a slotted spoon and keep on a plate.

4   Put the four pieces of pheasant in the casserole, skin side downwards, and brown them in the bacon fat, turning them over when they have become a nice golden brown. Then, add the whole button mushrooms and the miniature carrots and turnips and cook for 5 minutes.

5   Pour off the fat from the pan and pour in the armagnac. Cover and reduce by three-quarters of its volume. Add the stock, the red wine, the bouquet garni and the four strips of pig's trotter. Season lightly with salt and pepper and cook for 25 minutes, covered, in the moderate oven.

6   Add the miniature potatoes, the onions and diced bacon (3) to the casserole and return to the oven for a further 20 minutes cooking.

7   Meanwhile, cook the peas in boiling salted water for 15 minutes if they are fresh and for 6 minutes if frozen. Drain them in a colander.

Preparing the tomato liaison

8   Cut the unpeeled tomatoes in half and squeeze them in your hand to press out seeds and excess liquid. Put them in the liquidiser with the peeled garlic, 2 tablespoons olive oil, salt and pepper and blend until you have a smooth pink purée.

(continued on the next page)

Finishing and serving the dish

9   Take the casserole out of the oven and place over a gentle heat. Pour in the tomato mixture (8), stirring gently with a fork to mix it in thoroughly. Heat through but do not allow to boil. Scatter the peas over the surface and serve as soon as possible, either in the casserole or in a nice-looking dish.

Suggestions for the home cook

* The gelatinous texture of the pig's trotter helps to counteract the dryness of the pheasant.
* To make good eating, a pheasant should not be older than 12 months; an older bird will have hard, pointed spurs.
* If you are roasting a pheasant, ask the butcher to cut the leg tendons, which are particularly hard on the jaw, like those of the turkey. To keep the flesh moist, stuff it with a petit suisse blended in the liquidiser with the pheasant liver, a shallot, some herbs and seasoning and a teaspoon of armagnac. This stuffing can be used for all gamebirds.

84 Partridges on a Cabbage Bed

*Perdreaux sur un lit de chou 'A simple
and successful way of serving partridge'*

For four people

Main
ingredients
	4 young partridges and their livers
	salt and freshly-ground pepper
	4 rounds of French bread
	1 peeled clove of garlic
	4 thin slices of lean streaky
	    bacon for barding
	1 fat green cabbage weighing 2 kg
	    (4 lb 6½ oz)
	3 litres (5¼ pints) water and 30 g (1 oz)
	    coarse salt
	100 g (3½ oz) lean streaky bacon in 4
	    thin slices, each cut into 10 little
	    'lardons'
	1 litre (1¾ pints) water
	25 g (1 oz) butter
	2 tablespoons dry white wine
	2 tablespoons cold water

Equipment	1 trussing needle kitchen string 1 large stainless-steel saucepan 1 cast-iron casserole with lid

Preparing the partridges

1   Pluck, draw and singe the partridges if the game-dealer has not already done so.

2   Scrape the livers carefully to eliminate all the greenish traces of the bitter gall bladder, then crush them with a fork in a saucer.

3   Season the inside of the birds with salt and pepper, and put in each a slice of bread which has been rubbed lightly with garlic and spread with the liver paste (2).

4   Truss the birds neatly, season them all over with salt and freshly-ground pepper and bard their breasts with the bacon slices, held in place with string. The bacon will keep the flesh moist and prevent the skin from becoming too brown and drying out.

Preparing the cabbage

5   Cut the cabbage in four with a large knife, cut out the core, remove the coarser leaves, and take it apart. Wash the leaves in several waters.

6   Bring the 3 litres (5¼ pints) water and 30 g (1 oz) salt to the boil in the stainless-steel saucepan and blanch the cabbage leaves for ten minutes. Remove them with a slotted spoon and drain in the colander. Rinse the saucepan.

7   Put the 1 litre (1¾ pints) water in the saucepan, without salt, bring to the boil and blanch the bacon dice for 1 minute. Remove them with a slotted spoon.

Cooking the partridges

8   Preheat the oven to 170°C/335°F/Mark 3. Heat the 25 g (1 oz) butter in the casserole and cook the partridges, browning them all over, for 15 minutes over a brisk heat.

9   Take off the barding bacon (and keep it aside). Brown the breasts for 1 minute. Remove from the casserole, untruss them and keep hot between two plates in the heated oven with the door open.

Finishing and serving the dish

10   Pour the white wine and the 2 tablespoons of water into the casserole with the cooking juices from the partridges. Spread out the cabbage leaves (5) in the liquid and add the blanched bacon dice (7) and the whole slices of barding bacon (9). Turn it all over carefully with a fork to allow the juices to cover and permeate all the ingredients. Check the seasoning and simmer for 5 minutes, covered.

11 Place the partridges on this 'bed' and serve as soon as possible, directly from the casserole. Each guest helps himself to a whole partridge and has the pleasure of cutting it up himself.

Suggestions for the home cook

* Young partridges of from two to four months are the tenderest; the feathers at the wing-tips are still pointed at that age and get progressively more rounded as the bird ages. The claws and the beak are still flexible, the feet are delicate and yellow, becoming grayer with age.
* A partridge makes good eating two or three days after it has been shot; the muscles and flesh have relaxed sufficiently and, the flesh has not yet taken on that gamey taste – as unacceptable and disagreeable to the palate as the taste of farmed partridges.
* Young pigeons can also be cooked in this way.

85 Saddle of Hare with Beetroot

Râble de lièvre à la betterave 'Tender rosy hare with a Russian flavour'

For four people

Main ingredients	2 saddles of hare, weighing 400 g (14 oz) each 2 teaspoons of olive oil
Ingredients for the marinade	500 ml (scant pint) of red wine 1 large carrot and 1 onion cut into 1 cm ($\frac{1}{4}$ inch) mirepoix dice 1 small bouquet garni salt 8 peppercorns 8 juniper berries 2 cloves
Ingredients for the sauce and the garnish	350 g (12 oz) cooked beetroots, cut into very thin slices 2 tablespoons chopped shallot 2 tablespoons wine vinegar 200 ml ($\frac{1}{3}$ pint) double cream 1 teaspoon Dijon mustard 1 tablespoon freshly-chopped chives
Equipment	1 deep roasting-dish 1 small saucepan

One to three days in advance: preparing and marinating the hare

1   With a flexible knife, remove the membrane covering the saddles and discard it. Put the saddles in the deep roasting dish and cover them with the ingredients for the marinade – wine, mirepoix vegetables, bouquet garni, salt, peppercorns, juniper berries and cloves. Put the dish in the refrigerator and marinate for from one to three days, turning occasionally.

Cooking the saddles

2   Take the saddles out of the marinade with a slotted spoon and drain very carefully. Dry them on a cloth: if they are damp they will not brown properly. Season with salt and freshly-ground pepper. Preheat the oven to 250°C/480°F/Mark 9.

3   Transfer the marinade to a salad bowl straining it through a sieve so that only the liquid is retained.

4   Rinse and dry the marinade dish. Pour in the olive oil and put it over a brisk heat. Turn the saddles in the oil to brown them all over, then, put the dish in the hot oven and cook for 12 minutes.

5   Take the saddles out of the dish and keep them hot between two long dishes in the oven, turned down low and with the door slightly open.

Preparing the sauce and the beetroots

6   Spoon off two-thirds of the fat from the roasting dish, put it back on the heat and sauté the beetroot slices and 2 tablespoons of chopped shallot for 1 minute.

7   Add the 2 tablespoons of vinegar and 4 tablespoons of the strained marinade (3). Bring to the boil and reduce by three-quarters. Add the 200 ml ($\frac{1}{3}$ pint) cream and reduce by half. Add the mustard, taste for seasoning, and mix thoroughly. Do not allow to boil again. If the sauce is to be kept for any length of time, keep it hot in a bain-marie.

Finishing and serving the dish

8   Using a flexible knife, lift off the four fillets of meat from the tops of the saddles. Turn the saddles over and remove the four 'filets mignons' from underneath. Slice all eight pieces into fine esca-

(continued on the next page)

lopes, and fit them back on to the saddles as nearly in the original shape as you can manage.

9 Arrange the saddles in the middle of a long serving dish and place the drained beetroot slices all round. Pour the delicate pink sauce over the hare and sprinkle the dish with chopped chives.

Suggestions for the home cook

* Stripped of their membrane, the flesh of hares and rabbits may shrink and twist during cooking; to prevent this happening, puncture the spinal column in two or three places by placing the point of a sharp stout knife on the column, holding it with your left hand and banging it down with the palm of the right hand.
* You can try adapting this recipe for braised calves' liver. It is excellent and very original.

MEAT

86 Jacky's Lamb Charlotte

La charlotte d'agneau de Jacky 'Tender enough to eat with a spoon'

For four people

Main ingredients
1½ teaspoons olive oil
1 aubergine weighing 120 g (4¼ oz), unpeeled
1 tablespoon milk and 15 g (½ oz) fresh breadcrumbs
50 g (1¾ oz) meat from the shoulder of lamb
7 tablespoons whipping cream
salt and pepper

Ingredients for the lamb ragoût
350 g (12¼ oz) boned shoulder of lamb
10 g (⅓ oz) butter
100 g (3½ oz) each of carrots and onions, peeled and cut into 1 cm mirepoix dice
1 heaped tablespoon of chopped celery
2 peeled cloves of garlic
1 small bouquet garni
1 heaped teaspoon plain flour
3 tablespoons dry white wine
250 ml (scant ½ pint) stock made by dissolving ½ chicken stock cube in 250 ml (scant ½ pint) of water
350 g (12¼ oz) raw tomato pulp **(No. 99) or** peeled, deseeded and chopped tomatoes
2 large stoned black olives, cut into tiny dice
salt and freshly-ground pepper

Ingredients for finishing dish
2 tablespoons olive oil
20 very thin slices of aubergine, peeled
10 g (⅓ oz) softened butter for greasing the mould
30 g (1 oz) softened butter for enriching the gravy

Equipment   1 small oval dish
               1 liquidiser
               1 heavy-bottomed saucepan or casserole with lid
               1 medium-sized frying pan
               1 ovenproof bowl 15 cm (6 inches) across for moulding the charlotte

Preparing the forcemeat

1 Preheat the oven to 200°C/390°F/Mark 6. Brush the small cast-iron dish with olive oil, coat the aubergine with it and cook for 30 minutes in the moderate oven.

2 Soak the breadcrumbs in the milk in a bowl.

3 Meanwhile, take the 50 g (1¾ oz) meat from the shoulder of lamb and remove every shred of fat and muscle tissue from it.

4 Put the meat in the liquidiser and blend for 10 seconds. Add the soaked breadcrumbs and blend for a further 10 seconds. Scrape into a bowl and put in the refrigerator to rest for 15 minutes, together with the washed and dried container from the liquidiser which needs to be chilled for step 6.

5 Cut the cooked aubergine (1) in two lengthways, remove the flesh with a teaspoon and chop it with a knife. Season it with salt and pepper and put it into the refrigerator.

6 In the chilled container put the cream and the meat/breadcrumb mixture (4). Blend for 10 seconds and then pour off into a large bowl. Season with salt and pepper and fold in the chopped aubergine (5). Mix thoroughly with a wooden spatula and place in the refrigerator.

Preparing the lamb ragoût

7 Cut the remaining boned shoulder of lamb into eight pieces. Heat the 10 g (⅓ oz) butter in the heavy-bottomed saucepan and brown the meat on both sides over a brisk heat for 8 minutes.

8 Add the mirepoix dice of carrots, onion and celery, the garlic and bouquet garni and continue to brown for a further 8 minutes.

(*continued on the next page*)

9 Sprinkle on the heaped teaspoon of flour, stirring the meat and vegetables so that they are evenly coated; and cook for two minutes more.

10 Pour in the 3 tablespoons of white wine and boil for 20 seconds. Add the stock, the tomato, the diced black olives, salt and pepper and simmer, covered, for 40 minutes.

Finishing and serving the charlotte

11 Preheat the oven to 220°C/425°F/Mark 7. Heat the 2 table-spoons olive oil in the frying pan and when it begins to smoke put in the aubergine slices. Give them 4 minutes on each side, then drain with the slotted spoon and put to cool on a plate.

12 Brush the inside of a 15 cm (6 inch) charlotte mould with 10 g ($\frac{1}{3}$ oz) butter. Line it with 12 aubergine slices and spread them with a layer of forcemeat (6) $\frac{1}{2}$ cm ($\frac{1}{4}$ inch) thick.

13 Drain the ragoût – meat and vegetables – in a colander held over a second large bowl to catch the cooking juices. Remove the bouquet garni and dice the meat coarsely.

14 Fill the charlotte mould (12) with the mixture of chopped meat and vegetables and cover with the remainder of the forcemeat (6 & 12). Place the remaining eight aubergine slices on top and cook in a bain-marie for 1 hour in the oven.

15 Towards the end of this time, heat the cooking juices (13) without boiling them and whisk in 30 g (1 oz) butter, in pieces to enrich them. Give the pan a circular swirling motion to blend the sauce properly.

16 Unmould the charlotte on the serving dish and pour the juices round it. Serve as soon as possible.

Suggestion for the home cook

* Leftover meat from a leg of lamb or a roast of beef can be used for the ragoût.

Poultry, game and meat

Parslied Chicken **(No 74)** Veal Kidney cooked in its Fat **(No 88)** Veal Tournedos with
Chive and Cream Sauce **(No 87)** Grilled Duck with Herb Butter Sauce **(No 78)**

Woodcock in Red Wine **(No 82)** Saddle of Rabbit **(No 81)**
Pot-au-feu **(No 98)** Jacky's Lamb Charlotte **(No 86)**

Fresh Apricot Sauce **(No 125)** served with Honey Ice-Cream **(No 132)**
Claret Granita **(No 130)** Melon Sorbet **(No 129)** and fresh fruit

87 Veal Tournedos with Cream and Chive Sauce

Tournedos de veau à la crème de ciboulette
'A vegetable stuffing to keep the veal moist'

For four people

Main ingredients	1 piece of boned loin of veal (from the rib end of the loin) 640 g (1 lb 6½ oz) entirely free of fat and nerve fibre 40 g (1½ oz) butter
Ingredients for the vegetable stuffing	20 g (¾ oz) butter 35 g (1¼ oz) each of carrots, onions and button mushrooms, and 10 g (⅓ oz) celery, peeled and cut into small mirepoix dice salt and pepper 1 pinch of thyme 4 thin slices of fresh or preserved foie gras (optional) weighing 10 g (⅓ oz) each
Ingredients for the accompanying sauce	Cream Chive Sauce **(No 6)** 2 tablespoons of madeira 4 slices of truffle (optional)
Accompanying vegetables	Glazed Baby Vegetables **(No 101)**
Equipment	1 small heavy-bottomed saucepan 1 small sharp cleaver 1 small cast-iron casserole large enough to take 4 tournedos lying flat.

Preparing the vegetable stuffing

1   Heat the 20 g (¾ oz) butter in the small saucepan and soften the vegetables, without browning, in the following order: first the carrots, then after three minutes the celery and onion, then after a further three minutes the mushrooms. In this way the carrots will have 9 minutes cooking, the celery and onion 6 and the mushrooms 3. Season with salt and pepper and thyme, and allow to cool.

Preparing the tournedos

2   Cut the piece of veal into four equal tournedos 3 cm (1¼ inches) thick and weighing 160 g (5½ oz) each. Slit them horizontally to form a pocket. Season this pocket lightly with salt and pepper and fill it with the vegetable mixture (1) topped with a thin slice of foie gras, if you have it. Season the stuffed tournedos on both sides.

Cooking the tournedos

3   Heat the 40 g (1½ oz) butter in the casserole until it starts to colour and put in the tournedos. Let them cook and brown over a moderate heat for 4–5 minutes on each side; the inside of the pocket must be hot.

4   Preheat the oven to 180°C/355°F/Mark 4. Coat four hot plates or a serving dish with the Cream and Chive Sauce, place the tournedos on top and keep hot in a low oven.

5   Pour the 2 tablespoons of madeira into the casserole (4). Boil for 10 minutes, scraping up the caramelised juices with a fork. Pour the resulting syrupy juice over the tournedos and decorate each with a slice of truffle if available. Serve the dish with the Glazed Baby Vegetables **(No 101)** arranged in little bunches all round the meat.

Suggestions for the home cook

* You can recognise good veal by the rose-tinted white flesh shot with iridescence and also, if the carcase is displayed in the butcher's shop, by the fine white colour of the fat surrounding the kidneys.
* All kinds of sautéed veal cuts – escalopes, medallions, tournedos etc., should be cooked in utensils into which they fit quite tightly, if they are to remain juicy.
* The degree of heat is most important in cooking sautéed veal. Too fierce a heat will dry out the meat, too gentle a heat will turn it into boiled veal.
* This dish can be accompanied by fresh noodles.

88 Veal Kidney in its Fat

Rognon de veau dans la graisse 'Cooking a veal kidney so that it is tender, pink and silky'

For four people

Main ingredients	1½ tablespoons olive oil 4 veal kidneys encased in their natural suet
Ingredients for the vegetable garnish	350 g (12¼ oz) each of carrots and onions and 150 g (5¼ oz) white part of leeks, peeled and cut in 1 cm dice 2 tablespoons chopped shallot 1 unpeeled clove of garlic, crushed 1 bouquet garni
Ingredients for the sauce	1 teaspoon caster sugar 1 litre (1¾ pints) Algerian or Spanish red wine 8 tablespoons stock made by dissolving ¼ chicken stock cube in 8 tablespoons water 1 teaspoon Dijon mustard 25 g (1 oz) softened butter
Equipment	1 large flameproof casserole and lid 1 liquidiser 1 small saucepan

Suggestions for the home cook

* Provided you can keep them warm, you can cook the kidneys up to two hours in advance, giving you the time, if you feel so inclined, to prepare a more elaborate presentation. Blanch some handsome lettuce leaves and several strips of carrots and turnip cut with a potato-peeler. Then serve the kidneys, in their overcoats of fat, on a bed of lettuce decorated with highly-coloured vegetable ribbons, studded here and there with little sprigs of parsley.

(*continued on the next page*)

307

Cooking the kidneys

1 Preheat the oven to 220°C/425°F/Mark 7. Heat the 1½ table-spoons of oil in a large casserole and cook the mirepoix vegetables for 15 minutes without browning, stirring all the time with a fork. Add the shallot, crushed clove of garlic and bouquet garni.

2 Put the four kidneys, in their jackets of suet, on this bed of veget-ables. The fat allows a slow gentle cooking, keeping the flesh of the kidneys supple, silky and a rosy pink colour.

3 Cover the casserole and cook in the oven for from 45 to 50 minutes according to the size of the kidneys.

Preparing the sauce

4 Turn down the oven to 150°C/300°F/Mark 2. Remove the cas-serole from the oven, take out the kidneys with a slotted spoon and keep warm in a covered soup plate in the oven with the door open.

5 Put the casserole over a brisk heat, sprinkle the vegetables with 1 teaspoon caster sugar and cook them until they are a nice golden colour. Then pour off the cooking fat through a wire sieve, placed over a second bowl, in order to catch the vegetables. Put them back in the saucepan on a brisk heat and moisten with the red wine and stock. Lower the heat and simmer for 15 minutes, uncovered, until two-thirds of the liquid has evaporated.

6 Put the liquid, together with two heaped tablespoons of the cooked vegetables, in the liquidiser and blend for 1 minute.

7 Put this blended juice in the small saucepan over a low heat and beat in the mustard and the 25 g (1 oz) butter in pieces. Check the seasoning and keep warm in a bain-marie.

Finishing and serving the kidneys

8 While the sauce is reducing (5), remove the coating of fat from each kidney by hand, and carve the kidneys in very thin slices like roast beef. Arrange them in overlapping layers in a serving-dish or on heated plates and coat lightly with the sauce (7). Serve imme-diately.

89 Sweetbreads with Salsify

Ris de veau aux salsifis 'To do honour to a neglected vegetable'

For four people

Main ingredients	1 kg 200 g (2 lb 10½ oz) veal sweetbreads 2 litres (3½ pints) cold water 800 g (1 lb 12¼ oz) fresh salsify 1 litre (1¾ pints) cold water 1 tablespoon flour juice of 1 lemon 1½ teaspoons salt 60 g (2 oz) foie gras, fresh or preserved, cut in 4 thin slices (optional)

Ingredients for the vegetable garnish	50 g (1¾ oz) butter 350 g (12¼ oz) each of carrots and onions and 150 g (5¼ oz) white part of leeks, peeled and cut in mirepoix dice 2 tomatoes, peeled, deseeded and chopped (see **No 99**) 1 bouquet garni salt and pepper

---

Ingredients for the sauce	3 tablespoons dry vermouth 400 ml (¾ pint) dry white wine 400 ml (¾ pint) stock, made by dissolving ⅔ chicken stock cube in 400 ml (¾ pint) water 25 g (1 oz) butter

---

Equipment	2 large saucepans 1 large fireproof casserole with lid

---

One day in advance: preparing the sweetbreads and salsify

1 Soak the sweetbreads in a bowl under a slowly running cold-water tap for 3–4 hours. Blanch them by putting them in a saucepan with 2 litres (3½ pints) cold water, bringing to the boil and boiling for 3 minutes. Refresh in running cold water, drain, and remove the membranes and cut away any fibrous bits and pieces with a sharp knife.

2 Wrap them in a clean tea-towel and put beneath a weighted board in the refrigerator overnight to expel any remaining water and give them an even shape.

3 Wash the salsify and peel with a potato-peeler, holding the roots flat on the table by first one end and then the other. Cut them into 5 cm (2 inch) lengths and put in a bowl of water with a few drops of vinegar or lemon juice to prevent them discolouring.

4 When all the salsify is peeled, drain it and put to cook for 45 minutes in the second saucepan filled with the simmering cooking liquid known as a 'blanc', composed of a tablespoon of flour whisked into 1 litre (1¾ pints) cold water and seasoned with lemon juice and salt. Allow to cool and put in the refrigerator, still in their cooking liquid.

On the day: cooking the sweetbreads

5 Heat the 50 g (1¾ oz) butter in the casserole and put in the mirepoix vegetables, chopped tomatoes, bouquet garni and salt and pepper and the sweetbreads, seasoned with salt and freshly-ground pepper. Let them brown lightly all over for 10 minutes.

6 Add the 3 tablespoons vermouth, the 400 ml (¾ pint) white wine, bring to the boil and reduce for 5 minutes to drive off the alcohol. Add the stock, cover and simmer for 20 minutes.

7 Ten minutes before the cooking time is up, drain the salsify, remove the bouquet garni from the casserole and arrange the salsify round the sweetbreads on top of the vegetable garnish. Heat thoroughly.

Finishing and serving the sweetbreads

8 Remove the sweetbreads and keep them hot between two soup plates in a low oven with the door slightly open. Retrieve the salsify and keep hot on one side. Take out the mirepoix vegetables with a slotted spoon and spread them over four hot plates. If using foie gras: slit the sweetbreads horizontally to form a pocket, season the interior, and slide in the four thin slices of foie gras. Close up the sweetbreads and lay them on the bed of vegetables. Arrange the salsify prettily in little bunches round the meat, cover with foil and keep hot in a low oven while you make the sauce.

9 Strain the cooking liquid from the sweetbreads (7) through a wire sieve into a small saucepan. Place over a brisk heat, add the 25 g (1 oz) butter in pieces and reduce by a third to obtain a rich, creamy sauce. Pour this lightly over the sweetbreads and salsify and serve at once.

Suggestions for the home cook
* You can save time by cooking the sweetbreads as soon as they have soaked, without blanching; the sauce will only improve in flavour.
* The thankless task of peeling and cleaning salsify can be avoided by using tinned salsify, which is generally of very high quality.

90 Steaks Cooked Out of Doors

Steak en campagne 'A hot steak sandwich'

For two people

Main ingredients	2 pieces of beef (rib-steak or sirloin steak) weighing 250 g (8¾ oz) each salt and freshly-ground pepper 1 tablespoon olive oil 2 slices of home-made bread the size of the steaks 2 thick slices of streaky bacon weighing 50 g (1¾ oz) each
Accompanying sauce	40 g (1½ oz) Vintner's Butter **(No 91)** (optional)
Equipment	1 cast-iron grill with handles *or* a grill rack

1   Make a small fire with dry twigs and leaves. When it has caught properly add a few pieces of damper slightly mossy wood to damp the fire and make it smoke.

2   Put the *unsalted* meat on the grill and hold over the fire for 7 minutes on each side; this is not to grill the meat but to let it absorb the flavours of the woodsmoke. Remove and put on a plate.

3   Remove the damp logs and make a brisk fire with dry wood, including a few larger pieces, and wait about 20 minutes till the heart of the fire is glowing red. Put the grill over the heat.

4   Season the pre-smoked meat with salt and pepper and brush with oil on both sides, then place on the hot grill.

5   Put the slices of bread on the grill, at the same time, brown them on one side only and keep hot in a cloth.

6   Cook the steaks to your taste – rare, medium rare or well-done (*see page 35 for technique*). Two minutes before they are done, put the slices of bacon on the grill and brown for 1 minute on each side.

7   Put the cooked steaks on the un-grilled side of the bread. Spread each with a generous quantity of softened Vintner's Butter (if used) and cover with a slice of bacon.

The bread, grilled on one side, makes an almost waterproof dish for the steak, and the crumb catches all the savoury juices that run out of the meat. We thought up this recipe one October, while waiting in the shade of a small oak wood for the flight of the 'palombe' or wild dove.

Editor's note

In France the best bread for this is the pain de campagne – generous round loaves of slightly sour creamy-beige bread with a delicious flavour, baked in brick ovens and meant to keep for a week or longer. You could substitute rye-bread or home-made wholemeal bread.

91 Beef Cooked on Salt with Vintner's Butter

Côte de bœuf sur le sel au beurre vigneron
'Gros sel used as a grill'

For four people

Main ingredients	1 forerib of beef on the bone weighing 1 kg (2¼ lbs), trimmed by the butcher 1 tablespoon olive oil 600 g (1 lb 5 oz) coarse salt for grilling the steak salt and freshly-ground pepper
Ingredients for the Vintner's Butter	40 g (1½ oz) chopped shallots ¼ garlic clove, peeled and chopped 3 tablespoons dry white wine 250 g (8¾ oz) softened butter 1 tablespoon each of freshly-chopped parsley and chervil 1 teaspoon fresh lemon juice 1¼ teaspoons salt freshly-ground pepper 1 pinch of grated nutmeg
Equipment	1 oval roasting-pan 1 small stainless-steel pan 1 cleaver

Preparing and cooking the beef

1   Make sure the butcher gives you the third rib of the run of ribs, situated where the sirloin meets the forerib. Ask him to trim off all the bone except the actual rib itself. Flatten it slightly with the flat side of a cleaver.

2   Take the meat out of the refrigerator to warm up to room temperature. Brush both sides with oil.

3   Preheat the oven to 240°C/475°F/Mark 8. Put the salt in a thick layer in a roasting-pan and put in the hot oven. When it begins to crackle, after about 15 minutes, lay the meat on top and proceed as if for a straightforward grill (*see page 35 for technique*), allowing 12 minutes on each side. Halfway through grilling each side season with salt and freshly-ground pepper.

4   Remove the meat from the roasting-pan and let it rest for 15 minutes in the oven, with the door open, turning it twice, to relax the muscle fibres, spread the juices evenly through the meat, and generally achieve the desired tenderness. Meanwhile, prepare the Vintner's Butter.

5   Put the shallot, garlic and white wine in the small saucepan. Bring to the boil and reduce for 2 minutes until it is a moist purée. Cool by standing the base of the pan in cold water. With a fork stir in the 250 g (8¾ oz) butter in pieces, together with the chopped herbs, lemon juice, salt and pepper and nutmeg. Fold gently until you have a creamy butter.

Finishing and serving the beef

6   Place the rib of beef on a carving-board and carve it downwards into 8 slices. Season lightly with salt and freshly-ground pepper. Reconstitute the joint in as near to its original form as you can manage, on the serving dish and add 8 tablespoons Vintner's Butter (5), which will melt and flavour each slice deliciously. Serve as soon as possible.

Suggestions for the home cook

* The cut I prefer comes from a rather young and rather fat animal.
* Obviously, one can only salt the outsides and not the centre of a large piece such as a rib of beef, leg of lamb or large fish, before cooking, this is why I recommend carving into slices (or fillets for fish) and seasoning lightly just before serving.

92 Grilled Marinated Blade-Steak of Beef

Grillade de palette de bœuf à la marinade
'To ennoble and tenderise a little-known cut'

For four people

Main ingredients	800 g (1 lb 12¼ oz) beef in one piece, either blade steak or skirt, trimmed of all fat and sinew 1 tablespoon arachide oil salt and freshly-ground pepper 1 tablespoon freshly-chopped parsley
Ingredients for the marinade	3 tablespoons olive oil 3 tablespoons arachide oil 3 tablespoons red Algerian or Spanish wine
Ingredients for the beef sauce	150 g (5¼ oz) softened butter 15 g (½ oz) chopped shallot 5 tablespoons dry white wine 1 level teaspoon freshly-chopped tarragon 3 anchovy fillets ¼ garlic clove, chopped salt and pepper 2 level teaspoons mustard 2 teaspoons lemon juice 2 teaspoons armagnac 2 teaspoons Worcestershire Sauce
Equipment	1 small saucepan 1 liquidiser

One day in advance: marinating the beef

1   Put the beef in a shallow earthenware dish and cover with the ingredients for the marinade – olive oil, arachide oil and wine. Allow to marinate in the refrigerator for a minimum of 24 hours, turning after 12 hours.

Preparing the sauce

2   Heat 10 g ($\frac{1}{3}$ oz) of the butter in the small saucepan and add the shallot, the white wine and the tarragon. Simmer for 3 minutes, stirring with a wooden spatula. There should be 2 tablespoons of a moist shallot purée left.

3   Cool by plunging the pan in a basin half-filled with iced water.

4   Put the cooled shallot mixture into the liquidiser and add the 3 anchovy fillets, garlic, salt, pepper, and the 2 teaspoons each of mustard, lemon juice, armagnac and Worcester Sauce. Blend for 1 minute to obtain a smooth purée.

5   Add the remaining 140 g (5 oz) butter and blend for 2 minutes or until you have a light paste.

Cooking the beef

6   Heat either the grill on the cooker or, if using charcoal or a wood fire, the wire grill. Drain the marinated piece of beef and dry on a cloth. Brush it on both sides with 1 tablespoon arachide oil. Put on or under the hot grill and cook to your taste (*see page 35 for technique*).

7   When it is cooked, place the meat on a chopping-board and slice it into four large flat equal slices. Season with salt and freshly-ground pepper.

Serving the dish

8   Arrange the slices on four hot plates or a hot serving-dish and spread half the sauce (5) over them. Serve the remainder in a sauceboat.

(*continued on the next page*)

Suggestions for the home cook

* Less well-known and less tender but more tasty than rumpsteak or sirloin, I like to use this 'palette' or 'butcher's choice' as the marinade tenderises the meat and improves the flavour.

* By the same token, somewhat insipid but nonetheless worthwhile cuts like topside produce their flavour better if marinated before cooking.

* As it is served in this recipe the sauce is really a butter which melts on the slices of meat and 'lubricates' them. If you want to go further and make it into a hot rich sauce, you need only bring to the boil in a saucepan, 1 level tablespoon double cream and 2 tablespoons cold water, add the sauce and boil briskly for a few seconds, whisking as you do so. It will keep hot in a bain-marie until needed.

Editor's note

* Called a blade-steak in English or 'palette' in French, this piece of meat lies flat on the scapula or shoulder-blade of the animal. On a young steer it should be about 35 cm (14 inches) long 12 cm ($4\frac{3}{4}$ inches) wide and 5 cm (2 inches) thick.

A layer of connective tissue runs right through the centre of the steak: if this is carefully cut out you are left with two nice flat pieces of lean meat about 2 cm ($\frac{1}{2}$ inch) thick, which can be cut into steaks or left whole as in this recipe.

A good alternative, if the butcher has, as tends to happen, kept this piece for his own family, is a large piece of skirt-steak.

93 Fillet of Beef Cooked to Look like a Fish

Filet de bœuf en poisson 'An April Fool fish!'

For 10 people

Main ingredients	1 beef fillet weighing 2 kg 200 g (4 lb 14 oz), trimmed of fat
	200 g (7 oz) tinned truffles cut in very thin slices
	salt and freshly-ground pepper
	7 tablespoons arachide oil
	50 g (1¾ oz) butter
	1 handful flour
	150 g (5¼ oz) fresh (**No 118**) or defrosted frozen flaky pastry
	½ beaten egg

Ingredients for the herb sauce	7 tablespoons truffle juice from the tin
	250 g (8¾ oz) butter
	salt and freshly-ground pepper
	3 tablespoons each of freshly-chopped parsley and chervil

Equipment	kitchen string
	1 oblong roasting-pan
	1 rolling-pin
	1 baking-sheet
	1 small saucepan

One day in advance: preparing the fillet of beef

1   Make sure that the butcher trims off every scrap of fat and sinew, especially the loose flap which runs the length of the fillet. You should have nothing but the fillet itself, a long muscle in the shape of a torpedo.

2   Lay the fillet on the work-top parallel to the edge and slit it all along the middle of the side nearest you. Leave a 'hinge' so that when the fillet is opened out it looks like a fish – perhaps a kipper – which has been split open and flattened.

3   Using a small sharp knife, cut horizontal slits or grooves diagonally at regular intervals all the way along the two flat halves of the inside of the fillet on either side of the central 'hinge'. They should be made 3–4 cm ($1\frac{1}{4}$–$1\frac{3}{4}$ inches) long and 3 cm ($\frac{1}{4}$ inches) apart.

4   Slide two slices of truffle into each groove or 'buttonhole' so that little half-moons of truffle show in each one like the scales of a fish. Season with salt and freshly-ground pepper.

5   Carefully close up the fillet and tie up with string like a sausage, but not too tightly. Put the 7 tablespoons arachide oil in the roasting-pan, roll the fillet in it and keep overnight in the refrigerator.

6   If you are using frozen flaky pastry, take it out of the freezer and defrost at room temperature until needed the next day.

Cooking the fillet and constructing the head and tail of the fish

7   Take the fillet out of the refrigerator and allow it to come to room temperature. Preheat the oven to 250°C/490°F/Mark 9. Dot the fillet in its marinade, with 50 g ($1\frac{3}{4}$ oz) of butter in little pieces and roast in the oven for 30 minutes. Halfway through the cooking-time season the fillet with salt and freshly-ground pepper, then turn the meat and season the other side.

8   While the meat is cooking, flour the work-top lightly and roll out the flaky pastry. Cut out the shapes of a large fish's head and tail. Turn them over and place them on the baking-sheet, brushing the top with beaten egg. Trace the outlines of eye, mouth, gills and the tail fin with a sharp knife.

9 Remove the fillet from the oven and turn the heat down to 220°C/ 425°F/Mark 7. Put the fillet on a hot serving-dish and cover with a sheet of aluminium foil to keep hot.

10 Place the baking-sheet with the head and tail of the fish in the oven and bake for 15 minutes.

Preparing the sauce

11 Heat the truffle juice in a small saucepan and as soon as it boils start whisking in the 250 g (8¾ oz) butter in pieces, still boiling briskly. The sauce will thicken in about 2 minutes. Season with salt and pepper, add the chopped herbs and remove from the heat.

Finishing and serving the 'fish'

12 Untie the fillet and open it up again on the serving-dish. Place the pastry head at the thicker end and the tail at the narrower end. Season the meat again lightly with salt, and coat lightly with the herb butter, which will mingle with the truffle juices released during roasting. Serve as soon as possible.

Suggestions for the home cook

* The truffles can be replaced with neat slices of white button mushroom to simulate white scales.
* Unlike other cuts of beef, the fillet, with its muted flavour, is best taken from a beast killed not more than two days before.

94　Ox-cheek with Orange

*Joue de bœuf à l'orange 'The best of cuts for
a beef ragoût'*

For four people

Main ingredients	1 whole ox-cheek weighing 800 g (1 lb 12¼ oz), trimmed by the butcher 7 tablespoons arachide oil salt and freshly-ground pepper
Ingredients for the marinade	60 g (2 oz) button mushrooms, 120 g (4¼ oz) carrots and 150 g (5¼ oz) onions, peeled and cut into mirepoix dice 500 ml (scant pint) dry white wine 7 tablespoons freshly-squeezed orange juice 3 tablespoons freshly-squeezed lemon juice 1 small bouquet garni
Ingredients for the sauce and the garnish	1·5 litres (2½ pints) stock made by dissolving 3 chicken stock cubes in 1·5 litres (2½ pints) water 160 g (5½ oz) blackcurrants, fresh, tinned or frozen and defrosted 2 lemons 500 ml (scant pint) boiling water 2 oranges 1 tablespoon double cream
Equipment	1 casserole and lid 1 small saucepan 1 liquidiser

One day in advance: marinating the meat

1   Cut the ox-cheek into cubes 2½ cm (1 inch) square, each weighing about 30 g (1 oz). Put to marinate in a large bowl with all the ingredients for the marinade – diced vegetables, white wine, orange and lemon juice and bouquet garni. Mix the ingredients and moisten the meat thoroughly, cover and leave overnight in the refrigerator.

Cooking the ox-cheek

2   Remove the meat and diced vegetables from the marinade with a slotted spoon and dry the meat on a cloth or kitchen paper.

3   Heat the 7 tablespoons arachide oil in a casserole and brown the cubes of ox-cheek on all sides. Drain them with the slotted spoon and put on one side in a soup plate.

4   Put the drained vegetables in the oil in the casserole and let them colour very lightly. Do not let them brown too much. Blend the blackcurrants in the liquidiser for 2 minutes.

5   Replace the pieces of ox-cheek on the bed of vegetables and season with salt and freshly-ground pepper. Pour in the marinade (2) with its bouquet garni, the stock and the blackcurrant purée. Bring to the boil, cover and simmer for 1 hour 15 minutes or until tender.

Preparing the fruits

6   Meanwhile, peel the two lemons from top to bottom in strips with a potato-peeler. Then cut the ribbons of peel into very fine julienne strips 3 cm (1¼ inches) long. Plunge them into 500 ml (scant pint) of boiling water for ten minutes to blanch.

7   Peel the two oranges with the potato-peeler. Then remove the pith and skin from both oranges and lemons, with a small sharp knife and cut out the segments, sliding the knife carefully down the sides of each section close to the dividing membranes, so that the segments can be carefully lifted out. Catch and keep the juices as you do this.

Finishing and serving the dish

8   When the ox-cheek is cooked (5) remove the pieces of meat with a slotted spoon and keep hot between two soup plates in a low oven with the door slightly open.

(*continued on the next page*)

9 Pour the cooking juices, the vegetables from the marinade and the juice from the oranges and lemons (7) into the liquidiser and blend for 2 minutes to obtain a smooth purée.

10 Return the purée to the casserole, add the cream and boil for five minutes before putting back the pieces of meat and the juices they have yielded (8). Strew with the fruit segments (7) and the blanched lemon zests (6). Serve as soon as possible in the casserole.

Suggestions for the home cook

* Ox-cheek, to be good, must be taken from a young and well-covered beast – three years old at the most. This neglected cut is to my mind the best of all for braising, and is excellent for the classic 'bœuf à la mode' in place of the more usual, and dryer, cuts.
* 250 g (8¾ oz) of tagliatelle dressed with butter is an ideal accompaniment to this dish.

'Rillettes' of Beef

For a summer evening's meal you can cook the ox-cheek as described (5) and then shred it up with two forks on a chopping-board. Mix carefully with the sauce (10) and the fruit segments and add a tablespoon of freshly-chopped chervil. Put back in the casserole and chill overnight in the refrigerator. Serve your guests this marvellous 'rillettes' of ox-cheek with Chilled Light Watercress or Tomato Purée **(Nos 8 and 9)** and a variety of interestingly mixed salads.

95 Papa Guérard's Tripe

Les tripes à la mode de Papa Guérard
'Hearty and honest'

For four people

Main ingredients	1 kg 250 g (2 lb 12 oz) prepared tripe – (1½ lb double tripe and 1¼ lb honeycomb tripe) 1 calf's foot and 4 pig's trotters **or** 1 cow-heel, split lengthways but not boned 400 g (14 oz) onions and 300 g (10½ oz) carrots, peeled and sliced 2 cloves 2 garlic cloves, unpeeled 1 bouquet garni 200 ml (⅓) water 1 teaspoon of Arôme Patrelle (optional). (A type of caramelised colouring like gravy browning but made with onions) 1½ teaspoons coarse salt ½ teaspoon freshly-ground pepper 1 heaped tablespoon chopped shallot 7 tablespoons dry white wine 1 teaspoon calvados

---

Ingredients for the sealing paste	3 heaped tablespoons flour 6 tablespoons cold water

---

Accompanying vegetables	Potatoes Steamed with Bacon and Thyme **(No 110)**

Equipment	1 cast-iron casserole with lid 1 small saucepan

Preparing the tripe

1 Cut the tripe into 4 cm ($1\frac{3}{4}$ inch) squares with a sharp knife.

2 Put the calf's foot and trotters or cow-heel in a casserole, and scatter two handfuls of the sliced onions and carrots over the top, in equal quantities.

3 Put in a layer of double tripe, then more onions and carrots, the cloves and garlic and the bouquet garni.

4 Put in layers of tripe and vegetables, alternating the two sorts of tripe until the casserole is filled and all the ingredients are used up.

5 Mix the Arôme Patrelle, (gravy colouring), salt and pepper with 200 ml ($\frac{1}{3}$ pint) of water, pour over the tripe, put the casserole over a moderate heat and bring it to the boil.

Preparing the sealing paste

6 Mix the 3 tablespoons of flour and the 6 tablespoons of water in a bowl to obtain a thick dough with which to seal the lid of the ͵ casserole hermetically.

Cooking the tripe

7 Form this paste (6) into a fat ribbon and press down all round the top of the casserole to form an airtight seal when the lid is pressed on. Seal and cook over a low heat or in a low oven (170°C/335°F/ Mark 3) for 8 hours.

Finishing and serving the tripe

8 Just before the tripe is cooked, reduce the white wine with the shallot in the small saucepan until you have about 2 tablespoons of moist purée.

9 Open the casserole by sliding a thin knife between the lid and the edge of the casserole. Carefully lift out the calf's foot and trotters or cow-heel with a slotted spoon, bone them by hand, cut the flesh in 4 cm squares and return to the casserole.

10 Pour in the shallot purée (8) and the dash of calvados and simmer on a very low heat for 10 minutes, stirring with a fork. Replace the lid and serve in the casserole, accompanied by Steamed Potatoes with Bacon and Thyme **(No 110).**

Suggestions for the home cook

* There is only one secret to cooking good tripe. It must be scalded, blanched, scraped and cooked just as soon as the animal has been slaughtered, if it is to keep its succulent juiciness and do justice to a well-flavoured sauce. So make sure you buy it from a good and reliable butcher.

* The wine and shallot must not be added until the very end of the cooking process, partly to prevent the tripe discolouring but mainly to give the final touch of flavour and freshness to the dish.

* For me, the ultimate refinement of this recipe is to serve, as an accompaniment, a salad of raw truffles cut in fine slices and seasoned with salt, pepper, olive oil and lemon juice. You eat first a mouthful of tripe, and then a slice of truffle, and the effect is sublime.

***Editor's note**   In France the tripe in the charcuteries and tripe-shops is sold both fresh and cooked. The kind Papa Guérard uses in this recipe is fresh and needs several hours cooking. Outside France uncooked tripe is almost impossible to come by and it is always sold blanched and cooked. So, if you want to make this dish, cook the calf's foot, trotters or cow-heel for 6 hours, then put in the tripe and cook for a further $1\frac{1}{2}$ to 2 hours. (If you cook pre-cooked tripe for any longer than this it will disintegrate.)

96 Ham with Mushroom Purée

Jambon à l'os au coulis de champignons
'A simple but dazzling dish'

For four people

Main ingredients	20 g ($\frac{1}{3}$ oz) softened butter 4 slices of ham weighing 120 g ($4\frac{1}{4}$ oz) each and $\frac{1}{2}$ cm ($\frac{1}{4}$ inch) thick, cut from a York or similar ham on the bone 4 turns of the pepper-mill 3 tablespoons dry white wine
Ingredients for the accompanying sauce	40 g ($1\frac{1}{2}$ oz) fresh or frozen petits pois 250 ml (scant $\frac{1}{2}$ pint) water and 1 heaped teaspoon coarse salt for cooking the peas 10 g ($\frac{1}{3}$ oz) butter 250 g ($8\frac{3}{4}$ oz) button mushrooms, peeled, washed and chopped 1 level tablespoon chopped shallot 5 tablespoons dry white wine 7 tablespoons white port 250 ml (scant $\frac{1}{2}$ pint) double cream 50 g ($1\frac{3}{4}$ oz) fresh sorrel, picked over, washed and cut in fine strips
Equipment	1 long dish in ovenproof earthenware 2 stainless-steel saucepans

Heating the ham

1 Preheat the oven to 170°C/335°F/Mark 3. Spread the 20 g (¾ oz) butter in the ovenproof dish, put in the four slices of ham and season with salt and four turns of the pepper-mill. Pour in the white wine and cover with an airtight lid of foil.

2 Put the dish in the oven and let the slices of ham heat through slowly in the wine. Take care not to let it boil, which would make the meat shrink and toughen.

Making the sauce

3 Meanwhile, bring the 250 ml (scant ½ pint) water and 1 heaped teaspoon coarse salt to the boil in the first stainless-steel saucepan, and cook the peas for 15 minutes, if fresh, and for 6 minutes if frozen. Drain in a strainer and keep hot over a steaming saucepan of water.

4 Heat the 10 g (⅓ oz) butter in the second stainless-steel saucepan and soften the chopped mushrooms and the chopped shallot without browning for 2 minutes.

5 Pour in the 5 tablespoons dry white wine and allow to boil, uncovered, for about 4 minutes until all the liquid has evaporated. Next, add the 7 tablespoons white port, and then the 250 ml (scant ½ pint) cream, bring to the boil and reduce for 4 minutes.

6 Transfer the entire contents of the saucepan to the liquidiser and blend for 2 minutes until you have a smooth and foamy sauce.

7 Pour the sauce back into the saucepan, bring to the boil again, throw in the sorrel and boil for a further 25 seconds.

Finishing and serving the dish

8 Remove the earthenware dish from the oven and pour off the white wine into a bowl. Spoon the foamy mushroom and sorrel sauce round and over the slices of ham and strew with petits pois. Serve straight away in the cooking dish.

(*continued on the next page*)

Suggestions for the home cook ·

* When you have invited eight or ten guests, try and obtain a whole small Prague ham, which you can reconstitute round its bone after heating and before pouring on the sauce, to make an even more attractive dish.

* For a real feast the button mushrooms can be royally replaced with the same weight of morels (morilles) or millers (mousserons) or even truffles. If you choose truffles, you need only 80 g (2¾ oz) and the chopped shallot should be omitted. The rest of the recipe is the same.

* If you find yourself cooking a large ham for a party, say one of 7–8 kg (15½ lb–17½ lb), remember that it will be moister if you cook it for 6 hours at 75°C/167°F rather than for 4 hours at 90°C/194°F.

97 Tongue Pot-au-Feu

Pot-au-feu de langues 'The "locals'" pot au feu'

For four to six people

Main ingredients	1 ox tongue weighing 1 kg (2¼ lb), trimmed 1 calf's tongue weighing 600 g (1 lb 5 oz), trimmed 3 litres (5¼ pints) cold water salt and pepper 3 litres (5¼ pints) stock made by dissolving 4 chicken stock cubes in 3 litres (5¼ pints) water 1 onion, peeled and sliced into rings 1 carrot, peeled and sliced into rounds 1 small bouquet garni
Ingredients for the vegetable garnish	12 miniature carrots and 12 miniature turnips made from 150 g (5¼ oz) of each sort of vegetable cut into strips and 'turned' 6 small leeks, trimmed 6 very small potatoes, peeled 1 litre (1¾ pints) water and 15 g (½ oz) coarse salt 16 asparagus tips, fresh, peeled or tinned 6 unpeeled 4 cm (1½ inch) lengths of cucumber, deseeded salt and pepper
Accompanying ingredients	180 ml (⅓ pint) Fresh Tomato Sauce (**No 4**) coarse salt, mustard, gherkins, pickled onions
Equipment	1 casserole with lid 2 clean muslins or tea towels 1 small saucepan

Cooking the tongues

1 Three hours in advance, put the tongues to soak in a bowl of cold water, under a dribbling tap, or changing the water 3–4 times.

2 Drain the tongues on a cloth or kitchen paper and put them in the casserole. Cover with 3 litres (5¼ pints) unsalted water, bring to the boil and simmer, uncovered, for 30 minutes. Skim carefully and regularly throughout the cooking time, with a small ladle.

3 Drain the tongues and discard the cooking water. Remove the rough outer skin. Season them with salt and pepper, return them to the empty casserole and cover with 3 litres (5¼ pints) stock, the sliced onion and carrot and the bouquet garni. Cover and simmer on a gentle heat, or in a moderate oven (200°C/390°F/Mark 6) for 2 hours. Meanwhile, prepare the Tomato Sauce **(No 4).**

Cooking the vegetables

4 Thirty minutes before the tongues are cooked (3), add the miniature carrots and turnips and the leeks tied in a bundle, all tied up in a cloth. 20 minutes before the tongues are cooked, cook the potatoes in a small saucepan with 1 litre (1¾ pints) boiling well-salted water. 10 minutes before the tongues are cooked, add the asparagus and the pieces of cucumber, again tied up in a cloth, to the casserole.

Finishing and serving the dish

5 When they are cooked, drain the tongues and carve them into 5 mm (¼ inch) thick slices with a flexible knife. Reconstitute the tongues, as far as you are able, in the middle of the serving dish, season with salt and freshly-ground pepper and arrange the drained vegetables colourfully in little groups all round, alternating them with the pieces of cucumber standing up like little egg-cups, and crowned with tiny potatoes. Sprinkle with a little of the cooking stock and serve the dish at once. Hand the accompaniments – Tomato Sauce, gherkins, pickled onions and mustard, separately.

Suggestions for the home cook

* The cooking stock (3–6), after being carefully de-greased, can be served very hot in soup-bowls before the tongues, either accompanied by large slices of toast and grated cheese **or** enriched with a liqueur glass of red wine added to each bowl **or** a teaspoon each of cream and port and a whole egg per bowl. The egg will poach gently in the very hot stock.

98 The 'Pot-au-Feu' Pot-au-Feu

'The warming generosity of a universally well-loved dish'

For four people

Main ingredients	3 litres (5¼ pints) stock made by dissolving 3 chicken stock cubes in 3 litres (5¼ pints) water
	30 g (1 oz) coarse salt
	4 peppercorns
	600 g (1 lb 5 oz) flat rib of beef on the bone cut into four pieces
	500 g (1 lb 2 oz) ox-tail, cut into four joints
	½ onion, unpeeled, stuck with a clove
	½ onion, unpeeled, browned under the grill
	¼ head of celery, trimmed and washed
	1 whole head of garlic, unpeeled
	1 small bouquet garni
	300 g (10½ oz) fat salt pork
	1 litre (1¾ pints) cold water
	4 preserved ducks' legs **(No 80)**
	Freshly-ground pepper

Ingredients for the garnish	8 miniature carrots and 8 miniature turnips made from about 100 g (3½ oz) of each sort of normal-size vegetables, cut into strips and 'turned'
	4 small leeks, trimmed and washed
	80 g (2¾ oz) French beans, topped and tailed
	4 unpeeled 4 cm (1½ inch) lengths of cucumber, deseeded
	4 very small potatoes, peeled
	¼ young green cabbage, washed

Ingredients for	8 tablespoons Tomato Sauce (**No 4**)
the	8 large slices beef marrow, 1 cm ($\frac{1}{2}$ inch) thick,
accompanying	soaked overnight in cold water
sauce, etc.	250 ml (scant $\frac{1}{2}$ pint) cold water and $\frac{3}{4}$ teaspoon
	coarse salt
	15 g ($\frac{1}{2}$ oz) butter
	4 small slices French bread
	coarse salt
	horseradish sauce
	mustard
	gherkins
	pickled onions

Equipment	1 large earthenware marmite or stewpot
	2 medium-size saucepans, one with lid
	2 clean muslins or tea towels
	1 small saucepan

Cooking the meat and vegetables

1   Bring the stock, seasoned with salt and pepper, to the boil in a large earthenware marmite or stewpot and plunge in the beef, oxtail, 2 onion halves, celery, whole head of garlic and bouquet garni. Skim carefully as soon as the scum starts to rise to the surface and keep skimming at intervals as long as it is necessary. Lower the heat and cook very slowly, uncovered, for 3–3$\frac{1}{2}$ hours according to the tenderness of the meat.

2   Meanwhile, make the Tomato Sauce (**No 4**) and keep hot in a bain-marie.

3   One-and-a-half hours after starting to cook the meat, put the piece of fat salt pork in a medium saucepan, cover with 1 litre (1$\frac{3}{4}$ pints) unsalted water (the fat pork is already salty enough) and simmer, covered, for 1$\frac{1}{2}$ hours. 30 minutes before the meats (1) are cooked, add the miniature carrots and turnips and the leeks tied in a bunch, all tied up in a cloth, to the stewpot. 10 minutes before the meats are cooked, add the French beans and pieces of cucumber to the stewpot, again done up in a cloth. 20 minutes before the pork fat is cooked, add the potatoes and cabbage leaves to the saucepan in which it is cooking.

4 Then put a few ladles of the cooking liquid from the stewpot (1) in a second saucepan and heat the preserved ducks' legs for 10 minutes.

Finishing and serving the pot-au-feu

5 Put the soaked and drained slices of marrow in the small saucepan and cover with 250 ml (scant ½ pint) cold water and ¾ teaspoon coarse salt. Bring gently to the boil and remove the pan from the heat.

6 Butter the 4 slices of French bread with 15 g (½ oz) butter on both sides and toast to a golden brown. Drain the marrow slices with a slotted spoon and place them on the toast. Keep hot.

7 Remove the meats and the vegetables in their bags from the stewpot and the salt pork, cucumbers and potatoes from the saucepan, and drain. Slice the pork into four. Place a cucumber section in the middle of each plate like an egg-cup and place a tiny potato on top. Arrange the meats and vegetables around it in the form of a crown, and add a marrow croûton.

8 Sprinkle everything (except the croûton) with a little of the cooking liquid. Season with a few turns of the pepper-mill and serve the accompaniments – Tomato Sauce, coarse salt, mustard, horseradish, gherkins and pickled onions – separately.

Suggestions for the home cook

* When making pot-au-feu, you normally have to choose whether you want (a) a good strong bouillon at the end of the process, in which case you start the cooking of the meat (1) in cold water, or (b) flavoursome meat, in which case you start with boiling water, which seals in the juices. In this recipe, we start with boiling chicken stock (made with stock cubes and using fewer than the packet specifies) which provides both a well-flavoured bouillon and juicy, succulent meat.
* Carefully skimmed to remove every trace of fat, the bouillon can be served very hot in soup-bowls, before the pot-au-feu and accompanied by toasted bread and grated cheese **or** improved with a liqueur glass of red wine per bowl **or** enriched with a teaspoon each of cream and port and a whole egg, which will poach gently in the hot liquid.

Editor's note

The name of this recipe is taken from Michel Guérard's first restaurant, the famous Pot-au-Feu at Asnières.

VEGETABLES

99 Fresh Tomato Pulp

Tomate fraîche concassée

For four people

Main
ingredients

1   Raw Tomato Pulp
1·5 kg (3 lb 5 oz) fresh tomatoes
2 litres (3½ pints) water
salt and pepper

2 For cooked tomato pulp
1·5 kg (3 lb 5 oz) fresh tomatoes
2 litres (3½ pints) water
salt and pepper
1 teaspoon olive oil
2 finely-chopped shallots
2 cloves garlic, unpeeled
1 bouquet garni

USES

Raw tomato pulp
Freshwater Crayfish Sauce **(No 7)**
Chilled Crab Consommé with Chervil **(No 20)**
Truffled Lobster with Tomato and Basil **(No 54)**
Jacky's Lamb Charlotte **(No 86)**
Sweetbreads with Salsify **(No 89)**
Beetroot Purée with Wine Vinegar **(No 102)**
Artichoke and Asparagus Ragoût **(No 108)**

Cooked tomato pulp
Freshwater Crayfish Paupiettes with Thyme **(No 55)**

A Raw Tomato Pulp

1 Bring the water to the boil in a large saucepan. Remove the stalks from the tomatoes and plunge them into the boiling water for 15 seconds. Take them out with a slotted spoon and plunge them immediately in a basin of iced water to stop them cooking; this process is simply to make them easier to peel.

2 Peel the tomatoes with the help of a small knife, cut them in two. Press each half gently in hollow of your hand to squeeze out pips and watery juice.

3 Cut the tomato flesh in little dice or chop roughly with a large knife. Season with salt and pepper.

B Cooked Tomato Pulp

1 Follow steps 1–3 above.

2 Heat the olive oil in a heavy-bottomed saucepan and stew the chopped shallots gently. Add the raw tomato pulp, the unpeeled cloves of garlic and the bouquet garni and cook for 30 minutes half-covered, on a low heat until most of the moisture has evaporated.

3 Remove the garlic cloves, taste for seasoning, transfer the tomato pulp to an earthenware or stainless-steel container and keep in a cold place until needed.

100 Onion Purée with Grenadine

Confiture d'oignons à la grenadine
'An excellent way to cook onions'

For four people

Main *ingredients*	700 g (1½ lb) onions 120 g (4¼ oz) butter 1½ teaspoons salt 1 heaped teaspoon pepper 160 g (5½ oz) caster sugar 7 tablespoons sherry vinegar 2 tablespoons grenadine cordial 250 ml (scant ½ pint) coarse red wine

1 Peel and slice the onions thinly.

2 Heat the butter in the saucepan till it becomes deep nut-brown, beurre noisette but do not let it blacken. Throw in the onions, season with salt and pepper, and sprinkle with sugar.

3 Cover the saucepan, allow to soften and brown gradually for 30 minutes over a gentle heat. Keep an eye on them, and stir from time to time with a wooden spatula.

4 Add the sherry vinegar, the grenadine and red wine. Cook for a further 30 minutes uncovered, stirring regularly. This onion purée must cook very gently.

Suggestions for the home cook

* This purée can be served hot as a vegetable with hot dishes, or cold, when it is especially delicious with pâtés and terrines of meat, game and poultry.
* The grenadine is included to deepen its purple colour. If necessary, you can substitute blackcurrant cordial.
* An alternative version can be made by adding some well-washed sultanas, prunes, or small pieces of dried apricot to the onions at the same time as the sherry.

101 Glazed Young Vegetables

Les petits légumes glacés
'Sweet melting baby vegetables'

For two people

Main ingredients	4 baby carrots ⎱ with their green stalks 4 baby turnips ⎰ 4 medium-size new onions 800 ml ($1\frac{1}{4}$ pint) water 45 g ($1\frac{1}{2}$ oz) butter $1\frac{1}{4}$ teaspoons salt $2\frac{1}{4}$ teaspoons caster sugar freshly-ground pepper

Preparing the vegetables

1 Cut most of the green leaves off the carrots and turnips with a small knife, leaving 2 cm ($\frac{3}{4}$ inch) of 'topknot' formed by the base of the stalks. Leave 3 cm ($1\frac{1}{4}$ inches) of green shoot on the onions. Peel the carrots and turnips with a potato-peeler. Cut the roots off the onions and remove their outer skins. Wash the carrots and turnips in cold water and drain them in a colander.

Cooking the vegetables

2 Put the carrots in a saucepan which should be just large enough for them to lie flat without overlapping. Add 300 ml (generous $\frac{1}{4}$ pint) water, 15 g ($\frac{1}{2}$ oz) butter, $\frac{1}{2}$ teaspoon salt, $\frac{3}{4}$ teaspoon sugar and one turn of the peppermill.

3 Put the turnips and onions in another saucepan. Add 500 ml (scant pint) water, 30 g (1 oz) butter, $\frac{3}{4}$ teaspoon salt, $1\frac{1}{2}$ teaspoons sugar and two turns of the peppermill.

4 Put both pans on a low heat and simmer gently, giving the turnips and onions 18 minutes and the carrots 20 minutes. During this time, the water will evaporate almost entirely, leaving a thick and glossy syrup, which will glaze the vegetables.

5 To help the syrup cover and glaze the vegetables thoroughly, it is a good idea to shake the saucepans frequently with a swirling circular movement.

Serving the glazed vegetables

6 Arrange the vegetables prettily, according to their colours, on small heated dishes and place them next to the dishes they are to accompany.

Suggestions for the home cook

* During the winter baby vegetables may be replaced by miniatures, made by slicing, cutting up and 'turning' normal vegetables into little olive shapes. This means that celeriac can join the band.
* The choice of three vegetables – carrots, turnips and onions – which I have given here is not restrictive. You can add tiny leeks, French beans, petits pois, and so on.
* To glaze the vegetables 'à brun', you should let them cook for a further two minutes after all the water has evaporated, to give them an even brown colour.

102 Beetroot Purée with Wine Vinegar

Purée mousse de betteraves au vinaigre
'A deep rose-coloured sweet-sour purée'

For four people

Main ingredients	350 g (12¼ oz) cooked beetroot
	150 g (5¼ oz) onions
	1 teaspoon olive oil
	1 clove garlic, peeled and crushed
	3 tablespoons red wine vinegar
	50 g (1¾ oz) raw tomato pulp (**No 99**)
	salt and pepper
	1 tablespoon double cream
	7 tablespoons stock made by dissolving
	½ chicken bouillon cube in 7 tablespoons water

Equipment	1 liquidiser

1   Peel the beetroots and onions and cut them in very thin rounds.

2   Heat the olive oil in a saucepan and allow the onions and garlic to soften without browning. Let them cook until their moisture has evaporated – about 5 minutes – stirring with a wooden spatula to prevent them sticking.

3   Pour in the vinegar and deglaze the pan, then add the tomato pulp and the beetroot rounds. Season with salt and freshly-ground pepper. Cover, and cook on a gentle heat for 1 hour.

4   When the cooking is complete, purée everything in the liquidiser, having first added the cream and stock, to make a thick, light purée. Keep hot in a bain-marie until needed.

Suggestion for the home cook

* This somewhat unusual purée goes very well with game, replacing chestnut purée.

103 Celeriac Purée

Purée mousse de céleri-rave
'A striking and slightly exotic flavour'

For four people

Main ingredients	350 g (12¼ oz) celeriac 1 litre (1¾ pints) milk, cold salt and pepper 100 g (3½ oz) rice 2 tablespoons double cream

---

Equipment	1 liquidiser

---

1 Peel the celeriac with a small knife, and cut it into eight pieces. Put them in a saucepan and pour in the cold milk. Season with salt and pepper.

2 Place the pan on the heat and as soon as the liquid comes to the boil drop in the rice. Stir for 1 minute with a wooden spatula to ensure that the rice does not stick to the bottom of the pan, then half-cover and simmer for 20 minutes.

3 When the cooking is complete, drain the celeriac and rice in a colander placed over a bowl, so that the milk is saved. Purée the celeriac and rice in the liquidiser for 3 minutes, adding the cream. Then add 7 tablespoons of the cooking milk, to moisten the purée and give it a creamy consistency, and blend for a further minute. Taste for seasoning, and keep hot in a bain-marie until needed.

Suggestions for the home cook

* The use of rice rather than potato allows this purée to keep its proper celery flavour, while still becoming thick and creamy.
* A variant which I have recently tried is to replace the rice with 250 g (8¾ oz) of peeled and cored apples, added to the pan 10 minutes before the end of the cooking. It is subtle and delicious.

---

104 Watercress Purée

Purée mousse de cresson
'A beautiful green purée with a peppery taste'

For four people

Main	4 bunches of watercress
ingredients	1·5 litres (2½ pints) water and 20 g (¾ oz) coarse salt
	1 teaspoon lemon juice
	50 g (1¾ oz) butter
	4 tablespoons double cream
	salt and pepper

Equipment	1 liquidiser

1   Pick over the watercress, removing the tough stalks, and wash in running water. There should be about 250 g (8 oz) left.

2   Bring the water and salt to the boil in a large saucepan and blanch the watercress in it for 3 minutes. Drain in a colander and plunge immediately into very cold water to prevent it cooking any further and help to retain its colour.

3   Drain once more and purée for 2 minutes in the liquidiser.

4   Put the resulting purée in a small saucepan, add the lemon juice, the butter and the cream. Taste for seasoning and reheat gently, stirring thoroughly with a wooden spatula. Serve immediately.

Suggestion for the home cook

* Served immediately, this purée keeps its beautiful tender green. If it has to wait for an hour or more it will fade to a greenish yellow. You can, however, partially prepare the purée beforehand *and* keep its colour if you freeze it straight out of the liquidiser (step 3). The lemon juice, cream and butter are added when the purée is reheated.

105 French Bean Purée

Purée mousse de haricots vert
'To make the best of beans that are
no longer young'

For four people

Main ingredients	500 g (18 oz) fresh French beans of medium size 1·5 litres (2½ pints) water 35 g (1¼ oz) coarse salt 1 tablespoon double cream 1 tablespoon butter salt and pepper

Equipment	1 liquidiser

1 Bring the water and salt to the boil in a large saucepan and throw in the beans. Let them cook, uncovered, for 10 minutes at a galloping boil.

2 Drain and refresh them by plunging them immediately into very cold water.

3 Drain again in a colander and then blend for 2 minutes in the liquidiser until you have a smooth purée. Add the cream and blend for one more minute.

4 Heat the butter in a small saucepan until it just starts to brown and has ceased to 'sing' (beurre noisette). Add the bean purée, and mix thoroughly with the wooden spatula. When it has heated through, check the seasoning and keep warm in a bain-marie until needed.

Suggestions for the home cook

* The 'refreshing' of the cooked beans in cold water has two objectives: one, to stop them cooking any further, and two, to remove some of the salt from the deliberately over-salted vegetables. The salt serves to speed up the cooking process and to 'fix' the beautiful colour of the beans.

* As for Watercress Purée (**No 104**), you can make this purée partly in advance and still keep its colour by freezing immediately after puréeing in the liquidiser. The cream and butter are then added when you come to reheat the purée.

106 Leek Purée

Purée mousse de poireaux
'Smooth and succulent'

For four people

Main ingredients	1·2 kg (2 lb 10 oz) tender leeks 80 g (2¾ oz) butter 1 generous tablespoon double cream salt and pepper
Equipment	1 liquidiser

1   Using a small knife, cut off the tough ends of the leeks, together with the roots and all but a small proportion of the green parts. Then cut the leeks in four, lengthways, to make them easier to clean, and wash them several times in running water. Dry in a cloth.

2   Chop the leeks coarsely.

3   Heat 50 g (2¾ oz) of butter in a saucepan, and throw in the chopped leeks. Let them soften without browning. Season with salt and pepper and leave to cook gently, uncovered, for 30 minutes, stirring from time to time with a wooden spatula to prevent them sticking.

4   Purée the leeks for 4 minutes in the liquidiser to make a fine purée. Add the cream and blend for a further 1 minute.

5   Heat the rest of the butter in the small saucepan until it just starts to brown and ceases to 'sing' (beurre noisette). Add the leek purée, and stir thoroughly. Check the seasoning and keep hot in a bain-marie until needed.

Suggestions for the home cook

* It is necessary to purée leeks for longer than most vegetables in order to break down all the stringy little fibres. If they have not disappeared completely, it is best to push the purée through a wire sieve. You will lose about 20 per cent in the process.
* If you prefer leeks prepared in a somewhat more homely fashion, you should not purée them in the liquidiser but merely enrich them with the butter and cream immediately they have been cooked. Served in this way as a countrified 'jam' the leeks make a succulent accompanying vegetable.
* I do not agree that the leek is merely the 'poor man's asparagus'. With a Vinaigrette Gourmande (see **No 24**) it becomes magnificent; set off by a julienne of truffles, it is simply sublime.

107 Little Sweetcorn Pancakes

Petites crêpes de maïs 'Crisp kernels of corn in a herb-flavoured pancake'

For eight people – making 5 small pancakes per person

Main ingredients
100 g (3½ oz) flour
15 g (½ oz) fine salt
4 turns of the peppermill
1 whole egg and 1 egg yolk
250 ml (scant ½ pint) cold milk
50 g (1¾ oz) butter
100 g (3½ oz) tinned sweetcorn
1 tablespoon freshly-chopped chervil **or** parsley
3 tablespoons oil

Equipment
1 large heavy frying-pan

Making the pancake batter

1   Put the flour in a bowl and make a well in the middle. Sprinkle with salt and pepper. Break the egg into the well and add the egg yolk. Beat with a small wire whisk, pouring in the milk in a thin stream, until you have a smooth batter.

2   Heat the butter in a small saucepan until it starts to brown and ceases to 'sing' (beurre noisette). Mix it into the batter and whisk well.

3   Let the batter rest for 1 hour. Then add the sweetcorn kernels and the chopped herbs.

Cooking the pancakes

4   Lightly brush a large frying-pan with oil and heat it. Put in five separate tablespoons of batter, carefully spaced so that the small pancakes do not touch one another. As soon as they come in contact with the heat the undersides will colour rapidly, and all you have to do is to turn them over with a spatula and brown the other side.

5   Take them quickly out of the pan when they are done, and place on a hot buttered plate placed inside a low oven, with the door open.

6   Repeat the operation seven times. You will then have five little pancakes per person. They should be served on hot side-plates as an accompaniment to a main dish.

Suggestions for the home cook

* These pancakes can be served with drinks, but they are particularly good with poultry, especially duck, and with game.
* In order to retain their tender moist quality, it is best to cook them at the last possible moment.
* The batter can perfectly well be made in a mixer or liquidiser, and you will avoid all risk of lumps that way. You merely put all the ingredients in the mixer at once (including the previously prepared beurre noisette) and whizz for a minute or so. After blending, add the sweetcorn and herbs to the batter and let it rest for 1 hour.

108 Artichoke and Asparagus Ragoût

Ragoût d'artichauts aux asperges
'A crisp combination'

For four people

Main ingredients

12 small globe artichokes
½ lemon
1 kg (2¼ lb) medium asparagus
50 g (1¾ oz) softened butter
120 g (4¼ oz) lean bacon in four slices
    each cut into strips 1 cm (½ inch) across
60 g (2 oz) peeled and chopped onion
7 tablespoons dry white wine
250 ml (scant ½ pint) chicken stock made by
    dissolving ½ chicken stock cube in 250 ml
    (scant half pint) water
150 g (5¼ oz) raw tomato pulp **(No 99)**
1 tablespoon chervil sprigs
salt and pepper

Preparing the artichoke hearts and the asparagus

1 Cut the artichoke stalks off flush with the base and remove, by hand, the outer quarter of leaves.

2 Pare away the base of the artichoke with a small knife, to expose the heart.

3 Cut off the top of the artichoke, just above the choke, with a sharp knife: the choke is lightly covered with a few transparent violet-coloured inner leaves.

4 Eliminate the choke with a teaspoon, cut the heart in four pieces, then, in order to stop them going brown, rub the pieces thoroughly with a cut lemon. Prepare all the artichokes in the same way.

5 Peel the asparagus with a potato-peeler, working from tip to butt and holding the spears flat on the table by the butt. Wash the spears and cut them into three pieces 6–7 cm (2–2½ inches) long.

Cooking and serving the ragoût

6 In a cast-iron casserole, melt 20 g (¾ oz) of the butter, throw in the bacon strips and chopped onion and allow to soften without browning for 3 minutes. Add the artichoke pieces and the asparagus and stir with a wooden spatula.

7 Season very lightly with salt and pepper and add the dry white wine. Bring to the boil and allow to reduce by half. Add the stock and the tomato pulp.

8 Cook, partially covered, for 18 minutes, or until there is no more than 4 tablespoons of liquid left. Dot with the remaining 30 g (1 oz) of butter, cut in little pieces, and let it melt. Sprinkle with the chervil and serve in the casserole.

109 Potatoes in their Skins

Pommes à la peau 'Redolent of the earth'

For four people

Main ingredients
4 large waxy potatoes weighing 150 g (5¼ oz) each
1·5 litres (2½ pints) water
40 g (1½ oz) coarse salt
salt and freshly-ground pepper
80 g (2¾ oz) butter

Cooking the potatoes for the first time

1 Wash the potatoes scrupulously in cold water to get rid of every particle of earth and dry in a cloth. Do not peel.

2 Bring the water and salt to the boil in a large pan, or better still, in the lower half of a steamer. Put the potatoes to cook, in the boiling water or in the upper half of the steamer, for 30–35 minutes.

3 When the potatoes are cooked, drain them in a colander and allow to dry off for a few seconds.

Cooking the potatoes for the second time

4 Cut each potato into 8 slices 8–10 mm ($\frac{1}{4}$–$\frac{1}{2}$ inch) thick. Do not peel.

5 Lay the slices out flat on the work-top and season lightly with salt and freshly-ground pepper on both sides.

6 Heat a large frying-pan or two small ones over a brisk heat and melt the butter. When it begins to foam, put in the potato slices side by side without overlapping. Let them brown for about 2 minutes on each side.

Finishing and serving the potatoes

7 Away from the heat, and taking care not to break them, take the potato slices out of the pan one by one with a spatula. Place them in a vegetable dish, or in four small gratin dishes placed on saucers, and serve accompanying a main dish.

Mimi de Lamotte, gourmande friend, dreamed up this delicious recipe for a frugal evening. The skin of the potatoes, caramelising in the butter, permeates the whole dish with its flavour.

110 Steamed Potatoes with Bacon and Thyme

Pommes de terre vapeur au lard et au thym
'*A hearty country taste*'

For four people

Main
ingredients

160 g (5½ oz) smoked streaky bacon
4 nice large waxy potatoes weighing
    180 g (6¼ oz) each
½ teaspoon thyme
salt and pepper

Uses   Papa Guérard's Tripe **(No 95)**

---

1   With a small sharp knife, cut the bacon into eight equal slices.

2   Wash the potatoes meticulously and dry them, without peeling them. Cut them into half lengthways, and slightly hollow out the flat side of each half carefully with a teaspoon.

3   Sprinkle the insides of the potato halves lightly with salt, and put one bacon slice in each of the eight hollows. Sprinkle with thyme and give each one two turns of the pepper-mill.

4   Fill the lower half of a couscoussier or steamer with water. Arrange the potato halves in two layers in the upper part, cover and cook for 30 minutes over simmering water.

5   Serve in a hot dish, having again seasoned the potato halves very lightly with a little salt and a turn of the pepper-mill.

Suggestions for the home cook

* During the cooking, the bacon will give up some of its fat, impregnated with thyme and enrich the potato most appetisingly.
*You can put in some good sausages – for instance Cumberland sausages – or some chipolatas, on top of the potatoes in the steamer before you cook them, to make a substantial and charming dish.

111 Fried Potatoes with Gros Sel

Pommes frites au gros sel 'Good hefty fried potato chips'

For four people

Main ingredients	750 g (1 lb 10 oz) waxy potatoes 4 tablespoons goose or duck fat **or** lard 1 unpeeled clove of garlic 30 g (1 oz) softened butter ½ tablespoon coarse salt ½ tablespoon freshly-chopped parsley
Uses	Stuffed Geese Feet **(No 79)**

1   Peel the potatoes, then cut them lengthwise into four pieces, like the quarters of an orange. Drop them into a bowl of water as you go and keep the bowl under a running tap. Then drain them in the colander and dry thoroughly with a clean cloth.

2   Heat the fat in a casserole, and when it starts to smoke throw in the garlic and the quartered potatoes. Reduce the heat slightly and let the potatoes brown gently on all sides, turning them over from time to time with a wooden spatula. Cover, and cook for fifteen minutes.

3   Drain the potatoes with a slotted spoon and then put them into a deep dish. Pour off all the fat into a bowl, to be used again another time.

4   Return the potatoes to the casserole over a low heat, dotted with the butter, in pieces, which will gradually penetrate and impregnate them.

5   When the butter has been absorbed, sprinkle the potatoes with coarse salt, which will give them a slight crunch, and scatter on the chopped parsley. Serve immediately in the casserole or arranged round the dish they are to accompany.

Suggestions for the home cook

* You can prepare these fried potatoes beforehand. To keep them crisp, beat two egg yolks with a fork and pour them on the potatoes, still beating. Stir the potatoes well: do all this just before seasoning them with the salt and parsley. Put them on an ovenproof dish and keep them hot in a low oven (180°C/350°F/Mark 4) until you need them. As the egg yolk dries it forms a sort of carapace, which prevents the potatoes from going soggy.

112 Potato Purée with Parsley

Purée de pommes de terre au persil
'A countrified potato purée'

For four people

Main *ingredients*	800 g (1 lb 12 oz) potatoes 1 litre (1¾ pints) water and 15 g (½ oz) coarse salt 400 ml (¾ pint) milk 80 g (2¾ oz) softened butter 4 tablespoons freshly-chopped parsley

1   Peel the potatoes, wash and drain them and cut them into large pieces.

2   Put them in a medium-sized saucepan and add the cold water and salt. Bring to the boil, cover and simmer gently for 20 minutes. Avoid over-cooking, which makes the potatoes absorb water.

3   Bring the milk to the boil in a small saucepan.

4   Drain the potatoes in a colander, return them to the empty saucepan and crush them roughly with a fork, adding the butter in small pieces. The small lumps of uncrushed potato are what give this dish its character.

5   Return the saucepan to the heat and beat in the boiled milk gradually with a wooden spoon. The purée will gradually become lighter and creamier.

6   Mix in the parsley at the last moment and serve immediately.

Suggestions for the home cook

* The potatoes are best served as soon as they are ready.
* They can, if necessary, be kept hot in a bain-marie. To stop them drying out while they are waiting, smooth the surface and cover with a little milk.
* Never use a whisk when making mashed potatoes; they become glutinous and lose their flavour.

113 Fried Potatoes with Carrots

Poêlée de pommes de terre aux carottes
'Crisp, melting galettes of potato'

For four people

Main *ingredients*	120 g (4¼ oz) carrots 300 g (10½ oz) potatoes 120 g (4¼ oz) butter salt and pepper

Suggestions for the home cook

* Finely-shredded potato must be scrupulously washed to remove the starch, which might otherwise make it go sticky and discoloured.
* Although not strictly necessary, clarifying the butter prevents the formation of small burnt particles of milk solids during cooking; they are unpleasant both to look at and to taste.

Preparing the vegetables

1 Pare the carrots and potatoes with a potato peeler, wash and drain them.

2 Cut them into 5 cm (2 inch) lengths and cut them into very thin julienne strips, using the fine blade of the mouli-julienne.

3 Dry the carrot julienne in a cloth. Wash the potato julienne several times in cold water to eliminate the starch, then dry in a cloth.

Preparing the clarified butter

4 Melt 90 g (3 oz) of the butter in a saucepan over a very low heat – on no account let it boil. Skim it, and then very gently pour the hot butter into the bowl, leaving behind in the saucepan the white residue of milk solids. The butter in the bowl should be absolutely clear.

Finishing and serving the potatoes and carrots

5 Heat the remaining 30 g (generous 1 oz) in a second pan and cook the julienne of carrots, without browning, for 9 minutes. Season with salt and pepper and keep on one side in a warm place.

6 Season the potato julienne with salt and pepper. Divide half the clarified butter (4) equally between four individual ovenproof dishes; then using half the potato julienne, put a layer of it in each dish, pressing it down well with the back of a fork. Divide the carrot julienne between the dishes and finish with a layer of the remaining potato julienne. Pour the remaining clarified butter over each dish and press each galette again with the back of a fork.

7 Cook each one over a brisk heat for 5 minutes, then turn each galette over with the metal spatula. The underside should already be a pretty golden brown. Lower the heat and finish cooking the other side for 10 minutes.

8 Serve them as they are, in their little dishes, or place on four hot side plates.

114 My Gratin Dauphinois

*Mon gratin Dauphinois 'Cheese isn't
always indispensable'*

For four people

*Main
ingredients*

800 g (1 lb 12 oz) potatoes
2 teaspoons salt
3 turns of the pepper-mill
250 ml (scant ½ pint) milk
250 ml (scant ½ pint) double cream
½ garlic clove, peeled and very finely chopped
1 pinch of grated nutmeg
30 g (1 oz) butter

Preparing the potatoes

1   Peel the potatoes with a potato-peeler and slice them finely into very thin rounds. Dry them in a cloth, but do not wash them. Season them well, mixing in the salt and pepper with your hand.

Cooking the potatoes

2   Put the milk and then the potatoes into a saucepan, bring to the boil, lower the heat and simmer gently, covered, for 10 minutes.

3   Add the cream, the chopped garlic and the pinch of nutmeg, and continue simmering for 20 minutes, taking care that the potatoes do not stick to the pan.

Finishing and serving the dish

4   Preheat the oven to 180°C/350°F/Mark 4. Take out the potatoes with a slotted spoon and divide them between four small ovenproof dishes. Pour over the creamy liquid from the pan.

5   Dot the dishes with butter and finish by cooking them, in a bain-marie, for 10 minutes in the oven, to give them an appetising golden crust. Serve in their dishes.

Suggestions for the home cook

* I still have not discovered whether the faint but noticeable taste of cheese in this dish is due to some interaction between the cream and the starch.
* In any case, not washing the potatoes leaves intact their outer layer of starch, which makes a natural liaison with the milk and the cream and gives it a velvety texture.
* For incorrigible cheese enthusiasts, you can always scatter some grated cheese over the dishes just before they go into the oven to brown.

115 Spaghetti with Baby Vegetables

Ragoût de spaghettis aux petits légumes
'Spaghetti for a surprise occasion'

For four people

Main ingredients	200 g (7 oz) the finest available spaghetti 2·5 litres (4¼ pints) water and 50 g (1¾ oz) coarse salt

Ingredients for the vegetable garnish	1 cucumber of 300 g (10½ oz), peeled
	100 g (3½ oz) fresh ceps, cleaned, **or**
	  preserved 'au naturel'
	40 g (1½ oz) button mushrooms, cleaned
	1 artichoke heart, fresh **or** tinned
	1 litre (1¾ pints) water and 15 g (½ oz) coarse salt
	20 g (¾ oz) little peas, shelled fresh, **or**
	  frozen
	100 g (3½ oz) cauliflower florets
	30 g (1 oz) butter
	7 tablespoons arachide oil
	salt and pepper

Ingredients for the accompanying sauce	15 g (½ oz) dried morels and 15 g (½ oz)
	  fresh **or** preserved truffles **or** 50 g (1¾ oz)
	  button mushrooms
	3 tablespoons water
	1 tablespoon freshly-chopped chervil
	2 tablespoons double cream
	200 g (7 oz) softened butter
	2 tablespoons raw tomato pulp **(No 99)**
	salt and pepper
	1 teaspoon lemon juice

Preparing and cooking the vegetables

1 Cut the cucumber in five pieces and cut each into four lengthways. Trim these and 'turn' them into olive shapes, making 20 miniature cucumbers.

2 Cut the ceps, mushrooms and artichoke heart into 1 cm ($\frac{1}{2}$ inch) mirepoix dice.

3 Bring the water and salt to the boil in a saucepan and cook the peas for 15 minutes if fresh, 6 if frozen; the cucumbers for 6 minutes and the cauliflower florets for 4 minutes. Take them out carefully with a slotted spoon and drain in a colander.

4 Heat the butter and oil in a large frying-pan, and sauté all the vegetables (1, 2, 3). Season, turn off the heat and keep them in a covered pan.

Preparing the accompanying sauce

5 Wash the morels several times in cold water to eliminate any sand and put them to soak and swell for a few minutes in tepid water. Then, dry them carefully in a cloth and cut each in four vertical slices.

6 Cut the truffle into very fine julienne strips.

7 Bring the water and chervil to the boil in a small saucepan, and allow it to reduce by half. Add the cream, the 200 g (7 oz) of butter cut in small pieces, the truffle julienne, the sliced morels and the tomato pulp. Season with salt and pepper. Bring to the boil again and boil for 30 seconds. Add the lemon juice.

Cooking the spaghetti

8 Bring the 2·5 litres ($4\frac{1}{4}$ pints) water and 50 g ($1\frac{3}{4}$ oz) salt to the boil in a large pan. Throw in the spaghetti, broken in half over the pan. Stir with a wooden fork until the water boils again, to stop the pasta sticking together. Cook until just tender.

Finishing and serving the dish

9 Drain the sphaghetti in a colander and rinse under the cold tap to remove the starch. Return to the saucepan, and moisten with the sauce, mixing it in thoroughly with two wooden forks.

(*continued on the next page*)

10   Transfer the pasta to a large round heated dish and arrange the vegetables round the edge in a ring.

Suggestions for the home cook

*If you are having twenty guests, it may be easier to cook the pasta in advance. Follow step 8 exactly, cooking the pasta 'al dente', then place a large bowl under the colander to catch the cooking water, and drain the spaghetti. Rinse it immediately in cold water to stop it cooking, and set it aside until needed. When you want to serve it, simply boil up the cooking water again and plunge the spaghetti into it for 30 seconds. Then, finish the recipe in the normal way.

* The vegetables, also, may be poached the day before, then sautéd on the day.

Chocolate Marquise **(No 140)** Stuffed Apples with Almonds and Apricots **(No 137)**

Puddings and Pastries

Tart Apple Tarts **(No 138)** Caramelised Pear Pastries **(No 141)** Soufflé
Pancakes **(No 136)** Claret Granita **(No 130)**

PASTRIES

and

PUDDINGS

116 Sweet Flan Pastry

La pâte sablée sucrée 'A well-loved, amber-coloured, buttery pastry'

To make 500 g (18 oz) pastry

Main ingredients	150 g (5¼ oz) unsalted butter, softened to the temperature of the kitchen and cut into six pieces 75 g (2¾ oz) caster sugar 1 teaspoon vanilla sugar a pinch of salt 50 g (1¾ oz) ground almonds (optional) 250 g (8¾ oz) fine flour 1 egg ½ teaspoon cold water (optional)
Equipment	A food-processor A plastic bag

Suggestions for the home cook

* This pastry will keep extremely well in a sealed plastic bag, for up to eight days in the refrigerator and two months in the freezer. In the latter case, it should be removed from the freezer the day before it is needed and allowed to 'relax' for a night in the refrigerator, followed by an hour at kitchen temperature.

* It can also be used successfully to make delicious strawberry or raspberry flans or pear tarts in which the fruit is caramelised (see **No 141**). To do so, you simply roll out the pastry gently on a floured work-top, to a thickness of 1 cm (¾ inch), preferably in a regular round or square shape. Prick the surface with a fork to make sure it doesn't puff up and bake it blind in a medium oven (210°C/410°F/ Mark 7) for 20–30 minutes. When it has cooled, spread with a layer 1 cm (¾ inch) thick of crème pâtissière flavoured with kirsch or rum (see **No 122**). Then arrange the strawberries or raspberries on top and sprinkle with a raspberry purée (see **No 124**). If you have chosen pears they should be caramelised (see **No 141**).

A Using a food-processor

1 Put the pieces of butter, the caster and vanilla sugars, the salt, ground almonds (if used) and the flour all together into the bowl. Run the machine for 15 seconds.

2 Add the egg and blend for a further 15 seconds to allow the pastry to 'take' and become a coherent mass. If your mixture is on the dry side, add $\frac{1}{2}$ teaspoon of cold water.

3 Remove the pastry from the machine, flatten it slightly with the palm of the hand on the work-top and slide it into the plastic bag. Let it rest overnight in the refrigerator before use.

B Making the pastry by hand

1 Pat the flour into a mound on your work-top, sprinkle it with the caster and vanilla sugars and the salt and make a well in the centre.

2 Put the butter, cut in pieces, and the egg in the central hollow and start to mix them together, using the tips of the fingers of the right hand (unless you are left-handed!), at the same time using the left hand to work the flour methodically from the outer edges of the pile towards the centre. Then work the whole mass together with both hands, taking care not to treat the pastry too roughly.

3 When the ingredients have become a coherent mass, finish the pastry by crushing it with the palm of the hand and spreading it out with a long stretching movement on the *unfloured* work-top, to mix it really thoroughly.

4 Roll it up into a ball again, flatten it lightly and slide it into the plastic bag. Let it rest in the refrigerator overnight before use.

5 When needed, this pastry is baked in a medium oven preheated to 210°C/410°F/Mark 7.

117 Shortcrust Pastry

La pâte brisée 'The all-purpose pastry'

To make 500 g (18 oz) of pastry

Main ingredients	230 g (8¾ oz) flour
	20 g (¾ oz) skimmed-milk powder
	10 g (⅓ oz) caster sugar
	7 g (¼ oz) salt
	180 g (6⅓ oz) unsalted butter, softened to the temperature of the kitchen and cut into six pieces
	1 tablespoon of cold water
	1 egg
Equipment	1 food-processor
	1 plastic bag

Suggestions for the home cook

* This pastry can perfectly well replace flaky pastry in fruit flans. The inclusion of the egg gives the pastry the strength and elasticity it needs to absorb the fruit juices without becoming soggy.
* Don't be tempted to add more water than I have indicated in the recipe; it has the effect of making the cooked pastry dry and hard.
* Made without sugar, this pastry can be used equally effectively to make rustic dishes like homemade country pâtés and terrines, and meat cooked in a crust – for instance fillet of beef, a leg of lamb or a large, fresh, coarsely-cut sausage.
* The pastry will keep well for up to 8 days in the refrigerator, in a sealed plastic bag.

A Using a food-processor

1 Put into the bowl the flour, powdered milk, sugar, salt and butter. Blend for 15 seconds. Add the tablespoon of water and the egg, blend for a further 15 seconds to allow the pastry to 'take' and become a coherent mass.

2 Flatten the ball of pastry slightly and slide it into the plastic bag. Leave it overnight in the refrigerator: it will be suppler and easier to handle the next day.

B Making the pastry by hand

1 Put the flour in a mound on your work-top, sprinkle it with the powdered milk, the sugar and the salt, and make a well in the centre.

2 Put the butter, cut in pieces, and the egg in the middle of the pile of flour and start to mix them, using the tips of the fingers of the right hand (unless you are left-handed!) at the same time using the left hand to work the flour methodically from the outer edges of the pile towards the centre. Then, working the whole mass with both hands, add the tablespoon of cold water slowly.

3 When the ingredients have become a coherent mass, finish the pastry; crush it with the palm of your hand then spread it over the well-floured work-top, with a long stretching movement, to mix it really thoroughly.

4 Gather it into a ball again, flattening it slightly, slip it into the plastic bag and allow to rest overnight in the refrigerator before use.

5 When needed this pastry is baked in a medium oven preheated to 210°C/410°F/Mark 7.

118 Flaky Pastry

La pâte feuilletée 'A magic pastry'

To make 600 g (21 oz) of pastry

Main ingredients	250 g (8¾ oz) fine flour ⎫
	50 g (1¾ oz) butter, softened to the ⎪ for the
	temperature of the kitchen ⎬ basic pastry
	7 g (¼ oz) salt ⎪
	120 ml (scant ¼ pint) water ⎭
	250 g (8¾ oz) unsalted butter, ⎫ for the
	chilled ⎬ 'buttering-up'
	Several handfuls fine flour for flouring the
	work-top

Equipment	A food-processor
	A heavy knife
	A plastic bag
	2 sheets of plastic film
	A rolling-pin

See explanatory drawings on pages 378–9

Making the basic pastry

A   Using a food-processor

1   Put the flour, 50 g (1¾ oz) butter, salt and water in the bowl. Blend for 25 seconds so that the ingredients 'take' and form a coherent mass.

2   Remove the paste from the bowl, flatten it slightly with the hand and score the surface with the blade of a thick knife in a criss-cross pattern, in order to reduce the elasticity of the pastry.

3   Put it in a plastic bag and allow to rest for 2 hours in the refrigerator.

B   By hand

1   Put the flour in a mound on the work-top and make a well in it, put the salt and water in the centre and add the 50 g (1¼ oz) butter, cut into pieces.

2   Work all the ingredients gently together, using the tips of the fingers and taking care to incorporate the flour gradually, pushing it little by little into the centre of the pile.

3   Finish by working all the ingredients into a mass, flatten it slightly and score the surface as in A (2) above. Allow to rest for 2 hours in a plastic bag in the refrigerator.

'Buttering-up' the basic pastry

4   Take the 250 g (8¾ oz) of chilled butter out of the refrigerator and place between the two sheets of plastic film. Thump the butter with the rolling-pin to soften and flatten it, and then roll it out into a 15 cm (6 inches) square.

5   Flour the work-top lightly, roll out the basic pastry into a 25 cm (10 inches) square.

6   Place the flattened square of butter on the pastry so that it forms a diamond shape in the centre of the square.

7   Fold the four triangular corners of the pastry over the butter: the result will look like an envelope. The butter is now imprisoned inside the pastry.

(*continued on the next page*)

Folding the pastry

8   Flour the work-top again and gradually roll the buttered pastry away from you, taking care not to apply too much pressure, into a strip 25 cm (10 inches) wide and 50 cm (20 inches) long.

9   Fold the pastry back on to itself in three layers, making a new rectangle measuring 17 cm (7 inches) wide and 25 cm (10 inches) long. This is the first 'fold'.

10   Turn the rectangle through 90 degrees and roll it out away from you to make a strip 25 cm (10 inches) wide and 50 cm (20 inches) long. Then, as before, fold the pastry back on to itself in three layers; the rectangle has now had its second 'fold'.

11   Slide the pastry into the plastic bag and allow to rest for half an hour in the refrigerator.

12   Remove it from the refrigerator, and give it two further 'folds' in precisely the same way as described in steps 8, 9, and 10 above. As a result of this working, the pastry gains elasticity and strength; you must roll it out with great care, without using too much pressure on the rolling-pin, which would push the butter out through the pastry.

13   Slide the pastry once again into the plastic bag and allow it to rest in the refrigerator again for half an hour or more.

14   Half an hour before using the pastry for the chosen recipe, give it two final 'folds', using exactly the same method as before. This will bring the total number of 'folds' to six; the pastry is now ready, and is composed of layer upon layer of butter and pastry, which in a hot oven preheated to 220°C/425°F/Mark 7 will become marvellous translucent leaves.

To the lay eye, this pastry smacks of sorcery. By what strange process can a thin scrap of pastry swell and puff itself up to twenty times its original size? The secret lies in the recipe, which produces a piling up of hundreds of layers of butter alternating with hundreds of layers of pastry made from flour, butter, water and salt. When the flaky pastry is placed in the oven, each layer of butter becomes hot, fries and thereby lifts the layer of pastry immediately above it, creating a space between the layers; at the same time the water contained in the pastry turns into steam which tries to escape and helps puff up the 'leaves'.

Suggestions for the home cook

* What is the secret? All that is needed is that the basic pastry and the cold butter should be of a perfectly matched consistency. If, for example, the butter is harder than the pastry which surrounds it, it will, during the rolling-out, come out through the pastry when it is folded instead of staying in its separate layers, and things will go badly wrong when it is cooked. If, on the other hand, the butter is too soft, it will spread out under the pressure of the rolling-pin and won't stay in a clear-cut layer.
* To make really successful flaky pastry in the summer it is a good plan to cool the work-top half an hour before starting to make the pastry, by covering it with a large plastic bag filled with ice cubes.
* Flaky pastry can, immediately after the sixth 'fold', be cut up into 'feuilletés', tarts etc., which then can be frozen between sheets of plastic film. When they are needed, they can be transferred straight from the freezer to the preheated oven (220°C/425°F/Mark 7).
* It is also important, when cutting the pastry with a knife, to do it cleanly and carefully, without crushing it, which would prevent the pastry from rising properly, the different layers being stuck together and unable to separate during the cooking.

(*see illustration on next page*)

FLAKY PASTRY

FLAKY PASTRY

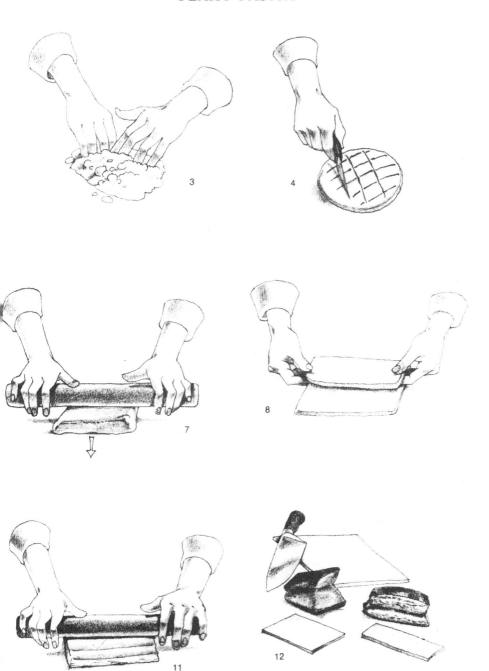

119 Choux Pastry

Pâte à Choux

For 800 g (28 oz) of pastry – making
approximately 30 puffs or éclairs

Main   120 ml (scant ¼ pint) milk
ingredients   120 ml (scant ¼ pint) water
1 teaspoon fine salt
1 teaspoon caster sugar
110 g (4 oz) softened unsalted butter
140 g (5 oz) flour
5 eggs
A powdering of icing sugar

Equipment   1 small thick-bottomed saucepan
1 bowl warmed with hot water
1 pastry-forcer with a 1½ cm (½ inch) nozzle
1 baking-sheet
1 sheet of silicone baking paper (bakewell)

Suggestions for the home cook

* The large amount of liquid (milk and water) used in this recipe turns into steam in the heat of the oven and 'blows up' the puffs, creating a hollow cavern inside.

* This recipe will be much more successful if you use the quantities and weights I specify and if you reduce them by half the result will be less light and less succulent. If this means you can't immediately use all the puffs or éclairs you have made, they can perfectly well be stored, loosely packed in a plastic bag, in the refrigerator for a week or in the freezer for one month. If you freeze them take them out the day before they are needed and let them soften for twenty-four hours in the refrigerator.

* Little puffs, filled with a mixture of diced cooked ham bound with fromage blanc and sprinkled with grated cheese or chopped fresh fine herbs, make good-looking, delicious hors d'oeuvres.

* Crème Chantilly **(No 121)** is the ritual filling for choux puffs. Spread them lavishly with it, once they have been cut in half.

1 Put the milk, water, salt and sugar and the butter into the small saucepan and bring to the boil.

2 As soon as it starts to boil, remove the pan from the heat, and gradually scatter in the flour in a fine shower, stirring it in with a wooden spatula.

3 Return to the heat and stir vigorously with the spatula for a minute, to evaporate some of the water and dry out the paste.

4 Transfer the mixture to the warmed bowl and mix in the eggs one by one, beating vigorously all the time with a whisk until the mixture is smooth and homogeneous.

5 Preheat the oven to 220°C/425°F/Mark 7. Slide the pastry into the forcing-bag, and according to your talents and experience, gently squeeze the bag and pipe the pastry on to a baking-sheet which should be lightly oiled, or better still covered with a sheet of bakewell paper. If you want puffs, pipe little round drops of pastry; for éclairs pipe little sausage shapes 10 cm (2 inches) long. Sprinkle the shapes with icing sugar.

6 Bake for 15 minutes in the hot oven, then reduce the temperature to 200°C/390°F/Mark 6 and bake for 15 minutes longer with the oven door propped open with a fork, in order to allow the escape of excess steam which would prevent them from rising properly.

7 Remove the baking-sheet from the oven and allow to cool. Then, if you want to use the puffs or éclairs immediately, cut them in half carefully with a serrated knife.

120 Baba and Savarin Dough

Pâte à baba ou à savarin 'Brain-child of King Stanislas Leczinski'

For 500 g (18 oz) dough or to make 4 large savarins, for five people each

Main ingredients	10 g ($\frac{1}{3}$ oz) fresh yeast 2 tablespoons tepid water 250 g ($8\frac{3}{4}$ oz) flour mixed thoroughly with 1 heaped teaspoon salt 3 eggs 7 tablespoons milk 10 g ($\frac{1}{3}$ oz) caster sugar 75 g (2 oz) softened butter 50 g ($1\frac{3}{4}$ oz) melted butter to grease the moulds
Ingredients for the syrup	250 ml (scant $\frac{1}{2}$ pint) water ⎫ 175 g (6 oz) caster sugar ⎬ syrup for one savarin 2 tablespoons rum ⎭ 3 tablespoons rum
Equipment	1 large china or stainless-steel bowl holding 2 litres ($3\frac{1}{2}$ pints) 4 savarin moulds 14 cm ($5\frac{1}{2}$ inches) in diameter
Accompanying sauces	Crème pâtissière **(No 122)** Crème Chantilly **(No 121)** Fresh Apricot Sauce **(No 125)**

Making the dough

1 Dissolve the yeast in the tepid water in a large bowl, mixing carefully with the whisk.

2 Add the flour and salt in a fine shower, add two of the eggs and start to mix the ingredients, working them well with a wooden spatula.

3 When the ingredients start to form a homogeneous mass, add the third egg, and, little by little, the milk.

4 Beat the dough energetically for about 10 minutes, lifting it with the wooden spatula in a continuous movement, until it becomes smooth and elastic.

5 Add the sugar, then the softened butter cut in pieces. Continue to beat with the spatula for 5 minutes to incorporate these two ingredients thoroughly; the dough will become very elastic and stretch without breaking.

6 Let the dough rest in the bowl covered with a damp cloth for 30 minutes; the yeast will cause it to rise. Plunge the spatula into the mass again, beat vigorously so that it sinks down, flatten it slightly and re-form it into a coherent mass.

Cooking the savarins

7 Brush the four savarin moulds with melted butter and divide the dough evenly between them.

8 Let the dough rise and swell again in the moulds, which should be kept at kitchen temperature, for approximately 30 minutes: the dough should rise to the top of the moulds. Preheat the oven to 200°C/390°F/Mark 6.

9 Put the moulds in the oven and bake for between 18–20 minutes. The savarins are cooked when the blade of a knife inserted into the middle comes out perfectly clean and dry. Unmould them immediately on to a wire rack so that the air can circulate around them for a few minutes. If you are only using one of the savarins immediately, the others can be placed, still warm, in individual plastic bags and stored in the refrigerator to keep them in perfect condition, or frozen.

Soaking the savarins

10 While the savarins are cooking, bring the water and sugar to the boil together in the saucepan, allow to cool slightly and add the two tablespoons of rum. (The quantities given are for only one savarin, so you will need to increase them if you are using more than one.)

11 Put the savarin in a deep round plate and ladle the syrup copiously over it, spooning up the liquid that collects at the bottom of the plate to pour over the top once again and thoroughly impregnate the savarin. (With a little practice, you will be able to plunge the savarin directly into the saucepan of syrup, so that it soaks it up right to the heart, then lift it out, somewhat cautiously, and place it on its serving dish. A savarin soaked in this way will swell to about one-third larger than when it came out of the oven.)

Finishing and presenting the dish

12 Sprinkle the savarin with the neat rum, and when it has been absorbed, lightly cover it with several spoonfuls of Fresh Apricot Sauce **(No 125)**.

13 Fill the hollow in the middle of the savarin with Crème Pâtissière **(No 122)** or Crème Chantilly **(No 121)** or, more simply, with a fresh fruit salad. Serve the remaining apricot sauce separately in a sauce-boat.

Suggestions for the home cook

* You must never allow a direct and simultaneous contact between the yeast, the salt and the sugar, because these two ingredients can stop the fermentation of the yeast.
* If the savarins are stuck fast in their moulds when you take them out of the oven, wrap them up in a tea-towel or kitchen foil. The moisture formed by the condensing steam will loosen them and make them easier to get out.
* The three remaining savarins, enclosed in plastic bags, can be kept in the refrigerator for twelve days, or for two months in the freezer, so long as they are put in while tepid to prevent them from going stale. If you have frozen them, you must remove them from the freezer the evening before they are to be used and allow them to soften overnight in the refrigerator.

Editor's note

We have specified whipping cream and double cream in the recipes in this section, where the author uses crème fleurette and crème fraîche, which are not easily found outside France. Whipping cream is lighter than double cream and whips to a comparatively greater volume. Maître Guérard distinguishes between crème fleurette and crème fraîche as follows:

I prefer 'fleurette' cream for this recipe, and it is nowadays far more easily obtained. It is in fact the 'crème fraîche' of French cooking, but sold before the thickening fermentations have started. So, though it has the same proportion of 'matière grasse' or fats, it is much runnier than double cream and has a more delicate, finer flavour, which enables one to make a particularly pristine Crème Chantilly. For the same reason I also specify it in many other of my Cuisine Gourmande recipes.

121 Crème Chantilly

'A white cloud of insubstantial cream'

To make 500 g (18 oz)

Main ingredients	500 g (18 oz) whipping cream, chilled
	50 g (1¾ oz) caster sugar, or better, icing sugar
	2 teaspoons vanilla sugar
	or
	400 g (14¾ oz) double cream, chilled
	100 ml (scant ¼ pint) cold water
	100 ml (scant ¼ pint) crushed ice
	50 g (1¾ oz) caster sugar, or better, icing sugar
	2 teaspoons vanilla sugar
Equipment	A large salad-bowl chilled in the refrigerator for an hour beforehand
	A small supple balloon whisk

1   Take the chilled cream and the salad-bowl out of the refrigerator. Put the cream in the bowl and add the sugar and the vanilla sugar.

2   Beat these ingredients for 2 minutes, using a supple movement of the wrist. Little by little the cream will 'mount' into an airy cloud, doubling in volume.

3   Then, beat rather faster for 30–40 seconds; the cream will continue 'rising' until it looks like egg white beaten to a soft snow and forms soft peaks on the whisk, and sticks between the wires of the whisk.

4   Stop beating immediately and decant the cream into a large earthenware cream-bowl if the cream is to be served on the side.

Suggestions for the home cook

* If the cream and the receptacle in which it is to be beaten are very cold the Chantilly will rise quickly and be extra light.
* If you use double cream instead of whipping cream, you should let it down with 100 ml (scant ¼ pint) of cold water mixed with the same quantity of ice crushed in a liquidiser. This will make the cream rise more easily.
* You *must* be careful to stop beating immediately the cream reaches the consistency of a firm snow (3). A few seconds over-beating will turn it into butter and whey.
* The finished Crème Chantilly will keep its consistency for from 6 to 12 hours in the refrigerator. If it has exuded a little water, a few turns of the whisk will restore it.

122 Crème pâtissière

'The essential cream'

To make 1 kg (2¼ lb) of cream

Main ingredients	½ litre (scant pint) milk half a vanilla-pod split in two lengthwise 150 g (5¼ oz) caster sugar 6 egg yolks 20 g (¾ oz) flour 20 g (¾ oz) cornflour
Equipment	1 heavy-bottomed saucepan
Uses	Fruit tarts (see **No 116**) Caramelised Pear Pastries **(No 141)** Millefeuille **(No 142)** Ali-Baba **(No 143)**

1   Bring the milk to the boil in a heavy-bottomed saucepan together with the vanilla-pod and 50 g (1¾ oz) of the sugar.

2   Meanwhile, put the egg yolks and remaining sugar in a large bowl. Whisk for one minute, until the mixture lightens and becomes gradually paler.

3   Gradually add the flour and cornflour in a fine shower, mixing them in delicately with the whisk.

4   Remove the vanilla-pod from the saucepan and add half the boiling milk to the bowl. Whisk vigorously and add the resulting mixture to the remaining half of the milk in the saucepan.

5   Return the saucepan to a brisk heat and whisk vigorously for a minute or two, taking care that the whisk goes right to the bottom of the saucepan to prevent the mixture sticking. Turn the cream into the washed and dried bowl.

Suggestions for the home cook

* If you aren't going to use the crème pâtissière immediately, film the surface with a little *unsalted* butter to prevent the formation of an unlovely skin.
* If you want a particularly succulent and melting crème pâtissière, replace the wheat flour with the same quantity of rice flour.
* Enriched with some plump sultanas soaked in rum, this cream is ideal for stuffing pancakes, which are heated for a few minutes in a hot oven and sprinkled with liqueur or spirit before serving.

123 Almond Cream

Crème d'amandes 'rich and voluptuous'

To make 250 g (8¾ oz) of cream

Main ingredients	50 g (1¾ oz) unsalted butter, softened 65 g (2¼ oz) icing sugar ⎫ mixed together 65 g (2¼ oz) ground almonds ⎰ very thoroughly 1 egg 1 level tablespoon cornflour 1 teaspoon rum
Equipment	1 liquidiser
Uses	Stuffed Apples **(No 137)** Ali-Baba **(No 143)**

1 Put the softened butter in the bowl and work it to a soft cream with the spatula.

2 Sprinkle in the mixture of icing sugar and ground almonds in a steady shower, beating all the time for about 2 minutes to keep the mixture light.

3 Add the egg and stir it carefully into the mixture to obtain a smooth and homogeneous cream.

4 Finally, add the cornflour and the rum and finish by stirring with a spatula. The cream is ready for use.

Suggestions for the home cook

*This cream can be kept for up to a week in the refrigerator, in a container sealed tightly with plastic film. Take it out half an hour before you use it to allow it to regain its smooth, supple consistency.

*You can also make up this recipe in a liquidiser, running it at the lowest possible speed. First blend the butter and sugar/almond mixture for a minute, add the egg and blend for a further 30 seconds, finally add the cornflour and rum and blend for 15 seconds.

*To make a simple and luscious pudding which uses this Almond Cream, cut a large brioche mousseline into big slices 2 cm (¾ inch) thick, spread them with a layer of almond cream a good centimetre thick, sprinkle with icing sugar and bake for several minutes on a metal baking-sheet in a hot oven (240°C/470°F/Mark 9) till they are a pretty pale golden colour. Serve immediately on hot plates.

124 Cold Fresh Raspberry, Strawberry or Blackcurrant Sauce

Sauce coulis de framboises, fraises ou cassis
'Useful fruit sauces to keep on hand'

For five people

Main ingredients	300 g (generous 8 oz) raspberries, strawberries or blackcurrants (fresh **or** frozen and thawed) 200 g (7 oz) caster sugar juice of 1 lemon
Equipment	A liquidiser
Uses	Melon Sorbet **(No 129)** Honey Ice-Cream **(No 132)** Raspberry Soufflé **(No 133)** Soufflé Pancakes **(No 136)** Apples stuffed with Almonds and Apricots **(No 137)** Ali-Baba **(No 143)**

1 Hull and pick over the fruit in a colander and if necessary wash them quickly in running water. Drain, and dry carefully with kitchen paper.

2 Put them in the liquidiser with the sugar and lemon juice and blend for 2 minutes.

3 If you like a very smooth sauce push the purée through a wire sieve with the back of a small ladle to eliminate any remaining seeds.

4 Pour the sauce into a sauce boat or earthenware bowl and chill before serving.

Suggestions for the home cook

* Like other fresh fruit sauces, you can keep these in an airtight plastic container for up to a week in the refrigerator or two months in the freezer. In the latter case, take the sauce out of the freezer the day before it is to be used and let it defrost overnight. Once unfrozen, whisk it well to restore its smooth texture.

* If you are using fresh blackcurrants, it is better to leave the little stalks on, and even to add a few blackcurrant leaves to intensify the flavour when you blend the fruit. Take care to sieve the sauce carefully after blending if you do so.

125 Fresh Apricot Sauce

Sauce coulis d'abricots 'Sharp and easily made'

For five people

Main ingredients	30 'ears' or halves of ripe fresh apricots, **or** apricots preserved without sugar 250 ml (scant ½ pint) water 100 g (3½ oz) caster sugar 1 vanilla-pod, split in two 1 tablespoon rum
Equipment	1 medium-sized saucepan A liquidiser
Uses	Light Pear Soufflé **(No 134)** Apples Stuffed with Almonds and Apricots **(No 137)**

1 Put the apricots, water, caster sugar and vanilla-pod in a medium saucepan and bring to the boil.

2 Allow to simmer gently, uncovered, for twenty-five minutes. The mixture will reduce by about one-third, giving a moist, thickish purée. Stir frequently as it cooks to prevent the apricots from sticking.

3 Take out the vanilla-pod, put the mixture in the liquidiser, add the tablespoon of rum and purée for two minutes.

4 Pour the sauce into a sauceboat or glazed earthenware bowl and, if it is to be served cold, chill in the refrigerator.

Suggestions for the home cook

* Like other fresh fruit sauces, you can keep this in an airtight plastic container for up to a week in the refrigerator or two months in the freezer. In the latter case, take the sauce out of the freezer the day before and let it soften.
* The sauce can be enriched by adding twelve Jordan almonds. Plunge them into boiling water for two minutes, refresh them in cold water and squeeze off the skins between your thumb and index finger. Then split them in two (for method, see page 421) and macerate for an hour in a spoonful of rum or kirsch before adding to the sauce.

126 Caramelised Peach Sauce

Sauce coulis de pêches au caramel 'For gourmands – a fine golden sauce'

For six–eight people

Main ingredients	750 ml (1¼ pints) water ⎫ 400 g (14 oz) caster sugar ⎬ syrup for cooking the peaches A vanilla pod ⎭ 3 unpeeled white peaches 100 g (3½ oz) caster sugar ⎫ 4 tablespoons cold water ⎬ caramel sauce 1 teaspoon lemon juice ⎭
Equipment	1 medium-size saucepan with a lid 1 small stainless-steel saucepan with a lid 1 liquidiser
Uses	Peach Charlotte **(No 139)** Ali-Baba **(No 143)**

Cooking the peaches in syrup

1 Put the water, the sugar and the vanilla pod into the medium-sized saucepan and bring to the boil.

2 Plunge in the peaches and let them simmer, covered, for about fifteen minutes.

3 Remove the peaches from the syrup with a skimmer or a slotted spoon and put them to drain and cool in the colander. Put the syrup, covered, in a cold place, and use it to poach other fresh fruits.

Preparing the caramel sauce

4 Put the sugar, 2 tablespoons water and lemon juice into a small saucepan, bring to the boil and simmer for about 5 minutes, when the caramel will have become a deep chestnut brown.

5 Give the saucepan a few brisk circular movements, to colour the sauce evenly.

6 Add the remaining two tablespoons of water to the caramel. Cover the pan immediately to protect yourself from the hot sugar spattering as it comes in contact with the cold water. (If you don't add this water the caramel will solidify as it cools.)

Finishing the sauce

7 Peel the peaches with a small stainless-steel knife and cut them carefully in half to remove their stones.

8 Blend the peach halves in the liquidiser for thirty seconds to obtain a smooth purée, add the caramel sauce and blend for a further fifteen seconds.

9 Pour the sauce into a sauce boat or earthenware bowl and chill before using.

Suggestions for the home cook

* Like other fresh fruit sauces (**Nos 124, 125**) you can keep this in an airtight plastic container for up to a week in the refrigerator or two months in the freezer. In the latter case, take the sauce out of the freezer the day before it is to be used and let it soften.
* In order to save time, you can of course use tinned peaches for this recipe.
* The sauce is equally delicious if the peaches are replaced by the same quantity of pears.

127 Chocolate Sauce

Sauce chocolat 'Simple to make and perfectly smooth'

For five people

Main ingredients	65 g (2¼ oz) unsweetened cocoa powder 175 g (6 oz) caster sugar 250 ml (scant ½ pint) water 25 g (1 oz) softened butter
Equipment	1 heavy-bottomed stainless-steel saucepan
Uses	Pears in syrup (*see* **No 141**) Honey profiteroles (*see* **No 132**)

1   Whip the cocoa, water and sugar in the saucepan with a wire whisk to obtain a smooth well-blended paste.

2   Bring to the boil and simmer for 3 minutes.

3   Add the butter, bring to the boil again, and simmer for 4 minutes, stirring constantly with the whisk to prevent the sauce sticking.

4   Lightly nap the pudding, which it is to accompany, with the sauce, or keep it hot in a bain-marie until needed.

Suggestions for the home cook

* If you do not use all the sauce you can store it, in an airtight plastic container, for a week to a fortnight in the refrigerator. Place it in a bain-marie, having first added a teaspoon of cold water, to bring it back to its former consistency, and reheat, whisking it well.

* I've tried every possible recipe for chocolate sauce, and this one is, I think, the easiest and best.

* A few pears cooked whole in syrup (*for method see* **No 141**) and placed round a few pretty oval spoonfuls of Honey Ice Cream (**No 132**) find their perfect accompaniment in this sauce.

* Chocolate sauce is also ideal for honey profiteroles (*see* **No 132**).

128 Coffee-Bean Sauce

Sauce aux grains de café 'The smoothness of crème anglaise and the flavour of coffee'

For five people

Main ingredients	250 ml (scant ½ pint) milk 75 g (2½ oz) caster sugar A teaspoon freshly-ground medium-fine coffee 3 egg yolks
Equipment	1 medium saucepan with lid
Uses	Chocolate Marquise (**No 140**)

1   Bring the milk and 35 g (1¼ oz) of the sugar to the boil in the medium-sized saucepan.

2   When the milk boils add the ground coffee. Cover, remove from the heat and leave to infuse for 15 minutes.

3   Meanwhile, put the egg yolks and the remaining sugar into a bowl and beat for a minute with a whisk, until the mixture lightens and becomes pale.

4   Add the coffee infusion (2) to the egg and sugar mixture in the bowl, beating vigorously.

5   Put everything back into the saucepan and let it thicken over a slow heat, without boiling, for about 6 minutes, stirring gently and continuously with a wooden spatula.

6   To test if the cream is perfectly cooked, remove the spatula with which you have been stirring it and run your finger across the coating of cream, making a channel. If the channel keeps its shape, the cooking and the thickness of the cream are perfect.

7   Transfer the cream to the washed and dried bowl without straining it. The presence of the ground coffee helps to give it its texture and consistency.

8   Allow to cool, stirring occasionally with the spatula to keep it smooth. You can speed up this process by putting the bowl in a receptacle half filled with cold water and ice cubes.

Suggestions for the home cook

* The cooking of the custard (5) should take place at less than 80°C/ 176°F. If it exceeds this temperature the egg yolks will coagulate and separate and the sauce will be ruined.
* If you do, by accident, boil and spoil the custard, put it in the liquidiser and blend for fifteen seconds to make it smooth again. If you don't have a liquidiser, put it in a bottle, put on the lid, and shake it as if you were mixing a cocktail.
* This sauce can be kept for two or three days in the refrigerator in a bowl sealed with plastic film.

129 Melon Sorbet

Melon en sorbet 'As fresh as a summer morning'

For six people

Main ingredients	6 small well-ripened melons weighing about 300 g (10½ oz) each 150 ml (¼ pint) milk 100 g (3½ oz) icing sugar 2 tablespoons white rum
Ingredients for the garnish	200 g (7 oz) wild strawberries 1 tablespoon caster sugar 1 tablespoon white rum 12 fresh mint leaves (optional) a few strawberry or other fresh leaves
Accompanying sauce	Fresh Strawberry Sauce (**No 124**)
Equipment	1 small saucepan 1 liquidiser 1 electric ice-cream maker (sorbetière)

Preparing the garnish

1   Put the wild strawberries, sugar and one tablespoon of rum to macerate in a bowl in the refrigerator.

Preparing the melons

2   Carefully decapitate the melons with a sharp knife, keeping the stalks attached to their little hats. Remove the flesh of the hats and reserve it in a second bowl.

3   Remove the seeds and surrounding fibres of the melons with a small spoon.

4   Then, with a soup-spoon, scoop out the flesh of the melons into the second bowl, leaving the gold and green skins intact.

5   Put the hollowed-out skins and the tops in the refrigerator.

Preparing the sorbet

6   In a small saucepan, boil the milk and icing sugar together. Allow to cool.

7   Blend the flesh of the melons in the liquidiser for 5 minutes to obtain approximately 600 ml (1 pint) of smooth and runny purée.

8   Add the cooled milk and sugar mixture and the 2 tablespoons of white rum to the melon purée and blend for 15 seconds more.

9   Empty this mixture into the electric ice-cream maker and run it until the mixture thickens and sets – 20 to 25 minutes approximately, according to the make of machine.

Finishing and presenting the dish

10   Remove the melon shells from the refrigerator, half fill them with the sorbet, scatter over it the macerated strawberries and fill to the top with the rest of the sorbet.

11   Put the hats on top, prettily decorated with mint leaves, if you have them.

12   Present the melons on a long dish, covered with strawberry leaves or other pleasant fresh foliage. Serve the fresh strawberry sauce separately in a sauceboat; it can be poured over the sorbet contained in each melon.

130 Claret Granita

Granité au vin de Saint-Émilion
'The frozen juice of the vine'

For six people

Main ingredients	200 ml (⅓ pint) water ⎫ for the syrup 200 g (7 oz) caster sugar ⎭ 1 × 750 ml (1¼ pint) bottle of red wine – preferably Saint-Émilion The juice of 1 orange The juice of 1 lemon 6 fresh mint leaves (optional)
Equipment	1 medium-sized saucepan 6 claret glasses

You don't need an electric ice-cream maker for this recipe, but it *must* be made a day in advance because the mixture of syrup, wine and fruit juice takes a long time to set and crystallize into flakes.

Preparing the syrup

1 Boil the water and sugar together for 1 minute in the medium-sized saucepan. Pour the syrup obtained into a bowl and allow to cool.

Preparing the granita

2 When the syrup is cold, add the wine, the orange and lemon juice and mix together with a small whisk.

3 Pour the mixture into a large flat dish or container and put it in the freezer or freezing compartment of the refrigerator. The shallow depth of the liquid allows it to set more rapidly.

4 During the course of the day, fork over the solidifying liquid regularly, scraping the crystals from the edges of the dish into the still-liquid central part. Continue until the whole is set into a mass of small light crystals.

Finishing and preparing the granita

5 Fill the 6 claret glasses with the granita, shaping it into a dome-shape with a spoon.

6 Arrange a few mint leaves prettily on top of each sorbet if you can obtain them.

Suggestions for the home cook

* You can dress up this granita with tinned white peaches or, in summer, well-ripened fresh peaches prepared in the following manner. Plunge them in boiling water for 15 seconds to make them easier to peel. Peel them, and cook for 15 minutes in 1 litre ($1\frac{3}{4}$ pints) of boiling water to which 600 g (21 oz) of caster sugar and a split vanilla-pod have been added. Cool them, and place a whole peach on top of each granita, stuck with two mint leaves, to look as if it is growing.
* In the winter, the orange juice in the granita base (2) can be replaced by mandarin or tangerine juice to give a new blend of flavours.

131   Bitter Chocolate Granita

Granité de chocolat amer 'Chocolate with iced coffee crystals'

For six people

Main ingredients	500 ml (scant pint) milk 100 g (3½ oz) caster sugar 100 g (3½ oz) cooking chocolate **or** 100 g (3½ oz) melted plain chocolate 100 g (3½ oz) unsweetened cocoa powder 250 ml (scant ½ pint) double cream
Ingredients for the coffee crystals	200 ml (⅓ pint) water 30 g (1 oz) caster sugar 1 heaped tablespoon of instant coffee
Equipment	1 medium saucepan 1 freezing tray 1 electric ice-cream machine 6 'flute' glasses, chilled in the refrigerator

A day in advance: preparing the coffee crystals

1 Bring the 200 ml ($\frac{1}{3}$ pint) water and 30 g (1 oz) sugar to the boil in the saucepan. Remove from the heat and whisk in the instant coffee thoroughly. Transfer the mixture to the freezing tray of the refrigerator and put it in the freezing compartment or freezer, stirring from time to time with the fork until the mixture sets and turns into small light crystals.

Preparing the chocolate

2 Next day, put the milk and 100 g ($3\frac{1}{2}$ oz) sugar in the saucepan and bring to the boil. Beat in the chocolate, broken into little pieces, with a small wire whisk.

3 Take 4 tablespoons of the sweetened milk and beat into the cocoa powder carefully, little by little, avoiding lumps. Then, pour the diluted cocoa into the milk in the saucepan and whisk thoroughly over a low heat.

4 When everything is thoroughly blended and melted, strain the mixture into a large bowl. Then, carefully fold in the double cream.

Finishing and serving the dish

5 Put the chocolate mixture (4) into the electric ice-cream maker and run for about 20 minutes, or until it has set and thickened.

6 Mix half the coffee crystals delicately into the chocolate ice with a fork.

7 Fill 6 champagne 'flutes' with the granita, forming each into a dome shape with a spoon and sprinkling the tops with the rest of the coffee crystals.

132 Honey Ice-Cream

Glace au miel 'A creamy ice with the bouquet of wild flowers'

For four people

Main ingredients	250 ml (scant ½ pint) milk 125 g (4½ oz) flower honey (avoid a variety which is dominated by one flavour, for instance acacia) 2 egg yolks 150 ml (¼ pint) double cream
Equipment	1 medium-sized saucepan 1 electric ice-cream maker

1 Bring the milk to the boil in the medium-sized saucepan, add the honey, whisking well with a small wire whisk, and bring back to the boil.

2 Meanwhile, put the two egg yolks into a bowl, whisk them for one minute, then add the cream, still whisking until well mixed.

3 Add the boiling milk-and-honey mixture and whisk vigorously.

4 Strain the mixture into a clean bowl and allow to cool.

5 Empty the cooled mixture into the electric ice-cream maker and run it for about 20–25 minutes, or until the mixture thickens and sets.

Suggestions for the home cook

* This beautiful creamy pale golden ice can replace vanilla ice-cream – as it used to.

* Red fruits – strawberries and raspberries – make good partners served with a fresh fruit sauce made from the same fruit (**No 124**).

* It is particularly good served with pears cooked in syrup and coated with chocolate sauce (see **No 141**).

* It can be used in the most delicious way to fill little miniature choux-pastry puffs or profiteroles, which can be bought ready-made or made at home (**No 119**). Slice the little puffs in half with a serrated knife, fill them with a teaspoonful of Honey Ice-Cream, close them up and serve them on a platter coated with hot Chocolate Sauce (**No 127**).

133 Raspberry Soufflé

*Soufflé aux framboises 'A particularly
luscious and melting soufflé'*

For six people

Main ingredients	360 g (12¾ oz) fresh or defrosted frozen raspberries 150 g (5¼ oz) icing sugar The juice of ¼ lemon 3 egg yolks 12 egg whites A pinch of salt 20 g (¾ oz) softened butter ⎫ 30 g (1 oz) caster sugar in a ⎬ for preparing shaker ⎭ the moulds

---

Accompanying sauce (optional)	Fresh Raspberry Sauce (**No 124**)

Equipment	1 liquidiser 6 small silver or white porcelain soufflé dishes 10 cm (4 inches) in diameter and 5 cm (2 inches) high 1 copper basin for whipping egg whites or 1 large bowl

---

*The secret of soufflés is, quite simply, that the egg whites are *not beaten too stiffly* – as so often happens. This means that they have reserves of strength which enable the soufflé to rise perfectly.

Preparing the raspberry purée

1   Blend the raspberries, 90 g (3 oz) of the icing sugar and the lemon juice together in the liquidiser.

2   When the mixture has become a smooth purée, add the egg yolks. Blend a further 15 seconds and turn the mixture into a large bowl.

Preparing the soufflé dishes

3   Brush the insides of the soufflé-dishes lightly but thoroughly with the softened butter. Sprinkle the buttered moulds with caster sugar, turn them upside down, and tap them lightly on the base to dislodge any extra sugar.

Preparing the soufflé mixture

4   Put the egg whites and the pinch of salt in the copper bowl or a large ordinary bowl, and whisk them with a hand or electric beater to a soft snow, taking care not to make them too stiff. Then, sprinkle on the remaining 60 g ($2\frac{1}{4}$ oz) of sugar in a fine rain, beating all the time.

5   Take a quarter of the egg whites and mix carefully with the raspberry purée, (2) using a spoon. Then, fold in the remaining egg whites, using a wooden spatula and lifting the mixture lightly to keep it airy.

6   Preheat the oven to 220°C/425°F/Mark 7. Fill the soufflé dishes to the brim with the mixture and smooth the tops with a metal spatula. Push the mixture away from the edges of the moulds with your thumb to enable the soufflés to rise more easily.

7   Cook the soufflés for 12 minutes in the oven and serve immediately. A Fresh Apricot Sauce (**No 125**) goes well with these soufflés, served separately in a sauceboat.

Suggestions for the home cook

* The layer of butter coating the dishes prevents the soufflés from sticking and allows them to rise smoothly and vertically. The sugar is used simply to give a slightly crunchy texture. Take care, therefore, that you don't touch the insides of the dishes with your fingers once they have been coated (3).

* If you want your soufflés to have a specially shiny appearance, dust them with icing sugar 3 minutes after you have first put them in the oven.

134 Light Pear Soufflés

Soufflé léger aux poires 'As light as a breeze'

For six people

<table>
<tr><td>*Main ingredients*</td><td>5 pears, well-ripened and weighing approximately 120 g (4¼ oz) each **or** 500 g (18 oz) of pears preserved in syrup
½ lemon
60 g (2 oz) caster sugar
1½ tablespoons pear liqueur
5 egg yolks
12 egg whites
1 pinch salt
2 tablespoons icing sugar</td></tr>
</table>

<table>
<tr><td>*Ingredients for cooking the pears*</td><td>1 litre (1¾ pints) water
100 g (3½ oz) caster sugar ⎱ syrup
1 vanilla-pod split lengthways ⎰
20 g (¾ oz) softened butter ⎱ for preparing
30 g (1 oz) caster sugar in a ⎰ the moulds
   shaker</td></tr>
</table>

<table>
<tr><td>*Accompanying sauce*</td><td>Fresh Apricot Sauce (**No 125**)</td></tr>
</table>

<table>
<tr><td>*Equipment*</td><td>6 small silver or white porcelain soufflé dishes 10 cm (4 inches) in diameter and 5 cm (2 inches) in height
1 copper bowl of the kind used for beating egg whites **or** a large bowl</td></tr>
</table>

Preparing the pear purée

1   Put the ingredients for the syrup – the water, sugar and vanilla-pod into a saucepan. Bring to the boil.

2   Peel and core the pears, rub them with the half lemon and cut them in quarters. Cook them in the syrup for 15 minutes, and then drain in a colander.

3   Blend the drained pears carefully for a minute in the liquidiser with 60 g (2 oz) caster sugar, the pear liqueur and the five egg yolks. Transfer the mixture to a large bowl.

Preparing the soufflé dishes

4   Brush the interior of the soufflé dishes lightly but thoroughly with the softened butter. Sprinkle the buttered dishes with the sugar in the shaker, then turn them upside down and tap the bases to dislodge any surplus sugar.

Preparing the soufflé mixture

5   Put the egg whites and the salt in the copper bowl or large ordinary bowl and whisk them to a soft snow with a hand or electric beater, without making them too firm. Towards the end of the operation incorporate the icing sugar, beating all the time.

6   Take a quarter of the egg whites and mix them carefully into the pear mixture with a spoon. Then gradually fold in the remaining egg whites, using the wooden spatula and lifting the mixture lightly to keep it airy.

Finishing and presenting the dish

7   Preheat the oven to 220°C/425°F/Mark 7. Fill the soufflé dishes to the top, and level the surface with the side of a metal spatula. Using your thumb, push the mixture away from the edges of each dish to enable the soufflés to rise more easily.

8   Cook for ten minutes in the hot oven and serve as soon as you take them out. A Fresh Apricot Sauce (**No 125**) served separately, is excellent with this dish.

Suggestions for the home cook

* A pinch of salt added to the egg whites dissolves some of the albumen contained in them, preventing them from becoming granular, and making them smoother.

* Rather than adding the pear liqueur neat (3) you can cut two ladies' fingers into six pieces, soak them in the spirit and introduce them into the soufflé mixture before filling the dishes. They will hold the delicious flavour of pear better.

135 Lazy Pancakes

Crêpes à la paresseuse

For five people

Main ingredients	100 g (3½ oz) flour 40 g (1½ oz) caster sugar a pinch of salt 1 egg 1 egg yolk the finely grated peel of ½ orange 250 ml (scant ½ pint) milk 50 g (1¾ oz) butter 2 tablespoons arachide oil to oil the pan
Ingredients for the filling	100 g (3½ oz) praline (a sticky mixture of caramelised sugar and grilled almonds and hazel nuts which can be bought at the confectioners or made at home) 120 g (4¼ oz) butter 1 tablespoon Grand Marnier **or** Cointreau
Ingredients for serving	50 g (1¾ oz) softened butter for buttering the plates 150 ml (¼ pint) armagnac
Equipment	1 or 2 heavy frying-pans or special pancake pans, 15 cm (6 inches) across 10 heat-proof plates

Preparing the pancake batter

1   Blend the flour, sugar, salt, whole egg and egg yolk and the orange peel in the liquidiser, adding the milk gradually and continuing to blend until you achieve a smooth cream.

2   Meanwhile, heat the 50 g (1¾ oz) butter in a small saucepan to form 'beurre noisette'. When it turns golden and ceases to sizzle all the water in it has evaporated.

3   When the milk has all been added to the batter (1) add the 'beurre noisette' to the liquidiser jar and blend for a further 15 seconds.

4   Pour the mixture into a large bowl and allow to rest for half an hour.

Preparing the filling

5   Rinse the container of the liquidiser and liquidise the praline, the 120 g (4½ oz) butter and the tablespoon of liqueur until you have a smooth mixture. Put it into a small bowl.

Cooking the pancakes

6   Brush the insides of the frying-pans lightly with oil. Stir the pancake mixture thoroughly.

7   Heat the pan over a medium heat, and, when it is hot, ladle a small amount of the batter, about 2½ tablespoons, into the centre, giving the pan a swift circular shake at the same time in order to spread the batter in a thin, even layer over the surface.   ·

8   Let the pancake cook for a minute to a light golden-brown on each side, sliding a metal spatula carefully underneath to turn it. When it is done, slide the pancake from the pan and pile on to a plate. Follow the same process to make nine more pancakes. You can use two pans to make two pancakes at once, but you must work quite fast and efficiently.

Finishing and serving the pancakes

9   When all the pancakes are cooked, lay them out on the worktop. Using the metal spatula, spread the surface of each with a thin layer of the praline mixture (5). Preheat the oven to 250°C/480°F/ Mark 9.

10   Brush ten heat-proof plates with butter, and place a pancake, praline side up, on each. Then when you wish to serve the pancakes, put half the plates in the hot oven for 30 seconds. Take them out, sprinkle each pancake with a tablespoon of armagnac, and serve. *Do not flame them.* When the guests have finished the first five, quickly heat and serve the remaining five.

Suggestions for the home cook

* The pancake mixture can be prepared the previous day: it will be necessary to whisk the mixture very thoroughly just before pouring it into the frying-pan in order to mix in the butter which has a tendency to rise to the surface.

* As the pancakes are heated through in a hot oven before serving, it is also possible to get most of your work done, and actually cook them, the day before. In this case, you should, after removing them from the pan, let them cool, laid flat on a table, or better still on a wire rack. When they are cool, pile them, flat, between two plates and put them in the refrigerator. The next day, take them out half an hour before serving, in order to allow them to warm up to room temperature.

136 Soufflé Pancakes

Crêpes Soufflées 'A showpiece for cooks'

For six people

For the *pancake mixture*	100 g (3½ oz) flour 40 g (1½ oz) caster sugar a pinch of salt the finely grated rind of half an orange 1 egg 1 egg yolk 250 ml (scant ½ pint) milk 50 g (1¾ oz) unsalted butter 2 tablespoons arachide oil to oil the pans

For the soufflé
mixture
	3 well-ripened pears weighing 120 g (4¼ oz)
	    apiece **or** the same weight of tinned
	    pears drained of their syrup
	½ lemon
	60 g (2 oz) caster sugar
	1 tablespoon pear liqueur
	6 egg yolks
	10 egg whites
	a pinch of salt
	50 g (1¾ oz) softened unsalted butter for
	    buttering the oven-dish
	icing sugar in a shaker

Accompanying *sauce*	200 ml (⅓ pint) Fresh Raspberry Sauce **(No 124)**
Equipment	1 liquidiser 2 small saucepans 2 pancake **or** frying-pans with thick bottoms, 15 cm (6 inches) across 1 copper bowl **or** a large earthenware bowl 1 large, long ovenproof dish

Preparing the pancakes

1   Follow the procedure in **No 135,** steps 1 to 4.

Preparing the pear soufflé mixture

2   Follow the procedure in **No 134,** steps 1 to 3.

Finishing the pancakes

3   When the pancakes are cooked, lay them out flat on the work-top.

4   In the centre of each, put 3 tablespoons of pear soufflé mixture.

5   Fold each pancake over, to form a half-moon shape like an apple turnover.

6   Preheat the oven to 220°C/425°F/Mark 7. Brush the ovenproof dish or a baking-sheet with softened butter.

7   Lay the ten filled pancakes on the dish, or baking-sheet, sprinkle them with icing sugar, and put them to cook in the hot oven for 6 to 8 minutes.

Serving the soufflé pancakes

8   Heat 6 flat plates. Take the dish out of the oven, slide each pancake out with the metal spatula. Lay two on each plate and surround them with Fresh Raspberry Sauce **(No 124)**.

Suggestions for home cooks

* Before attempting this recipe it is wise to practise making the Light Pear Soufflé **(No 134)** several times. It won't be long before it is child's play and then you can amaze your friends and make them quite green with envy.
* The cooking time may seem rather short, but it really is long enough. The golden rule for soufflés is that they should always be soft and moist inside.

137 Apples Stuffed with Almonds and Apricots

*Pommes bonne femme à l'amande
d'abricot 'Beautiful apples, plump and tender'*

For four people

Main ingredients	8 fresh or dried almonds ⎫ 4 whole dried apricots ⎪ for stuffing 1 level teaspoon caster sugar ⎬ the apples 2 tablespoons rum ⎭ 4 apples weighing 200 g (7 oz) each – either russets or Golden Delicious 8 heaped teaspoons butter 8 heaped teaspoons caster sugar 8 tablespoons water
Accompanying sauce	200 ml ($\frac{1}{3}$ pint) Fresh Apricot Sauce **(No 125)**
Equipment	1 round or oval enamelled cast-iron plate

Suggestions for the home cook

* The 4 teaspoons of sugar added half-way through the cooking time (9) can be replaced by the same quantity of Almond Cream **(No 123)**.
* You can use soft fruit, in summer, instead of the almonds and apricots. For instance: strawberries, raspberries or stoned cherries. In this case, serve the apples with a Fresh Raspberry Sauce **(No 124)**.
* In the summer, this simple and delicious pudding can be served chilled.

Preparing the fruit filling

1   If the almonds are fresh, shell them and remove the soft inner skin with a small vegetable knife. If they are dried, plunge them for two minutes in boiling water, refresh in cold, and squeeze each one between thumb and index finger to remove the skin.

2   Whether they are fresh or dried, cut them in half lengthwise across their width.

3   Wash the dried apricots under the cold tap and cut them into little dice 1 cm ($\frac{1}{2}$ inch) across.

4   Let the diced apricots macerate with the almond halves in the rum and caster sugar for 1 hour.

Preparing and cooking the apples

5   Using a potato-peeler, peel the apples carefully, leaving the stalks on. Decapitate them with a small knife, and keep the little tops on one side.

6   Core the apples with an apple-corer and fill the hole with the macerated almonds and apricots.

7   Arrange the stuffed apples on a flat enamelled iron oven-dish, sprinkle them with the liquid in which the apricots were soaked, put a good teaspoon of butter on the top of each, and finally, put their 'hats' on top.

8   Preheat the oven to 220°C/425°F/Mark 7. Sprinkle each apple with a teaspoon of caster sugar. Pour 8 tablespoons of water round the apples and dot the dish with the 4 remaining teaspoons of butter.

9   Bake for 30–40 minutes in the hot oven. The apples should be perfectly cooked, but must not fall apart and turn into jam. Half-way through, baste the apples with their juice, and sprinkle each with a second teaspoonful of sugar. At the same time, put the Fresh Apricot Sauce (**No 125**) to heat through in a bain-marie.

Finishing and serving the dish

10   Take the dish out of the oven, pour over the apricot sauce and serve to your guests.

138 Tart Apple Tarts

Tartes fines chaudes aux pommes acidulées
'Light apple tarts'

For four people

Main ingredients	8 small russet or Golden Delicious apples, approximately 1 kg (2 lb 4 oz) apples the juice of one lemon a handful of flour 400 g (14 oz) fresh or frozen flaky pastry **(No 118)** 200 g (7 oz) softened butter 120 g (4¼ oz) caster sugar
Accompanying cream	Crème Chantilly **(No 121)**

Suggestions for the home cook

* If you have no flaky pastry you can make this recipe very well using Shortcrust Pastry **(No 117).**
* Following the same techniques of 'nourishing' the fruit with butter and sugar during the cooking, you can, according to the season, also make delicious tarts of stoned cherries, halved apricots, peaches, pears and so on.
* You can freeze uncooked tarts, prepared up to step 7 with the chosen fruit, and put them straight in the preheated oven, without defrosting, when they are needed. The cooking time – 30 minutes – is the same. In this event avoid soft fruits like strawberries and raspberries because they are too juicy, and tricky to freeze.

Preparing the apples

1   Peel the apples with a vegetable-peeler, cut them in half and cut out pips and the horny parts around the core. Then cut each half into little crescents $1\frac{1}{2}$ cm ($\frac{1}{2}$ inch) thick. .

2   Put them in a bowl and sprinkle with lemon juice (to prevent them from discolouring), mixing them round with your hands.

Preparing the pastry bases

3   Lightly flour the work-top.

4   Divide the flaky pastry into four equal parts of 100 g ($3\frac{1}{2}$ oz) each. Make four little balls and flatten them with the rolling pin to form four discs 17 cm ($6\frac{1}{2}$ inches) wide and 2 mm thick. (If you do not feel confident of success with this method, roll out the pastry a little more, put an upturned saucer on each piece and trim round the edge with a small knife.)

5   Put the pastry rounds on a wetted baking-sheet, and preheat the oven to 220°C/425°F/Mark 7.

6   Using a small knife, draw a concentric circle 1 cm ($\frac{1}{2}$ inch) in from the edge of each round, incising the pastry to a depth of 1 mm ($\frac{1}{16}$ inch). This operation allows the edge of the tart to rise properly and form a border.

7   Within this inner line, arrange the apple crescents moistened with lemon juice in the form of overlapping petals, so that they cover the pastry completely. Dot each tart with 25 g (1 oz) of butter and sprinkle with 15 g ($\frac{1}{2}$ oz) caster sugar.

Cooking and serving the tarts

8   Bake for 30 minutes in the hot oven. Half-way through the cooking dot the rest of the butter on the tarts and sprinkle them with the remaining sugar.

9   When they are cooked the tarts will be a beautiful golden colour and the apples caramelised. Serve immediately on hot plates, either plain and natural or with an accompaniment of your choice, perhaps Crème Chantilly (**No 121**) or more simply with fresh cream served separately in a sauceboat.

139 Peach Charlotte

Charlotte aux pêches 'A pudding for yesterday's children'

For eight people

Main ingredients	5 leaves of gelatine (10 g ($\frac{1}{3}$ oz)) 500 ml (scant pint) milk 1 vanilla-pod split lengthways 200 g (7 oz) caster sugar 5 egg yolks	for the charlotte cream

2 peaches in syrup
18 sponge fingers
250 g (8$\frac{3}{4}$ oz) whipping cream

Accompanying sauce — 500 ml (scant pint) Caramelised Peach Sauce **(No 126)**

Equipment — 1 charlotte mould 18 cm (7 inches) across and 10 cm (4 inches) deep

Preparing the charlotte cream

1 Soak the gelatine in a little cold water to soften and swell.

2 Bring the milk, vanilla and 100 g (3½ oz) of sugar to the boil in a stainless-steel saucepan. When the milk starts to rise in the pan remove from the heat, cover and leave to infuse for 5 minutes.

3 Meanwhile, put the egg yolks and the remaining 100 g (3½ oz) of sugar in a bowl. Beat for 2 minutes or until the mixture lightens and pales.

4 Remove the vanilla-pod and add the milk gradually, whisking rapidly all the time.

5 Put the mixture back in the saucepan, return to a low heat and allow to thicken without boiling, stirring gently with a wooden spatula all the time. It will take 6–8 minutes. The cream is perfectly cooked and of the right thickness when a channel traced with your finger in the cream clinging to the back of the spatula holds its shape.

6 Transfer the hot cream immediately to a clean bowl and add the drained leaves of softened gelatine, which will dissolve in it.

7 Allow the mixture to cool, stirring from time to time to keep it smooth. You can speed up the cooling by putting the bowl in a container half-filled with cold water and ice cubes.

Preparing the fruit garnish and the mould

8 Drain the peaches and cut them into 2 cm (¾ inch) dice.

9 Line the interior of the mould with sponge fingers, smooth side out and tightly packed one against the other. Trim the biscuits level with the top of the mould.

Preparing the whipped cream

10 Take the chilled bowl out of the refrigerator, put the 250 g (8¾ oz) cream in it and whisk gently for one minute, then more rapidly for about 5 minutes (*for the method see page 387*) until the cream is the consistency of stiffly beaten egg whites.

(*continued on the next page*)

Finishing and serving the dish

11 Add the diced peaches to the charlotte cream (7), which, now that it has cooled, has started to thicken. Pour the whipped cream on top and fold it in delicately with the wooden spatula, lifting and turning it lightly to aerate the mixture thoroughly.

12 Fill the biscuit-lined mould with this mixture and allow to chill for an hour and a half in the refrigerator.

13 Turn out into a deep dish and top generously with the Caramelised Peach Sauce **(No 126)**.

Suggestions for the home cook

* Peaches can be replaced with pears, strawberries or raspberries, or even with apples, which should be cut into dice, cooked for a minute in syrup, drained and macerated with a tablespoonful of Calvados.
* Charlottes benefit from being prepared a day or two in advance and kept in the refrigerator.

140 Chocolate Marquise

Marquise fondante au chocolat

For five people

Main ingredients	145 g (5 oz) plain eating chocolate 7 egg yolks 250 g (8¾ oz) caster sugar 300 g (10½ oz) softened unsalted butter 165 g (5¾ oz) unsweetened cocoa powder 500 g (18 oz) whipping cream ⎰ for the 50 g (1¼ oz) icing sugar ⎱ Crème Chantilly 14 sponge fingers 1 small coffee cup of strong cold, black, unsweetened coffee

---

Accompanying sauce	Coffee-Bean Sauce (**No 128**)

Equipment	1 bowl, chilled in the refrigerator 1 charlotte mould 17 cm (6½ inches) in diameter 1 long porcelain serving plate, chilled

---

1 Let the chocolate melt in a small saucepan in the bain-marie or in a lowish oven (170°C/335°F/Mark 3).

2 Beat the egg yolks and sugar in a bowl for about 2 minutes until the mixture becomes light and pale.

3 Add the melted chocolate, gently folding it in with the wooden spatula, turning and blending the mixture well.

4 In a second bowl work the softened butter with the whisk, until it becomes smooth and soft. Add the cocoa powder gradually, whisking to create a homogeneous cream.

5 Add the cocoa/butter mixture to the egg yolk/chocolate mixture and whisk together thoroughly.

6 Using a balloon whisk, and the chilled bowl, make a Crème Chantilly **(see No 128)** with the cream and icing sugar. Tip this Chantilly over the chocolate mixture and work everything together briskly with the whisk to obtain a perfectly blended mixture.

7 Brush the finger biscuits with the cold coffee, and line the bottom and sides of the mould with them,

8 Pour in the chocolate cream, and put in the refrigerator for 2–3 hours before serving, to become firm.

9 Turn out on to a chilled oval serving-dish and surround with the Coffee-Bean Sauce which goes especially well with this dish.

Suggestions for the home cook

* It is inevitable that, when the chocolate cream and the Crème Chantilly are mixed together (6) the mixture will collapse and shrink a little. It is the complete fusion of the two creams which makes the final result so melting and luscious.
* You can have fun spiking the cream with tiny strips of preserved oranges **(see No 144)** and little pieces of finger biscuit soaked in a rum syrup.
* To make an unusual festive pudding, slide a fine slice of frozen Marquise, without the sponge fingers, into a diamond of Flaky Pastry **(No 118)** which has been cut in half after leaving the oven. It can be sumptuously accompanied by a Coffee-Bean Sauce **(No 128)**, served separately in a sauceboat.

141 Caramelised Pear Pastries

Feuillantines de poires caramélisées 'The lightest of airy delights'

For four people

Main ingredients	200 g (7 oz) fresh **or** frozen Flaky Pastry **(No 118)**
	1 litre ($1\frac{3}{4}$ pints) water $\Big\}$ to soak the pears
	1 lemon
	4 very ripe pears weighing 120 g ($4\frac{1}{4}$ oz) apiece (Doyenne de Comice, William, Beurre Hardy, etc.) **or** pears preserved in syrup
	1·5 litres ($2\frac{1}{2}$ pints) water
	200 g (7 oz) caster sugar $\Big\}$ for cooking the pears
	1 vanilla-pod split in two
	1 handful of flour
	1 beaten egg for glazing the pastries

Ingredients for the garnish	4 tablespoons Crème Pâtissière **(No 122)**
	4 tablespoons whipping cream, chilled
	1 level tablespoon caster or, better, icing sugar $\Big\}$ for the Crème Chantilly
	1 pinch vanilla sugar
	1 teaspoon pear liqueur
	4 heaped tablespoons caster sugar

Equipment	1 salamander (optional)
	1 chilled bowl
	1 saucepan
	1 cloth
	1 baking-sheet

One day in advance: prepare the Flaky Pastry (No 118) and the Crème Pâtissière (No 122)

Preparing the fresh pears

(If you are using tinned pears, start at step 4)

1   Put the cold water in a bowl and add the juice of half the lemon.

2   Peel the pears with a vegetable-peeler, cut them in half, cut out the pips and the horny bits round the core. Rub all over with the second half of the lemon to prevent them discolouring, and plunge them as you do so into the lemon-flavoured water.

3   Make the syrup by boiling the 1·5 litres (2½ pints) of water, sugar and vanilla-pod in the saucepan. Reduce to a simmer and poach the drained pear halves, completely covered by a folded cloth placed over the top of the pan, for 15 minutes. Allow to cool.

Making and cooking the pastries

4   Preheat the oven to 220°C/425°F/Mark 7. Flour the work-top lightly, roll out the flaky pastry to a square shape approximately 12 cm (5 inches) square and 4 mm (⅕ inch) thick.

5   With a large knife, cut the square into four equal smaller squares 6 cm (2½ inches) square.

6   Place them, turned upside down, on a baking-sheet. To glaze them, brush them with beaten egg, taking care that none trickles over the edge, as this would stop them rising properly. Bake for 12–15 minutes.

Preparing the Crème Chantilly

7   Chill a bowl in the refrigerator, put in the cream, icing sugar and vanilla sugar and whisk slowly for 1 minute with a balloon whisk, then more rapidly for approximately another 5 minutes (*for the method see* **No 121**) until the cream has the consistency of stiffly-beaten egg whites.

Finishing and serving the dish

8   Make the salamander red-hot over the gas flame (or heat the gas or electric grill). Heat four plates or one long serving-dish.

9   Whisk the Crème Pâtissière and the pear liqueur together to a smooth cream.

10 Drain the pear halves (keeping the syrup for poaching other fresh fruit) and slice them into the finest slices with a small knife.

11 When they are cooked, take the pastries from the oven and slice them through with a serrated edged knife. Put the bottom halves on the hot serving plates or serving dish.

12 With a metal spatula, spread the top of each of the upper halves with a tablespoonful of Crème Pâtissière, place two finely-sliced pear halves in two overlapping layers on top. Sprinkle with a tablespoonful of caster sugar and place beneath the white-hot salamander or red-hot gas or electric grill until the sugar caramelises.

13 Spread the bottom halves of the puffs with a large tablespoonful each of Crème Chantilly, and cover with the pear-covered tops. Serve immediately.

Suggestions for the home cook

* If you have no whipping cream you can make the Crème Chantilly with 2 tablespoons of double cream thinned with 2 tablespoons of cold water.
* To make successful Crème Chantilly and avoid turning the cream into butter it is essential that the cream, water (if used) and the bowl should be very well chilled. Do not whip for too long.
* If you do not have an iron salamander with a handle, of the kind used by French pastrycooks, you can use any flat piece of iron 5 or 6 cm (about 2½ inches) across, part of an automobile spring for instance, or the hinge of a shutter.
* If you haven't a salamander or efficient overhead grill, you can replace the pears in syrup with sliced preserved oranges, which don't need caramelising.

142 Millefeuille with Crème Chantilly

Millefeuille à la crème légère 'A thousand-and-one layers'

For four people

Main ingredients	a handful of flour
	360 g (12¾ oz) fresh or frozen Flaky Pastry **(No 118)**
	250 g 8¾ oz) Crème Patissière **(No 122)**
	80 g (2¾ oz) whipping cream, chilled ⎫
	10 g (¼ oz) caster or, better, icing sugar ⎬ Crème Chantilly
	⎭
	30 g (1 oz) icing sugar in a shaker
Equipment	1 baking-sheet
	1 bowl, chilled in the refrigerator

Suggestions for the home cook

* Flaky pastry often tends to shrink in the oven. To avoid this, it is best to cut out the three rectangles the day before, and let them rest overnight in the refrigerator, protected by plastic film.
* When strawberries and raspberries are in season you can add 250 g (8¾ oz) of one or both of these fruits to the Crème Chantilly in step 8. Keep a few on one side to decorate the top of the millefeuille.
* You can have fun making a criss-cross or 'quadrillage' pattern of caramel in the icing-sugar coating by laying on a thin steel skewer, heated to white-hot in the fire or gas flame.

Preparing the millefeuille

1　Preheat the oven to 220°C/425° F/Mark 7. Lightly flour the work-top and roll out the flaky pastry into a large rectangle 20 cm (8 inches) by 45 cm (18 inches) and 2 mm (1/12 inch) thick.

2　Using a heavy knife, cut the pastry cleanly into three rectangular strips 15 cm (6 inches) by 20 cm (8 inches).

3　Brush the baking-sheet with water, lay the 3 strips of pastry on it and prick the surfaces all over with a fork. This stops the pastry 'puffing' too much during the cooking.

4　Bake for 20 minutes in the hot oven (in two batches if your oven won't hold a baking sheet large enough to take the three pieces of pastry at once).

5　Remove from the oven and allow to cool on a wire rack; the pastry should be a beautiful hazelnut brown.

Preparing the cream

6　While the millefeuilles are cooking, make the Crème Pâtissière (**No 122**) and let it cool rapidly, stirring and aerating it well with a whisk.

7　Take the chilled bowl out of the refrigerator, add the single cream and the icing sugar and beat with a small wire whisk for 1 minute, then more rapidly for a further 5 (*for the technique see* **No 121**) until the cream is the consistency of egg-whites whipped to a soft snow.

Finishing and serving the dish

8　Add the Crème Pâtissière (6) to the Crème Chantilly (7) and fold the two together carefully with a wooden spatula, using an upwards motion to aerate the mixture and retain its light texture.

9　With a metal spatula, spread half the resulting cream on one of the strips of millefeuille. Place the second millefeuille, spread with the rest of the cream, on top, and cover with the third and last mille-feuille, smooth side up. Sprinkle the confection lavishly with icing sugar, to give an even white coating. Place it on a serving-dish and slice it carefully with a serrated knife in front of your guests.

143 Ali-Babas

'A baba with forty flavours'

For eight to ten people

Main ingredients	65 g (2¼ oz) candied orange peel 30 g (1 oz) assorted crystallised fruits 30 g (1 oz) sultanas 250 g (8¾ oz) uncooked Baba Dough **(No 120)** 25 g (¾ oz) melted unsalted butter for buttering the moulds
Ingredients for the syrup	500 ml (scant pint) water 350 g (12¼ oz) caster sugar 7 tablespoons rum
Ingredients for the garnish	500 g (18 oz) Crème Pâtissière **(No 122)** 250 g (9 oz) Almond Cream **(No 123)** 80 g (2¾ oz) icing sugar in a shaker
Accompanying sauces	Fresh Raspberry Sauce **(No 124)** Caramelised Peach Sauce **(No 126)**
Equipment	2 round Genoese moulds (deep tins with sloping sides) 14 cm (6 inches) in diameter

One day in advance: preparing the dough

1 Cut the candied orange peel and the crystallised fruits into, respectively, squares and cubes 1 cm ($\frac{1}{2}$ inch) square, with a small sharp knife.

2 Rinse the sultanas in cold water and drain them in a colander.

3 Put the baba dough into a large bowl and incorporate the candied peel, crystallized fruit and sultanas with the wooden spatula.

4 Allow the dough to rest for 20 minutes at room temperature. The yeast in it will cause it to rise.

5 Push it down with a wooden spatula, flatten it and form into a coherent mass.

Cooking and soaking the Ali-Babas

6 Brush the insides of the two genoese moulds with melted butter and divide the dough between them. Leave to rise a second time at room temperature, for about 40 minutes, until the dough rises to the top of the moulds. The fruit will slightly slow up the process. Preheat the oven to 200°C/390°F/Mark 6.

7 Bake for 18–20 minutes in the oven, turn out immediately and put them, upside down, to cool slightly on wire racks for a few minutes.

8 While the Ali-Babas are cooking, boil the water and sugar together in the saucepan. When it reaches boiling point, and the sugar is thoroughly melted, take off the heat, allow the syrup to cool slightly, and add the rum.

9 Put the cake rack over a large deep dish and moisten the Ali-Babas lavishly with the warm syrup, using the small ladle to scoop up the syrup which accumulates at the bottom of the dish and pour it over the Ali-Babas again. They should be completely saturated right to the centre with the syrup. Put to rest on their wire racks in the refrigerator overnight.

(continued on the next page)

On the day: finishing and serving the Ali-Babas

10   Preheat the oven to 200°C/390°F/Mark 6. With the serrated knife, cut the Ali-Babas carefully in half across the middle, spread the Crème Pâtissière evenly on the two bottom halves in a thick layer and replace the two tops.

11   With a metal spatula, cover the filled and re-formed Ali-Babas completely with a thick coating of Almond Cream, warmed to room temperature.

12   Sprinkle them liberally with icing sugar to form an even coating, and place them on a baking-sheet. Bake for 10 minutes to glaze them nicely; they should remain white, but be lightly marbled with gold shadows.

13   Put the Ali-Babas on the serving plate, put them to chill in the refrigerator and serve accompanied by a Fresh Raspberry Sauce **(No 124)** or Caramelised Peach Sauce **(No 126)**, handed separately in sauceboats.

Suggestions for the home cook

* As for all savarins, you can perfectly well keep Ali-Babas for 12 days in the refrigerator or 2 months in the freezer, provided you seal them in plastic bags when they are still warm from the first cooking stage (step 7) to prevent them going stale. If you freeze them, take them out of the freezer a day before they are to be soaked and leave to soften overnight in the refrigerator before proceeding with step 8.
* On the other hand, Ali-Babas are even better eaten 2 or 3 days after they have been finally glazed in the oven. All the different flavours ripen to make a perfect whole.

144 Eugénies

Les Eugénies 'Candied orange robed in bitter chocolate'

For four people

Main ingredients	2 oranges weighing 200 g (7 oz) apiece
	3 litres (5¼ pints) of boiling water, used in three stages of 1 litre (1¾ pints) each
	500 ml (scant pint) cold water
	650 g (1 lb 7 oz) caster sugar
	150 g (5¼ oz) cooking chocolate
	60 g (2 oz) unsweetened cocoa powder

Peeling the oranges

1   With the small sharp knife slice both ends off the oranges so you can sit them comfortably on the work top. Then, cut the skin from top to bottom in strips 3 cm (1 inch) wide taking great care that no white pith comes away with the orange peel. (The peeled orange can be used for some other purpose – juice, for instance, or a fruit salad). Cut the peel strips into diamonds of roughly the same size – about 3 cm (1 inch) or 4 cm (1½ inches) across.

Crystallizing the orange peel

2   Put 1 litre (1¾ pints) of water to boil in a saucepan, then plunge in the orange-peel squares for 3 minutes. Refresh them in cold water, and repeat twice more, using fresh water each time. (This is to remove as much bitterness as possible from the peel.) Drain the peel in a colander.

3   Empty and rinse the saucepan and put in the 500 ml (scant pint) of cold water and the sugar. Bring to the boil, stirring constantly with a fork to dissolve the sugar and add the drained orange peel. Cook for 3 hours on a low heat; the surface of the liquid should be barely shivering.

4   Take out the orange-peel squares with a skimmer and lay them on a wire rack to drain off excess syrup. Let them dry out in the air for 3 hours.

(*continued on the next page*)

Coating the orange peel

5   Cut the chocolate into small pieces with a sharp knife. Let it melt slowly in a second saucepan standing in a bain-marie at about 30°C/ 85°F stirring continually with a wooden spatula to make it really smooth.

6   Lift up the squares of candied orange peel one at a time on a fork, without piercing them, and dip them in the melted chocolate.

7   Put the coated squares on the cake rack to allow the chocolate to set a little, and then, after a few minutes, roll them thoroughly in the plateful of cocoa powder so they are completely coated with it. Let them cool in the cocoa and pick them out with your fingers, shaking each piece gently to dust off any excess cocoa.

8   Pile them in a crown on a plate covered with a white paper doily, and offer as an extremely elegant accompaniment to coffee at the end of a meal.

Suggestions for the home cook

* You can perfectly well prepare these sweets in advance, and store them for a week in the refrigerator, completely buried in cocoa powder.

INDEX

Bold numbers indicate recipe numbers